The Courage of Common Men

Texans Remember World War II

Stephen Neal Manning

Republic of Texas Press

Library of Congress Cataloging-in-Publication Data

Manning, Stephen Neal
    The courage of common men: Texans remember World War II /
    [interviewed by] Stephen Neal Manning.
        p. cm.
    Includes bibliographical references and index.
    Contents: We plummeted like a rock out of the sky / Charles Harper—They
    died in my arms and I couldn't help them / Matias Rodriguezl—It's a little hard
    to go to sleep at night / Robert Louis Lanier—Didn't they know they weren't
    supposed to shoot at me? / James McKernon Jones—For Christ's sake,
    they're killing people all over the place / Harry Haines—What the hell are they
    applauding for? / Bill Dallas—They're not gonna get me, it's gonna be
    somebody else / Manuel Palmer—Three years of degradation and human
    bullshit / Charles Clinton Green—Ninety percent of what I know I learned
    aboard submarines / Rufus Roark—I woke up to see a rifle muzzle pointed in
    my face / Ira Simpson—I went to many places I never would have gone / John
    T. Ferguson—It was not love at first sight / Robert and Virginia Gibeson—
    Shells from the Japanese fleet splashed around us / Ron Vaughn—It seemed
    like a million years, even though it was only two / Joe Leeah—The Japs made
    them dig their own graves / Thornton Hamby—Things don't change overnight /
    LuQuincy Bowers—One-man show: pilot, navigator, bombardier / Rip Collins—
    We never shirked a duty / Lloyd Groce.
    ISBN 1-55622-838-4 (pbk.)
    1. World War, 1939-1945—Personal narratives, American.
    2. World War, 1939-1945—Veterans—Texas—Interviews. I. Title.

D811.A2 M282 2001
940.54'8173--dc21

                               00-051731
                               CIP

Printed in the United States of America

ISBN 1-55622-838-4
10 9 8 7 6 5 4 3 2 1
0101

All inquiries for volume purchases of this book should be addressed to Wordware Publishing, Inc., at 2320 Los Rios Boulevard, Plano, Texas 75074. Telephone inquiries may be made by calling:
(972) 423-0090

Contents

Acknowledgements

Several people gave me invaluable help in completing this book, by putting me in touch with veterans, providing information, or gathering photographs: Dennis Brand and Ben Dupree of the American Legion, Linda Groce Boze, Charles Groce, Harry W. Haines III, Bob Leffert, C.J. Newman, Mateo Pruneda, Janette Rodrigues of the *Houston Chronicle*, Glynis Sakowicz, Ira Simpson, and Sarah Walker of the Tarrant County Black Historical and Genealogy Society.

I thank Ginnie Bivona at Wordware's Republic of Texas Press for her infinite patience and her confidence in me. I thank the members of the Dallas/Fort Worth Writers Workshop for helping me make the book better, for example Jimmy Butts for some crucial advice on the format for the book and Mackey Murdock for some well-timed words of encouragement.

I've tried to make my mother, father, and brother proud with this book. I have mischievously kept the whole thing a secret so I can surprise my parents by mailing the book to them when it comes out. My mother has been known to ask me bluntly over the telephone, "When are you going to write a book!?" Well, Mom, here it is.

Most of all, I want to thank my wife, Maria, for her rock-solid support and encouragement.

Introduction

I'm not sure how my obsession with World War II was born. Maybe it happened because I grew up on military bases overseas at the height of the Cold War. Jet fighters streaked over my high school in England a dozen times a day, annoying my teachers but delighting me. Ever since I've been fascinated by our military and its history.

Having lived a third of my life in Europe and traveled extensively, I've seen first-hand how our way of life and standard of living stack up against the rest of the world. I'm sure it's difficult for many people who grew up in the United States not to take for granted that the water should always be hot when you want to take a shower. The phone system should always work the first time you try to make a call. The grocery store should be open no matter what hour of the night you want to shop. We're so used to it, most of us never stop to wonder where all this comfort and prosperity came from.

I had just begun a career in journalism when 50th anniversaries of legendary events rolled around on the calendar, and I had the opportunity to meet in person those who had been in places and survived experiences I could only read about and try, with inadequate means, to imagine. I listened to stories from men who'd been at Pearl Harbor, Normandy, Iwo Jima.

One day, I was happily at work on one of my war projects, interviewing a veteran who'd been a prisoner of the Japanese. The man was full of stories and eager to tell them, and ending the interview proved difficult. The afternoon dragged on. I had a feeling the man did not often have a receptive audience. So I shut up and listened and learned a thing or two.

I saw the man out the door and returned to my desk, and a lady in the newsroom said to me, "I feel sorry for you, having to listen all day to old men telling war stories. *Who cares?* That was fifty years ago!"

I mumbled a polite reply, but thought to myself, if that woman had been *listening*, and heard the story I just heard, her attitude would be different.

Her sniping failed to puncture my enthusiasm, but her question, "Who cares?" stuck with me. I knew she spoke for most people born after the end of the war. For people of my generation and the ones that preceded and followed it, World War II is ancient history, rarely revisited. Nothing I know about it was learned in school; my history classes always ran out of time at the end of the semester before we got to it.

The distance in time doesn't change the fact that we live in a world forged by the generation that won World War II. We are what we are, and we have what we have, because of them. We lead comfortable lives with little to complain about—though that hardly stops us. True adversity is a stranger to us. We have more jobs than people to fill them—how wondrous that must seem to those who grew up during the Depression! Cell phones, sport utility vehicles, shopping malls, the Internet—all this had to come from somewhere.

It comes from the time when quiet, unassuming men left ordinary lives behind, traveled to faraway places with strange-sounding names, and risked everything. Our future was almost stolen from us, but they saved it. Our world could have been very different if not for them. Many of them are still with us, and one lives not far from you, perhaps on your street. Perhaps next door. In this book, nearly twenty veterans from across Texas share their stories.

This is not a history textbook full of dates and statistics. It's the view from ground zero: individual experiences and their effect on the people who survived them.

Many of these veterans on these pages have lived in Texas all their lives; the others got here as fast as they could. All would object strenuously to my calling them heroes in the title. I'm sure they would argue they just did their job. I would remind them how big that job was.

You may find some of the incidents described here unbelievable. The tennis ball on Iwo Jima, the man who says he was too dumb to be afraid of combat, and the assertion that you're too *busy* during combat to be afraid, have all been challenged by readers. My response: Yes! Exactly! These are incredible stories, and I find some of them hard to believe myself.

But these veterans were there, and these are their memories.

Charles Harper
Fort Worth

I knocked on Charles Harper's security door on a cozy side street in west Forth Worth and waited. Excitement tickled the back of my neck. Bombers had long captured my imagination. As a gunner aboard B-29s, Harper experienced at least two ordeals of a kind few men survive to tell about. I had so many questions I wanted to ask him.

The inner door opened and I peered through the bars into the darkened interior. Harper stood in shadow, steadying himself on a walker. He sized me up through spectacles, smiled and unlocked the security door.

"Welcome," he said shyly as we shook hands.

"I've been looking forward to meeting you," I said, stepping into the foyer.

A bright-faced woman emerged from the living room and extended a hand, introducing herself as Alta Fay, his wife. "Are you Steve?" she asked, grinning. "You're so ...*young!*"

I laughed. "Yes, ma'am. That's what the publisher said, too."

Harper turned his walker toward a side door and said, "Let's go into my office and talk."

Yellowed newspaper articles with pictures of Harper back before his hair turned white hung in frames on the walls, telling of his work as owner of Harper's Bluebonnet Bakery and his

Charles Harper

involvement in civic organizations. A large folding display with pictures of airmen and B-29s occupied one corner. A world map punctured by color-coded pushpins documented Harper's travels. I recognized my own little office in his. My eyes gravitated toward the pins marking Brazil, Africa, India, Burma, places we would soon discuss. An unruly sprawl of books and papers claimed every inch of space on three tabletops that surrounded Harper's swivel chair, leaving room only for a keyboard, printer, scanner, and a large monitor. He eased himself into the swivel chair and I sat in a soft chair opposite the outside table, knowing we would get along just fine. I was in the presence of a fellow computer geek.

He watched as I inserted a fresh tape into the miniature recorder, turned it on, and set it on the desk in front of him. I already knew how I wanted to open the conversation.

"You had a lot of bad luck with airplanes during the war," I said.

He chuckled. "Yes, I had a long string of close calls. It seemed like the planes I got on just didn't want to stay in the air. In fact, I don't travel by air anymore. I've given up on it. If I have to go across the country to a reunion or to visit relatives, I drive."

"But airplanes attracted you at one time," I said.

"Yes. I volunteered for the Army Air Force. I preferred to enlist and have a choice rather than be drafted and not have a choice. I thought the Air Force would be more glamorous than the other branches. Besides, I'd never been in an airplane before! But I had trouble on those things right from the start."

"What was the first mishap?"

"On the second flight of my life, a B-25 Mitchell, a twin-engine bomber, carried me and four other young airmen between bases. When it approached the runway at Omaha, I sat in the midsection with the other passengers, listening to the pilot get his instructions from the air traffic control tower. It sounded like it was going to be a routine landing, but then I heard the engines sputter and gasp. The plane, already in a controlled descent, suddenly plummeted like a rock out of the sky. I never heard the sound of the landing gear lowering. The plane plopped down on the ground and plowed a path through six inches of snow covering a cornfield, barely missing a row of large trees.

"The plane ground to a halt. I wanted out of that plane, but snow and soil blocked the exit. You see, in a B-25 the crew entered and exited from a hatch in the bottom of the fuselage, which worked fine as long as the plane was standing up on its landing gear. But the plane landed on its belly, so we were stuck in there. Did I mention I have claustrophobia?

"The only way out was to crawl through the dark bomb bay up to the cockpit and climb through the pilot's escape hatch. Once I got out I looked back at this unfortunate aircraft resting on its belly in the snow, nowhere near the runway. Crewmembers stood around, scratching their heads and debating what happened. It turned out the flight engineer accidentally shut off the fuel transfer in mid-air."

"Not exactly the glamour you expected."

"No, it wasn't. But I didn't have the sense to get out of flying right then and serve the country from the ground.

"I was assigned to be part of the crew of a brand-new type of airplane, the B-29. My newly formed crew finished 300 hours of bombing runs and gunnery practice in Clovis, New Mexico, and then we went up to Herington, Kansas, to pick up our very own Superfortress. My position on the plane was central fire control. I sat in a rotating chair under a small scanning dome on top of the plane, behind the wings. From there I remotely controlled two gun turrets, one on top of the plane behind the cockpit, and another on top of the plane right behind my bubble."

"What did you think of the B-29?" I asked.

Charles Harper's crew poses in front of the B-29. Harper is at front row left.

"It was a hell of an airplane, the most advanced plane in the air at that time. Unlike the early B-24s and B-17s, which were open to the outside air and exposed their gunners to freezing temperatures and forced them to use oxygen masks at high altitudes, the B-29 had a pressurized and heated cabin. It kept its crews comfortable at altitudes of 30,000 feet or higher. The remotely controlled gun turrets made our job much easier than, for example, a waist gunner on a B-17, who had to rely on his own muscle to move the guns around. I just rotated in my seat and aimed at Japanese fighters with a computing sight, and the turrets followed my every move. The gunners could even switch command of the turrets back and forth at will to train the maximum possible number of guns on an enemy plane.

Charles Harper in his gunner's scanning dome on top of his B-29 Superfortress.

"My crew's commander was Capt. John Townsend, a pilot who liked to wear sunglasses during 3 A.M. flight briefings." He laughed. "But he was a good pilot. Once we had our plane we began the trip around the world to our base in India. The thought of finally getting to join the fight against the Japanese excited me, it excited all of us. We were ready.

"But the excitement soon evaporated! As the plane gained speed for takeoff, I heard a *thud* and the plane shook violently. I braced myself as the B-29 careened off the runway and rolled through a barbed wire fence, blowing out all its tires. I climbed out to learn a jackrabbit had hopped out in front of the plane and collided messily with a blade of the No. 3 prop. I would have to wait a little longer to fight the Japs. We had to stay overnight while maintenance men replaced the damaged propeller and tires."

"So that's already two mishaps before you even reached the war," I said.

"Oh, but that was just the beginning," he said. "Our journey took us to Florida, Puerto Rico, British Guyana, and then Natal, Brazil. For the next leg of the trip we had to cross the Atlantic Ocean to Accra in Africa. The plane cruised high above the ocean through a beautiful, clear night, and I could look up and stare at the bright stars from the central fire control seat. But my peaceful night ended when I heard concerned voices on the plane's intercom.

"The flight engineer, Forrest Newman, told the pilot, 'We've got a problem.' I listened closely to the conversation that followed. A vital part in the fuel transfer system had shattered, and we had no way to move fuel from the central tanks into the wing tanks, where it could feed into the engines. Despite having full tanks, suddenly we had a fuel crisis. We had already traveled far out over the Atlantic, too far to return to Brazil.

"Capt. Townsend asked the navigator, Bob Leffert, to find the nearest airstrip, and Leffert found Roberts Field in Liberia. With some difficulty this late at night, Howard Keene, the radio operator, got someone at Roberts Field to answer his call and told them we needed to make an emergency landing. Roberts Field warned us off, because even though we had CAVU conditions (ceiling and visibility unlimited) where we were, a heavy thunderstorm blanketed the field, reducing visibility to zero. They said Townsend would not be able to find the runway."

"What were you thinking at this point?" I asked.

"I was well aware other B-29s had been lost because of this same problem with the fuel transfer system. The B-29's cutting-edge technology still needed a lot of kinks worked out. I reflected that here I was in trouble on an airplane for the third time, and I still hadn't gotten to fight any Japs!"

"What did the pilot do?"

"He informed us he would continue on to Roberts Field, storm or no storm. We couldn't make it to any other airstrip. As we crossed the coast of Africa, I saw and heard the No. 3 engine sputter and spark, out of gas. Flight engineer Newman feathered the prop. Before long, dark clouds engulfed the plane and I couldn't see a thing except the lightning bolts that lit up the sky. Townsend told us he planned to make a pass over the runway and if he couldn't see it, he would order us to bail out. Right into the middle of the storm!

"Three minutes out, the No. 1 engine died, leaving us with only two more. I stared down through the clouds, trying to see runway lights. We all did. Suddenly, the rain stopped and a gap in the clouds opened up, and there it was! Townsend didn't miss his chance. He dropped that plane down fast and placed it expertly right on the end of the runway. The plane jolted as the tires hit the pavement, and we rolled down the runway, and within seconds I saw the No. 4 engine give out, and before the plane reached the far end of the runway, rain came down again in buckets. If we hadn't spotted the runway right then, we would have missed our chance. I looked down from my bubble and saw a 'Follow Me' Jeep come out to meet us in the rain and guide us to a parking spot. I was mighty glad to see that Jeep!

"A few days later the base personnel got the pump repaired and we continued on our way. I got to see Accra and then Khartoum, where I saw a long camel caravan marching alongside a river." He smiled at the memory. "That was a fascinating sight for a wide-eyed boy from Texas! When we got to Aden in Arabia, I had the chance to do some sightseeing with Bob Leffert, the navigator, and we both took a camel ride.

"We flew on to Karachi and then to Dudkhundi, India, a small town 90 miles south of Calcutta. There we joined the 444th Bomb Group, part of the 58th Bomb Wing. The Americans had established a makeshift B-29 base with hangars made of canvas supported by steel frames. The temporary hangars

Charles Harper (right) and Bob Leffert take a camel ride while sightseeing in Aden.

Charles Harper sightseeing in Calcutta.

only covered the nose section of the big bombers; their wings and tails stuck out. Dudkhundi was a hot, dusty, flat, barren place surrounded by rice paddies. We lived in tents and had no amenities, nothing to help pass the time. I made several trips into Calcutta with my buddies and was delighted to see trains carrying hundreds of Indians crowded onto the tops and sides of the railroad cars, just like you see in the movies.

"I couldn't wait to get in the air and drop bombs on the Japs. None of us could. That was what we were there for. Our first target was to be Rangoon, Burma. Bomber crews had to take a 'checkout pilot' along with them on their first combat mission, and the checkout pilot assigned to us, Thomas Welch, wanted to go in his own plane, which bore the nickname *Maiden U.S.A.* So we left our own plane at the base and headed out over the Indian Ocean on a warm, sunny, breezy day. We flew along as part of a large formation. I don't know how many bombers.

"An hour away from Rangoon, I heard the frantic words *'Fighters! Fighters!'* burst over the intercom. The words came from our tail gunner, Sigmund Kohn, Sig we called him. I spun around in the scanning dome, searching the sky for enemy planes. Below me, the left and right gunners were asking, 'Where? Where?' Then I realized what Sig was actually shouting: *'Fire.'*

"The pilot's voice came over the intercom: 'I'm depressurizing the plane. Blattner, go check back there!' Bill Blattner, the left gunner, rushed back through the radar room and opened the door leading out of our compartment back toward the tail gunner's position. An acrid smell bit into my nostrils and I realized it was smoke. Blattner shouted into the intercom, 'The whole rear of the plane is in flames!'

"I looked down between my knees and saw smoke swirling into the compartment. I waited to hear the pilot's voice through the intercom, but he didn't respond. Blattner returned to our compartment, unable to reach Kohn in the thickening smoke.

The air quickly grew unbreathable, grating against my windpipe and making me cough. Thick, black smoke rolled around me."

"What was going through your mind at this point?" I asked.

"I was afraid we would fall to the earth. I had a picture in my mind of the fire eating all the way through the tail section and chopping the plane into two pieces, way up there in the sky. I heard the bomb bay doors creak open and felt the plane bounce upwards a little as the bombs fell clear of the plane; the bombardier had released them into the Indian Ocean so the fire wouldn't set them off. A queasy feeling of weightlessness told me the plane was descending quickly toward the ocean. Looking up through the bubble, I saw the other bombers in the formation rising above us and receding into the distance, continuing toward the target.

"Below me the navigator, Bob Leffert, entered the gunners' compartment from the tunnel that followed the length of the plane over the bomb bays. He said, 'The intercom is dead, so Townsend sent me back here to tell you we're going to ditch. We need to get into position for a crash landing.'

"Leffert told us later he'd witnessed a spirited debate in the cockpit between the commander, Townsend, and the checkout pilot, Welch, about what to do. Welch wanted to bail out, in fact copilot Ed McClendon got so far as to drop the nose wheel so the cockpit crew could jump out through the nose wheel door. But Townsend overruled Welch and decided to land the plane in the water. This was despite the fact that nobody had ever successfully ditched a B-29. The plane always broke in half in the midsection, right about where I sat, and disappeared beneath the waves in seconds, taking the crew with it."

"What did you think about the decision to ditch?" I asked.

"I was glad for it," Harper said. "If we had bailed out, we'd have been scattered across miles of ocean, with very little chance of anybody finding us. This way, whatever happened we would go through it together."

"What did you have to do to prepare for ditching?"

"I climbed down from the central fire control pedestal, which was a wide, round metal stand with a platform that supported my rotating chair. I sat with my back against the bomb bay access door, and my legs pointing toward the pedestal, my knees slightly bent. My eyes stung and watered. Leffert sat down next to me. Breathing became a struggle, and I started to choke. I wondered if I'd last until the plane hit the water. The next thing I knew an oxygen mask pressed against my face, and I took in a wonderful breath of clean, soothing air. I saw Leffert next to me, waiting for his turn. I filled my lungs with air, and when I saw Leffert start to gag, I gave the mask back to him and watched his face light up with relief as the clean air washed through his body. We shared the mask back and forth all the way down.

"The smoke grew so thick I could no longer see left gunner Blattner and right gunner James Farrell even though they were only feet away, waiting in the same compartment for impact. I heard the crash of shattering glass and realized one of the gunners had taken a fire-axe and smashed through the dome I usually sat under, hoping to clear out some of the smoke. It didn't help. I wished we had safety belts to hold us in place during the landing. I wondered about the tail gunner, but with the intercom dead and the rear of the plane in flames, we couldn't do anything to help him. We'd have to meet up with him in the water.

"The plane slammed into something unbelievably hard, convulsed horribly, and slammed into it again. The bomb bay access door blasted open, throwing me across the compartment like a rag doll. Water filled my world in an instant, surging around me at waist level, and sprayed through the compartment like a squall, drenching me. The central fire control pedestal snapped in two, and its top half rammed into the bulkhead where I'd been sitting just a second earlier."

Harper paused, deep in thought.

"Townsend dragged the tail in the water to slow the plane down. He was very skillful and set it down as easy as he could. It was still like hitting a brick wall, but he did a great job."

"What did you do next?"

"The one thing on my mind was to get out of the plane as fast as possible. I fought to get back on my feet. I could taste salt on my lips. The other men scrambled to find a way out. Everything was happening at once and it's kind of a blur to me now. But Leffert tried the radar room door, saw the tangled mess of equipment that had broken loose to block the way to the rear hatch, and turned back into our compartment, screaming, 'We can't go that way. Get the hell out of here now!'

"Blattner tried to climb up through the shattered scanning dome, but he stopped about halfway through and shouted, 'Help me out of here! I'm stuck!' The canteen hanging off his belt was snagged on the gun sight. Leffert gave a mighty swing of his fist and *flattened* the canteen, unsnagging it! That's what adrenaline will do for you. Once Blattner's feet disappeared through the hole I tried to go out the same way. But I had a slightly larger frame, and I couldn't fit through. So I stood there in the water a moment, looking for the next best way out. I really wanted to use the rear exit behind this compartment, but water and tangled equipment filled that section. I thought about it, and decided no. I couldn't bring myself to go under that water without knowing what I'd find back there or how long it would take.

"Then Leffert grabbed me and shouted, 'Take the tunnel, Harper!' I climbed into the round, padded tunnel that passed over the bomb bays toward the cockpit and crawled as fast as I could to the sunlight visible at the far end. Thank heavens, the water had not risen high enough to enter this tiny crawlspace. My back rubbed against the padding above me. For the second time in my life I had to hunt to find a way out of a crashed plane. This was not good for my claustrophobia.

"I made it into the front compartment, which was partially flooded, and climbed out the pilot's escape hatch. I'm pretty sure I was the last man off the plane. I jumped into the ocean, went under the surface and bobbed back up to see the majestic bomber floating intact, its four propellers and high, curved tail sticking up out of the water. The impact had twisted the tips of the propeller blades back almost 90 degrees.

"I heard the voices of the other crewmembers behind the wing, which floated at water level. I climbed up onto its leading edge and crossed over to the trailing edge, and found the crew gathering in two bobbing life rafts. James Farrell, the right gunner, sat in one of the rafts and I wondered how he'd gotten there because I hadn't seen him get out. Bob Leffert also sat in a raft, apparently unaware of the gruesome lacerations he had on both shins. He'd cut himself while climbing through the shattered plexiglass dome. Two men helped me aboard a raft, and I collapsed, glad to be out of the water."

"What happened to the tail gunner?" I asked, afraid I already knew the answer. The way Harper looked away and lowered his voice was informative.

"We quickly paddled the rafts back around the horizontal stabilizer to look for him. It was a shocking sight. The fire had consumed a large section of the tail, rudder, and stabilizers. I mean those sections were gone. Burned away. Vaporized. The tail gunner's compartment was an incinerated, empty shell. Sig Kohn was missing. We scanned the waves behind the plane, but saw no sign of him.

"Somebody asked, 'Do you think he bailed out, or did the fire get him?' and another man replied, 'If the fire got him, there's absolutely nothing left of him.' We never found out for sure.

"The *Maiden U.S.A.* showed no signs of sinking any time soon, so we tied our rafts to the left wingtip and waited. I hoped the plane would hold together and stay afloat, because with it sitting there next to us we'd be much easier to spot from the air. With the checkout pilot along for the ride, but the tail gunner missing, we had eleven men on two five-man rafts. I got to ride on the raft that held six men."

"Did you have a radio?" I asked.

He nodded. "That was our first order of business, to try to make radio contact with somebody. So we began our long, frustrating torture of wrestling with survival equipment that simply didn't work as advertised. Our emergency kit included a 'Gibson Girl' radio—"

"What's that?" I asked.

"Oh, that's right, that was before your time. A 'Gibson Girl' was a lady who had a voluptuous figure with an extremely narrow waistline. The radio was named after them because of its curved shape, which allowed a person to clutch it between his legs and hold it steady while cranking the handle to send out a signal. It needed an aerial antenna to get out a signal. We had a balloon and a hydrogen generator. In theory, if we inserted the tip of the generator into the water, the generator would fill the balloon with hydrogen, and the balloon would rise into the air, carrying the antenna with it. In practice, the balloon did inflate but it just floated pathetically on top of the water. It was too weak to lift the antenna.

"Next we tried the box kite, but after assembling the kite eleven grown men working together couldn't get the kite to fly." He shook his head ruefully.

"But we didn't give up. We rigged the oars together and lashed the antenna to the end, and men in both rafts held the oars up, hoisting the antenna as high as we could. Then Capt. Townsend started cranking the handle. No signal went out. I could see Townsend was getting frustrated. He cranked harder, but still no signal. Townsend kept cranking harder and harder until the handle jammed. He gave it a real good crank to loosen it and the damn thing broke off in his hand! He tossed it into the ocean, firing off a string of curses."

"You must have been pretty upset," I said astutely.

He nodded. "That was when I started to comprehend how isolated we truly were. We bobbed up and down in two tiny little rafts on the endless surface of the ocean, with nothing but the B-29 to keep us company."

"What were you and the other men saying to each other?"

"We started to talk about our situation, what best to do. One of the men asked, 'Do you think anybody heard the SOS Howard sent out before we ditched?' and another asked, 'Think the Japs are out looking for us?' The right gunner, James Farrell, was moaning in severe pain. He'd been thrown around pretty hard by the impact. I remember them saying he might have a broken back.

"We floated helplessly next to the plane for several hours, waiting for something to happen. I just sat there in kind of a daze. Suddenly gunfire cracked in my ears, snapping me back to alertness. My heart pounded and we all started looking around.

"'What is that?' somebody asked. 'Who's shooting?' We didn't see anybody out there but us. There it went again. It sounded just like a bullet ricocheting. Sharp, threatening sounds. We heard it again and again. It took us a while to realize the sounds were coming from the plane, and it wasn't gunfire at all. The plane was popping its rivets!"

"You're kidding," I said.

"The waves had been buffeting, stretching, and pulling the airframe for hours, and now the forces at work on her were ejecting rivets like machine gun bullets. The little missiles flew in every direction, and before long they started splashing in the water around our rafts. I started to worry this might not be the best place to be right now. Then, sure enough, a rivet ricocheted off our raft's rubber skin. That was enough for us. Somebody shouted, 'We need to get out of here!'

"We untied the rafts as fast as we could and paddled to a safer distance. From there we watched the plane struggle to hold together. Still she resisted sinking.

"Then I heard a very welcome droning in the distance and turned to see a B-29 approaching at low altitude. She was the *Lady Marge*, one of the bombers returning from the mission to Rangoon. She circled overhead and dropped cans of fresh water and K-rations, along with a note that told us our position had been reported and help was on the way. Of course, there was no telling how long it would take for help to arrive. But thanks to the extra supplies we didn't have to worry about imminent death from starvation or thirst. The *Lady Marge* and all the other bombers roared on into the distance and disappeared.

"I felt the wind shift and looked back at the *Maiden U.S.A.* I sensed the strain would be more than she could bear. The plane dipped its nose under, stuck its tail in the air and slipped beneath the waves in four seconds. And we were alone."

"Did the plane make a lot of noise as it went under?"

"No, it was surprisingly quiet. Some equipment floated back up to the surface and we found more emergency kits. We cut up a parachute and covered our bodies with the pieces to protect our skin from sunburn. The other men wrapped smaller pieces of parachute around their heads, but I didn't have to do that because, for some reason, I was the only crew member who kept his cloth flight helmet on when we abandoned the plane.

"We took off our shoes to avoid damaging the rafts and settled down to wait for the promised rescue. A couple of the men tried to use the fishing gear in the survival kit, mostly to pass the time and keep their minds off things, but that equipment proved useless too. The wind strengthened, the water grew choppy, and a lot of the men got seasick.

"Finally night fell, and in the darkness we heard a plane fly high overhead. We immediately started to debate whether we should send up a flare. It was risky, because Japanese territory was only 100 miles away. We had no way of knowing who was in that plane. But some of the men said we needed to get off these rafts as soon as possible, even if it meant capture. Capt. Townsend decided to go ahead and do it. The flare shot up into the sky and floated slowly down, but the pilot of the plane either didn't notice or didn't care.

"By the next morning I was wondering whether I'd ever get off this little raft. We had no room to move, and nothing to do. At the other end of my raft, Bill Blattner, the left gunner, had a survival knife out for some reason and accidentally stuck the blade right through the skin of the raft. Air whistled out of one of the raft's three compartments, and the end of the raft began to collapse."

"Why in the world did he have a knife out?" I asked in disbelief.

"I don't know." Harper shook his head, looking downward. "No legitimate reason."

"What did you do?"

"At first we cussed him out pretty good, called him all kinds of foul names, asked him, 'Are you trying to kill us all?' Then we realized we needed to save the raft! The men at that end fumbled with the repair kit, all the while shouting at Bill."

"Were you able to help with the repairs?"

"No, I couldn't do anything but watch. I was at the other end, and I had no room to move, we were packed in like sardines. I saw a flurry of hands as they worked desperately to patch the hole. Somebody kept shouting, 'Fix it! Fix it!' It made my skin crawl and my hair stand up on end to think of being dumped into that ocean with nowhere to go. I hugged that raft pretty tight. It was the only thing separating me from that water. I looked over at the men on the other raft, but there was nothing they could do either. I just tried to avoid looking at the water that was lapping against the raft only inches away. I wanted more than anything not to end up treading water in it again.

"Someone spread glue on a rubber patch and they placed the patch over the hole. They pumped air into the raft and we watched to see what would happen. The part of the patch covering the hole stretched like an inflating balloon and broke. The raft continued to sag.

"My heart threatened to hammer its way through my chest. The men tried again with the same results, growing more and more frantic. There was no room for us on the other raft. We had to have this one.

"After several tries someone hit upon the idea of using several patches, one on top of the other. We used the pump again, watching desperately. This time, it held."

"Wow," I said. "What did you say to Blattner then?"

"We really let him have it. Some of the men got pretty rude. But Blattner was beside himself with guilt, you know. He felt just as bad about it as anybody else did."

"Can you tell me specifically what they said to him?" I prodded.

Harper shrugged, smiled coyly, and glanced away, unwilling to repeat the words. "We said about what you'd expect, I guess," was all he would say. "He wasn't very popular for a while."

"What else happened that day?"

"That made for an exciting morning, but once we had that crisis behind us, time seemed to slow to a halt. We just floated there. Boredom and depression took hold of all of us. I wondered why one of the Navy's Catalina patrol planes didn't come out to pick us up. It was taking an awfully long time for somebody to come get us."

"How rough was the sea?"

"We had three-foot seas. It didn't seem to me to be too rough to land a flying boat, but maybe it was. Some of the men tried again with the fishing gear but still didn't have any luck. We still had supplies of food and water, but we just couldn't help dwelling on why nobody had come out to rescue us. We looked for things to talk about to keep our minds busy, and we started speculating about what caused the fire."

Harper looked grim. "We think Sig Kohn might have been smoking back there and started the fire that killed him. We don't know that for a fact. But we suspect that's what happened."

For a long moment he said nothing, distracted by some distant memory.

"I thought that day would never end. Nothing to do, nowhere to go, just sitting there under the sun. But sometime after dark, I heard a commotion among the other men and looked up to see searchlights far off in the distance. We debated what to do again. 'They might be Japs! Do we put up a flare or not?'

"We could hear boat motors getting closer. But we were so close to Japanese territory, the boats could easily be the enemy. But Capt. Townsend said we couldn't stay out there forever. Farrell needed medical attention for his back, and Leffert for the lacerations on his legs. The captain made his decision and fired the flare gun, and we waited.

"The boats rushed toward us and came to a stop right in front of us, shining their searchlights in our eyes. Townsend yelled, 'Who are you?'

"And we heard a voice with a British accent say, 'The Royal Indian Navy!'

"These motor launches were tiny boats, maybe 35 feet in length, but they looked grand as battleships to us. Their only armament was one two-pound gun mounted on each stern. Those crews took a big risk patrolling that close to

Japanese-held shores to find missing airmen. The men on one of the boats helped me climb aboard, and a sailor pushed a steaming mug of tea into my hands.

"I met a man on the boat named Frank Worth, a combat photographer from London who came along for the ride. He couldn't get pictures of the actual rescue in the dark, so he asked us all to re-enact it the next morning. So we got back in the rafts and the Indians pulled us back aboard the boats again, this time with the camera rolling. Worth made a newsreel out of it that showed in theaters in India."

A sly smile grew on his face. "Care to see it?" he asked softly.

"You've got it?" I asked, excitement creeping into my voice.

"Yes. I've kept in touch with him, and he sent me a copy last year. I can play it for you right here on my computer."

I eagerly left my seat and stood behind him, watching over his shoulder as he clicked the mouse. A small window popped open on the screen and I saw, in white block letters superimposed over a globe, the words "Indian News Parade." Martial sounding music blared. The next screen displayed the title, "DRAMATIC RESCUE IN ENEMY WATERS BY THE ROYAL INDIAN NAVY."

Then, a high-pitched, fast-paced narrator's voice with a sharp British accent began the story:

"*Sailing with the RIN on night patrol, Midshipman Worth got these close up pictures of the rescue of American airmen.*" A B-24 filled the screen. "*A Liberator bomber probes through the night,*" the narrator said. "*While aboard ship, every man is alert. Ship and aircraft both signal that they see something.*" The camera closed in on a sailor scanning the sea with binoculars.

"*Up go flares, revealing at last the lost airmen, who for three days were the object of a relentless search.*" The rafts came into view on the water, far in the distance. "*In tiny rubber dinghies, the airmen were small enough to be hidden in the trough of a wave.*

The alertness of the RIN has saved them from a slow and terrible death on the waters."

We watched the flickering black and white images as the two rafts floated up beside the Indian patrol boats, which were shockingly small. They must have been crowded on the trip back to shore. The airmen waved happily at their rescuers.

"Their spirits are high," the narrator intoned, *"probably with relief at their rescue. But they've not got the strength to climb aboard unaided. Willing hands help them in."* The sailors pulled the haggard-looking airmen aboard. The Americans wore strips of cloth around their heads.

"Look!" Harper said, his voice hushed. "There I am. That's me, the only one wearing his flight helmet." He pointed at a figure obscured behind other men. The young Harper came into full view, grinning from ear to ear as an Indian sailor grabbed his hand and pulled him off the raft. The flight helmet made him easy to spot among all the heads wrapped in parachute cloth.

"Hot coffee sets the blood once more coursing through their veins," the narrator continued. *"They've got an amazing story to tell, and the most exciting part for them is their rescue at a moment when they'd made up their minds they had made their last trip."* The camera followed one of the boats as it headed off toward the horizon. *"Once again, the little ships of the RIN have done a big job, and they've done it in true ... naval ... style!"* With that resounding finish, the screen faded to black.

"That's really something," I said, feeling connected to a distant era. I'd seen black and white newsreels before, films so ancient surely they had nothing in common with the present. But now I had watched one while the subject breathed next to me. This wasn't just abstract talk about history. World War II sat right in front of me.

"Want to watch it again?" he asked, grinning up at me.

I nodded. "Absolutely."

Afterwards he continued his story. "The boats carried us north to a British base in northern Burma. Admiral Louis Mountbatten's flagship was anchored there, and so was a hospital ship. James Farrell and Bob Leffert ended up on the hospital ship for treatment, but the rest of us got wined and dined like royalty on Mountbatten's ship before we returned to Dudkhundi! Those two were pretty sore about missing that." He laughed.

"Since the plane we ditched was the checkout pilot's, my crew still had our own perfectly good B-29. Before long we took off on our second mission. Leffert had rejoined the crew by then."

"Did your B-29 have a nickname?" I asked.

"No. Unlike a lot of American bombers, ours never had a name. Leffert tried a couple of times to get us to agree on one, but we never could reach a consensus. He wanted to call her the *Maiden U.S.A.* after the plane we ditched, but it never happened."

"Tell me about your second mission."

"The target was Bangkok, Siam. We reached the initial rendezvous point a few minutes too late and missed joining up with our squadron. So Capt. Townsend joined formation with the next squadron coming up behind and said we'd go drop our bombs with them instead.

"The formation approached a huge rail yard. I heard the bomb bay doors creak open and felt the plane float upward as the bombs fell. Capt. Townsend banked the plane, and I got a clear view of the railroad tracks and railcars going up in smoke and flame below us."

"Did Japanese fighters attack you?"

"I was watching for enemy fighters but saw none during the bombing run. For that matter, I saw very little flak. But after we finished the run, I heard the bombardier shout a warning from up front, and I looked up to see several Zeros swooping in on the formation, straight ahead. They seemed to be focusing on my plane. Sure enough, they were! They came in one after the other. At least four. Maybe six. I swiveled in my chair, aiming my sight at the first fighter, and the two top turrets followed my movement. I fired a burst at it, and it zoomed down below my plane, where I couldn't see it.

"In the back of my mind I could hear the bombardier, Joe Evans, shouting something into the intercom, but I didn't know what he was talking about. I didn't have time to think about it, because I already had the second plane in my sights. I fired again, and by the time it passed by I was already aiming at the third plane. I don't know why they came at us in a straight line like that. Evans kept shouting things, he was real excited about something, but I was concentrating too hard to pay attention.

"I don't remember all the details of the battle. It became a blur. I would aim, fire, swivel, aim, fire. No time to think or keep score.

"Then a Zero came in from high at 2 o'clock, aiming its nose at our fuselage and heading right toward me. I stared right into its prop and gun barrels and fired the guns. The Zero kept coming, streaking incredibly close with muzzles flashing. It shot holes in the skin of the bomber, running from just behind the cockpit down the length of the tunnel towards me. At the end of the trail of machine gun bullets, a 20mm explosive shell punched through the plane three feet in front of my bubble and exploded. My chest took a big wallop and shrapnel sprayed up and down my left side, from my ankle up into my crotch and along my arm. It turned my elbow into a bloody pulp. The Zero screamed directly overhead, no more than thirty feet away."

Harper spoke more and more slowly and softly as he ventured into this part of the tale. "I don't remember a whole lot about what happened next," he said.

"What's the next thing you do remember?"

"I was lying flat on my back on the floor. The other gunners must have pulled me down from the pedestal. At first I thought I was lying in the bunk in the radar compartment, but in fact someone just put a cushion under my head. My back felt wet. I vaguely remember Frank Quinn and Bill Blattner hovering over me, telling me things like 'You're gonna be OK.' They dumped a lot of sulfa powder on my wounds. I was bleeding a lot.

"Bob Leffert came back through the tunnel and said, 'The damned intercom is out again.' Then he saw me. Here's where Leffert's version of the story and mine are a little different. Leffert says he found Bill Blattner holding a morphine syringe with a shaky hand, trying to work up the courage to stick it in my leg, but he was afraid he'd hurt me and couldn't bring himself to do it. Leffert says he looked down at my shredded leg and told Blattner, 'He's in so much pain already he won't give a damn about a needle!' and he grabbed it and jabbed it in me."

"What's your version of the story?" I asked.

Harper shook his head. "I don't remember them *giving* me any morphine. If they did, it didn't help with the pain one bit."

"What else do you remember?"

"I floated in and out of consciousness a lot. I felt them doing things to help me, like wrapping the wounds on my left leg in gauze. Leffert says they didn't have to cut off the pant leg because it was already missing. They reassured me and tried to keep me comfortable. After a while my bleeding slowed down and Leffert said, 'Looks like the shrapnel didn't hit any arteries.'

"I remember Leffert asked me, 'Does your chest hurt, Charles?' and I thought about it and said, 'Well, yes, as a matter of fact it does.' I looked down to see the front half of my flak jacket blown off, with bits of metal visible inside. Leffert says the 20mm shell hit me square in the chest."

"What else do you remember?"

"I woke up in a long, unfamiliar room full of beds. I couldn't move my left arm. I looked down and saw a cast on it. Wounded men lay in bed after bed, and doctors and nurses moved back and forth. I had no idea where I was, but people spoke in British accents. I heard people calling the nurses 'Sister,' and thought it was strange; to me the word 'sister' was a casual, slangy thing, not something you'd say to a nurse.

"Someone, a doctor or a nurse, told me I was at Cox's Bazaar, a British base in northern Burma. My crew had dropped me off there for medical treatment before continuing on to Dudkhundi. I found out that while I was unconscious the British doctors removed a large number of metal fragments from my body."

"How did you like the British hospital?"

"Didn't care for it. They served the worst food I ever ate in my life, powdered eggs and such that I simply could not eat. The only thing they had that I could get down was canned tomatoes and Jello. I begged for a transfer to the American hospital in Calcutta, and after about two weeks I persuaded them to let me go. The best thing about returning to an American base was that I got to have a 'Co-Cola' in a little six-ounce bottle. I had a fellow go over to the PX to buy six bottles for me! That was a treat.

"I eventually returned to Dudkhundi, still recuperating. My left arm was in bad shape. Even now I can't bend it all the way. Doctors have been removing shrapnel from my body for the rest of my life. The most recent operation was in 1998, when an X-ray revealed nineteen fragments still inside me."

"Did you go on any more missions?"

"It took me quite a while to recuperate. But rather than just lying around the barracks I decided to help out at the base's gunnery school, running 16mm training films of enemy aircraft while gunners tracked them in simulators. Then I found out the 444th Bomb Group would soon move to a new base at Tinian in the Mariana Islands. From there the planes would be able to reach mainland Japan and even Tokyo itself. The CO had to decide what to do with me, so he called me into his office to talk.

"I knew the CO had something weighing on his mind. It was common knowledge on the base that he'd already forced one young man to go back to his crew, and that young man went out on a mission and didn't come back. The commander knew I'd gotten off my duff to help out at the gunnery school even though I wasn't fully recovered from my wounds.

"He asked me, 'Well, what do you want to do, Harper?'

"I said, 'I don't know, sir. What do you think we ought to do?'

"He thought about it a moment and said, 'I'll tell you what, Harper. You can do one of two things. You can go back to your crew and go to Tinian with us, or you can go home.'

"I thought about it real hard. I'd had a lot of close calls. I already had two Purple Hearts. An offer like this did not come along very often.

"So I said, 'Sir, I'm not trying to get out of anything. But if it's really all the same to you, I think I'll go home.'"

He fell silent, staring off into space.

"There's something I want to ask you about," I said. "Bob Leffert, the navigator, says you shot down at least four Japanese fighters before you got hit. But you didn't make any mention of that. Is it true?"

"Oh," he said, shaking his head dismissively, "everything happens so fast in that kind of situation. The fighter's only in your line of sight for a few seconds before it passes by, and you immediately look for the next one to shoot at. Everything's a blur. I honestly can't tell you I shot down any fighters. I don't even know for sure that I managed to *hit* any."

Leffert had told me the bombardier, Joe Evans, saw the planes go down in flames one after the other and shouted about it into the intercom. But Harper had nothing more to say about it. Who knows what really happened? I had seen before how two men could experience the same battle and come away with irreconcilably different memories. If Harper really did single-handedly save his crew from a formation of enemy fighters, he felt no need to take credit for it.

I reached forward and turned off the tape recorder.

"Thank you," I said.

He showed me around the house; I followed slowly as he guided himself with the walker. In one room a framed Purple Heart hung on the wall. In another room hung a cloth map of Japan and surrounding waters Harper had taken from the raft. His wife brought out a leather jacket that bore a bright white patch on the back with big, bold Chinese lettering.

"This message was in case we had to bail out over China," Harper said. "It says something along the lines of, 'Don't shoot. I am an American. I am on your side.'"

He looked at the patch skeptically and remarked, "If you ask me, it just gave them a good target."

I remembered to ask if I could borrow a photograph of him from the war years. He found a framed portrait of a handsome, dark-haired man in uniform and handed it to me. The years had wrought great changes, and I had to look for the resemblance. But it was there.

We stepped momentarily onto the redwood deck in his back yard, overlooking a pool. "I built this deck a long time ago," he said. He pointed to the two square openings in the center of the deck struggling to hold their own against the inexorable growth of the oak trees they contained. The thickening trunks were starting to push the redwood frames around the holes out of place.

"I planted those trees in the early sixties," Harper said, frowning at the way they strained against their confinement.

"Seemed like I left plenty of room for those scrawny little things when I built the deck around them. Look at them now."

I thanked him again for taking the time to talk to me. He saw me to the door and I walked out toward the street. Down the street I saw a carefree girl no more than seven riding in circles on a bicycle. I glanced down at the smiling face in the portrait, and the thought struck me that the difference in age between Charles Harper and myself was more years than I had been alive.

Charles Harper
today

Matias Rodriguez
Kerrville

"I never expected to be in the war," Matias Rodriguez told me in his relaxed and gentle voice. We sat in his comfortable living room in the peaceful Hill Country town of Kerrville, where eight generations of the Rodriguez family have lived since 1829. The Baptist minister's son-in-law, Danny, sat nearby, listening curiously, and his wife listened from the kitchen.

"When Japan attacked Pearl Harbor, I was only sixteen. I figured the war would be over by the time I was old enough to serve. But it was just getting started. The minute I graduated from high school I went into the service. That was June 1943. I joined the 28th Infantry Division, which was made up mostly of older men from the Pennsylvania National Guard, and I was assigned to the 110th Infantry Regiment as a medic.

"In April 1944, General Eisenhower came to inspect our division at Swindon, England. He looked us over and decided we were up to the task of making the Normandy landing on the first day. We were all set to do it. But for some reason he changed his mind two weeks before the invasion and sent the 29th in our place. I consider that providence, because I might not be here to do this interview with you if I had made that landing.

31

Matias Rodriguez in 1943.

"We crossed over the channel on D+23 and saw the destruction on Normandy Beach. We traded places with the division that had made the landing for us, the 29th, at St. Lo. They had been almost totally wiped out. I remember seeing three dead Germans lying in the street my first day there. We took over the 29th Division's positions at night so the Germans wouldn't see our movements.

"I was as green as you can be, nineteen years old. Didn't know a thing. A buddy and I heard a plane go over, didn't think anything of it, didn't even look up as we walked across a field. And then we heard this long whistle. A German plane dropped a bomb right over us. It hit right there in the middle of the field, picked me and the other guy up, and hurled us through the air. I fell to the ground, shaking all over."

Rodriguez' voice became faint and he averted his eyes. His son-in-law perked up, watching him intently. "I heard my buddy making an awful gurgling noise. I didn't understand the meaning of the noise, so I crawled over to him. Shrapnel had hit him all over, cut his belly open, and spilled out his insides.

"I was lucky to be a medic rather than a combatant," Rodriguez said softly. "I did my best to help the wounded. It was tough, seeing those boys I couldn't help." He shook his head solemnly, looking away from me again. "They died in my arms and I just couldn't help them. The ones that survived had their arms and legs all torn up. All we could do there was give them the most basic first aid, just try to keep them alive a little longer, take their names, and send them back to the field hospitals.

"I believe in providence, you know. I'll tell you why. We were there in the Hurtgen Forest..."

"You were in the Battle of Hurtgen?" I exclaimed. I hadn't known this. The little-known bloodbath in November and December of 1944 wasted American lives in an unnecessary offensive through a thick, treacherous forest. The thought of sitting next to someone who had been there made the hair stand up on the back of my neck.

"Yes, I was there."

"Can you ... can you describe it?" I hoped I was not asking too much.

After a time, Rodriguez said, "Hurtgen Forest was beyond words. You can't put a battle like that into words. The destruction, the chaos ... I saw guys blown up, and there was nothing I could do. In two weeks I learned the sound of every tank, every gun the Germans had. It was an amazing thing to see, artillery shells disintegrating those huge trees. Men lying there wounded, screaming and hollering. Figures advancing toward you in the woods. Tanks coming around the bend. Man-to-man combat, desperate, one-on-one fighting. So much happening all at once, I can't begin to describe it."

By now I had learned to recognize when a veteran would go no farther, so I resisted the temptation to press for more details. Instead I waited for him to resume the story.

"Four of us spent fifteen days crouching in one little foxhole, trying not to get killed. One day I just had to get out, to relieve myself, you know. I went behind a tree. It was snowing, it had snowed two weeks without stopping, every tree was white. Pardon me for saying this, but I had my pants down." His face reddened slightly.

"All of a sudden I heard an 88mm shell whistling and I knew, I just *knew* I was in big trouble. I grabbed my pants and dashed back to the foxhole, but I couldn't get there in time, so I hit the ground. That shell hit six feet in front of me, and I stared at it, waiting for it to explode.

"It was a dud."

Everybody laughed, relieved. I understood why he became a preacher after the war.

"How did you deal with the stress of a battle like that?" I asked, riveted.

"I did my job and that was it. Whatever I could do to help those boys. I tuned out everything that was happening around me as much as I could.

"Meanwhile, the Germans were accumulating all their best troops and weapons for one last effort to break us, get to our ports, and take our supplies. On Dec. 16, the first day of the Battle of the Bulge, they took me prisoner.

"I was in Clerf, a little Belgian village near the borders of Luxembourg, Germany, and France. Our battalion headquarters had set up in a railroad station. I was there with fifteen other men, including Bernie, a Jewish boy, and an Italian Catholic lieutenant named Dellagardi. The three of us, a Jew, a Catholic, and a Baptist, were always together, and we were together when we got captured. Not a shot had been fired for weeks, and all of a sudden the Germans threw everything they had at us and just ran over the Americans. Our division was out there getting wiped out. The Germans captured almost entire regiments. Our captain told us they were making a last, desperate push.

"The Germans overran the whole village that night. A whole bunch of them burst into the station and surrounded us. It happened so quickly, we didn't even put up any resistance. Our infantry was already gone. I had a German pistol I had found, and the captain whispered to me, 'Get rid of that! Don't let them see you with any captured German equipment.' So I hid it.

"The next morning they started us on the march back behind the lines. Hundreds of us walked four days in the snow, with no food. The only way we got water was by putting snow in our mouths. But it's amazing how you can survive. Survival is the strongest thing in a human being.

"On the fifth day they put us aboard a train and took us deep into Germany. About that time the weather cleared up, allowing our aircraft to go up, and one of the first things our pilots did was attack German trains, trying to stop the flow of supplies.

Our own planes strafed the train we were riding on, killing some of our boys. I got lucky, they didn't hit me.

"The Germans took us to a camp at Ziegenhain, outside Kassel, where we stayed until the end of the war. The Germans starved us almost to death. I got down to 110 pounds. They only fed us a piece of black bread and a bowl of soup every day. We got very weak, very thin, especially the boys who'd been kind of big beforehand. I remember one guy named Potts who was originally 220 pounds, and he went down to 120 pounds. Just skin and bones.

"One thing that helped me survive was, I never smoked. The Red Cross packages we got always had cigarettes along with the food. The other soldiers saw cigarettes as something to smoke, but I saw them as money to spend. I used to give my cigarettes to a German, and he'd bring me powdered milk and dried food.

"One night the Germans took us out on a work detail to fill bomb craters at a rail yard. I had four Chesterfields in my pocket; you're too young to remember those, but they were a type of cigarette that was very popular with the GIs. I said to a guard, 'Cigarette?' He said, 'Ja, Ja!' And took it. The next night we went out to the rail yard again and here comes this German guard with a big cheese sandwich for me! We got to be sort of buddies. That helped me a lot.

"All my buddies were addicted to nicotine. It's the hardest thing to get away from, I don't care what anybody says. Once there was a cigarette butt on the ground, and two men saw it at the same time and dived for it. 'I saw it first! No, it's mine!' And I'm not exaggerating, they got into a fistfight over this little butt. Things like that happened, even between buddies. Addiction will do that to you."

"How did your captors treat you?" I asked.

"They didn't beat us up or anything like that. Matter of fact, the Germans liked us better than the English did. But they were strict. I remember two boys broke into the kitchen. They hit the guard over the head with an axe handle and knocked him out cold. The Germans used dogs to trace them back to the American section of the camp. They took all 110 of us outside, lined us up, and set a machine gun right in front of us. They said, 'It was two of you. If you don't come out, we'll gun you down.' And these two guys stepped out. They put them in solitary confinement. If the guard had died they probably would have killed them.

"The camp had four towers with 50mm machine guns. One night a boy from Pittsburgh tried to escape, and a German guard shot him, just riddled him with bullets. The next day an American plane flew over our camp. We waved handkerchiefs at him until he realized it was a prison camp. He passed over real close, checking us out. A German guard took his machine gun and tried to knock the plane down. Big mistake. That pilot circled back, headed right for that tower and dropped a bomb. Killed thirteen prisoners, including two Americans.

"The night before we were liberated we could hear artillery and tanks fighting nearby. The ranking American prisoner, a colonel from the 101st Airborne told us, 'Don't you leave the barracks tonight. Nobody goes outside. If you do, you're gonna get shot.' The next morning a big tank rolled into camp, smashed right through a gate, flattening the fence. We were liberated on April 2, 1945."

"Did your buddies survive?" I asked.

"Yes, they both made it. I don't see how Bernie survived, being Jewish. The Germans separated all the Jewish prisoners from us and I never saw them the whole time I was in camp. Another Jewish boy I knew by the name of Shapiro didn't make it out.

"We flew back to a hospital in France. One of the boys was so desperate to eat, the second night at that hospital he went down to the PX and ate doughnut after doughnut after doughnut, and he died. His system couldn't handle it.

"We got on a hospital ship to return home. Before we left some men came and told us, 'General Eisenhower would like to meet with you. He wants to interview some former POWs. Those of you who would like to stay for that, we'll put you on the next ship out.'"

"Did you meet him?" I asked eagerly.

He shook his head. "I said, 'I'm not waiting for anyone. Take me home!'"

Matias Rodriguez is now a Baptist minister in Kerrville.

Robert Louis Lanier
Sulphur Springs

It may be the most famous single moment of the war: six Marines pushing a proudly flapping American flag into the rocky summit of Mount Suribachi. That event, immortalized in a legendary photograph and an imposing monument, is recognizable even to those who know little else about World War II. I was excited to get the chance to talk to someone who was there and saw it happen.

"I sat waiting in the dark, surrounded by Marines, occasionally glancing up at the white-hot shells streaking overhead," Robert Lanier told me. "The battleships out there lit up the night every time they fired off a salvo.

"The captain of our company gathered us together to tell us our mission. We'd been speculating about it for weeks. He stood in the middle of a circle of us on the open deck of our LST (Landing Ship Tank). I knew there were a lot of other ships around us but had no idea how many."

I looked it up later. More than 800 ships took part in the invasion.

"The captain finally gave our destination a name," Lanier said. "And when he did, it was a place we'd never heard of. He said, 'Men, we're going to Iwo Jima,' and he told us this ugly little scrap of land was vital because it had airfields. Our bombers that got shot up over Japan and couldn't make it back to their

R.L. Lanier (center) with two buddies before the Iwo Jima landings.

base at Saipan needed a place to make emergency landings. It was Iwo or the ocean."

"Did the captain tell you what to expect when you hit the beach?" I asked.

"I remember him standing there speaking to us, outlined by moonlight. He reassured us the island had been bombed for weeks," Lanier said. "What defenders remained had dug in and were hiding from the bombing in their caves. Nobody knew how many still lived, but it couldn't be that many.

"He said we'd head in for the beach at daylight. He told us how we would go about capturing the airfields. My regiment, the 27th Marines, would cross the island to the other shore, turn north, and head for the airfields. The 28th Marines would

Christmas – 1944

"I'll be home for Christmas in 19??"

R.L. Lanier sent this picture home to his family in 1944.

cross the island at the same time and then turn south toward Mount Suribachi. Together we would cut the island in two."

"He made it sound so simple," I observed.

"And that's what I thought at the time," Lanier agreed. "I heard all this and said to myself, 'That doesn't sound like too big a deal.' After all, we had trained hard for months specifically for this day."

"So you felt ready for what was about to happen?"

"Yes, but I was young. I didn't really understand what was about to happen. It had taken long months of training, in the hills around San Diego and on the beaches of Hawaii, to bring the 5th Marine Division to this point. The training was hard, and it hardened us. The Marine Corps aimed to strip off the recruit's individuality until only a soldier remained. The Corps didn't want you having your own thoughts, it wanted its own thoughts filling your mind.

"I'll always remember one drill sergeant, his name was Fronfelter, who got into my face and shouted, 'Lanier, one person couldn't be as stupid as you are! You must be twins!' I sorely wanted to plaster the man. But I remembered the advice of a recruiter back home: 'Keep your nose clean, do what you're told, and you will survive boot camp.' So I survived. I wasn't very happy at the time, but now I think the training the Marines put me through was great."

"What kind of gear did you carry into battle?" I asked.

"I had a backpack carrying at least fifty pounds' worth of the bare necessities for survival: a poncho, a shovel for digging fox-holes, a canteen, some C rations to eat, hand grenades, and as much ammunition as I could carry. And I held the weapon I hoped was going to keep me alive: I was a BAR man. The BAR is the Browning Automatic Rifle, a heavy machine gun normally supported by a bipod. But we took off the bipod for this invasion to fool the Japs into thinking it was just an M-1 Garand. The BAR could fire one shot at a time, or it could empty its clip all at once, the perfect tool for mowing down infantry charges. I'd seen what the gun could do back in training and decided this was the weapon I wanted to carry into battle. Other men carried the M-1, which was highly accurate but was only a semi-automatic, which means only one bullet fired for each pull of the trigger. With the BAR, I felt I had a better chance of coming back alive."

"How did you pass the time waiting?"

"The men played cards and dominoes or read letters from home. Some of us curled up inside the amtracs, the amphibious vehicles, and slept. Others chatted about what they would do when they got home. All of us expected to return home, of course.

"The sun climbed up over the horizon the morning of Feb. 19, 1945, and we went in. I was in the first wave. Thirty of us crammed into an amtrac. I watched the little vehicle's rear doors close and heard the engine roar to life. The LST's rear doors swung open and the amtrac moved with a jerk, rolling out the back of the ship into the water. We left the protective cover of the ship and chugged in toward the shore.

"The amtrac was open to the sky, and the Navy men operating it warned us to keep our heads down or we'd have casualties before we ever reached the beach. I waited, focusing on the rear doors. Soon those doors would open and we would rush out around the rear of the vehicle."

"I always thought the landing craft opened in the front," I said.

"You're thinking of a Higgins boat," he said. "Those came in later waves, but we were in amtracs. So we had a few extra seconds of cover.

"Nobody spoke as we drew closer to shore. We heard enemy fire. Bullets whistled past and mortar shells screamed overhead and crashed into the water. Some landed pretty close. The noise grew louder every second.

"We were told to arm our weapons and get ready. The amtrac crunched against the shore, got traction, and rolled up into the sand. It stopped and I stared at the rear doors, ready to rush out and search for cover. The doors didn't open. Meanwhile I could hear the bullets and shells all around us. Still the doors didn't open.

"Finally one of the Navy men yelled, 'The sand is jamming the door! Get over the side ... now!' I didn't have to be told twice. We knew the amtrac was a sitting duck for Japanese artillery, and we didn't intend to hang around for their spotters to notice us. So we all bailed out. One boy put a leg over the side and started screaming that he'd been shot in the leg. I made it out, dropping six feet into the black sand, which shifted loosely under my feet. It was slow going in that sand. I struggled to move forward, but my boots sank and slipped."

"What was going through your mind?"

"One overwhelming thought: I had to keep moving and find some cover. It would be suicide to stay there in the open. Sand erupted into the air all around me. I looked around for shelter and found it in the craters that seemed to be everywhere because of the massive bombing our planes had done to the island. Marines crowded into every depression, trying to get organized. Enemy fire was intense. Time was of the essence; we had to make it inland before the next wave of Marines came in behind us, or we'd have total chaos with all those men trapped together on the beach.

"I lay in a crater with five or six other men, including my immediate superior, a corporal by the name of Hoffman. I'd trained with him for months. One minute Hoffman was speaking, alive, the next he was dead. A bullet smacked into his head between the eyes, right in front of me.

"One of the Marines yelled, 'There's a goddamn sniper shooting at us!' We got as low to the ground as we could, in case the sniper tried again. I was in shock, I couldn't believe

Hoffman was dead, couldn't believe one of us was already gone so quickly. We hadn't been on that island 15 minutes. How the hell did that Jap sniper manage it? Hoffman's eyes had been just barely sticking over the edge of our hole. If he'd moved slightly in either direction, that bullet would have hit *me*.

"How did it make you feel?" I asked.

Lanier thought about it. Even after all these years, the pain of the memory was evident in his voice. "I suppose it should have made me mad. After all, we were Marines, and we were supposed to react with fury at things like that. But at the time I was overcome with grief. I had to carry out the grim duty of spiking Hoffman's M-1 into the ground by the tip of its bayonet, removing the helmet from his head and hanging the helmet on the butt of the rifle. This would serve as a marker so corpsmen could later find the body and remove it from the beach."

I considered asking him to describe the scene more fully, but something in his voice made me think twice. He had to remove the helmet from the head of a man who'd been shot between the eyes with a high-powered rifle. It didn't take much imagination to realize how grisly it must have been.

"Did you say any words for him, or anything like that?" I asked.

"No. That was all we had time for. I didn't want to leave him there. It *hurt* to leave him there. But we had to keep moving."

"What did you do next?"

"Slowly, precariously, we began to move inland. We were fighting that awful sand as much as enemy fire. The men took turns advancing, rushing forward and then dropping to the ground to cover the next group that jumped up and pressed ahead."

"What was the island like?"

"There wasn't much to see. It was a wasteland. It was a sulfur island, in fact the name Iwo Jima means sulfur island, and the smells of sulfur and smoke from the explosions mixed in the air. The sun baked the sand so hot it burned my hands. The months of bombing had blasted away the trees and bushes until there was no natural cover to speak of, only charred, twisted stumps. And I saw no animals. Not even a bird. If birds ever lived there, the bombing thoroughly removed them.

"On the southern end was Suribachi, an ugly, extinct volcano, 546 feet high. Wherever we were on the island we could see it. Aside from that and the airfields to the north, the island didn't have much in the way of landmarks. You wouldn't think there could be an army of Japs out there, but they did a brilliant job of hiding themselves. Twenty thousand of them, armed with heavy artillery, mortars, Nambu machine guns, and rifles. They didn't have much food, but they were well stocked with ammunition."

"How much trouble did you have crossing to the other side of the island?"

"It was slow going. Time and time again the Japanese pinned us down. But tanks eventually started coming ashore, and the ones that managed to make it off the beach helped us break through. I always half-expected a bullet or a grenade to find me at any moment as I inched my way across the island. My perspective had changed drastically since before the landing, when I told myself it wouldn't be such a big deal!

"Japanese soldiers popped up everywhere. Strangely enough, some Japs seemed unaware an invasion was happening. They'd come up out of a hole in the ground, casual and routine, and find themselves facing U.S. Marines. We'd react quickly and shower them with bullets."

"Did you ever hit them?"

"I'm not sure," he said. "In those situations so many of us would fire, I never knew whether my bullet was the decisive one. I remember one Jap ambled out of a cave yawning, without his rifle, looking like he'd just been taking a nap. But he was a combatant. We shot him."

"How much progress did you make your first day?"

"It took almost the entire day to cross from the east shore to the west. When we got there, a lot of men went down to the beach and immediately got pinned down by Japanese machine gun fire coming from a pillbox. But I had stayed up off the beach behind cover, and I opened up with my BAR, sending a hail of bullets right into the pillbox. The machine gun fire stopped, at least temporarily, and the men scrambled back up off the beach. Once they'd found safer positions, they all started shooting at the pillbox. Then a tank arrived, and just to make sure the job was done, it torched the pillbox with napalm while we cheered.

"Now that we had achieved our first objective of splitting the island in two, we had the rest of the island to conquer. It was only eight square miles of land. Little did we know it would take more than a month.

"You know, it was strange enough in the daytime, with that slippery sand, the burnt landscape, and Japs sneaking around underground. But at night it got even stranger." He stopped, thinking about something.

"How do you mean?" I asked.

"At night, flares constantly flew over the island, lighting the ground and exposing enemy movements. I'd hear the taunting voices of Japanese soldiers floating over me as I tried to rest in my foxhole. In their Japanese accents, speaking in broken English, they would cry, 'Help me! I'm a Marine. I'm hurt. I need you to come get me.' Of course none of us ever fell for it.

"When that trick didn't work, the Japanese might resort to a banzai charge. That was when I came closest to Japanese soldiers. I'd stare out past the perimeter, straining to see what was going on out there. Figures would materialize from the darkness, twenty-five to fifty men at a time, and rush toward me and my buddies in our line of foxholes. I opened fire with my BAR, and the same would happen all up and down the line. I could see muzzle flashes dancing back and forth in the dark. The Japs moved in, hollering, twenty feet, fifteen feet, closer. Big men, not small like the stereotype. At least they looked big to me at the time.

"One Jap ran up within three feet of my foxhole and fell to the ground, so full of bullets he was dead when he landed. Then everything was quiet. But I didn't move. None of the Marines did. We didn't leave the safety of our foxholes to investigate. Only when the sun rose would we see the mass of Japanese bodies just outside our line."

"The charges must have frightened you quite a bit," I prodded.

"Yes," he said thoughtfully. "I knew damn well the Japanese men expected to die all along when they did it. Those charges were suicide missions, pure and simple. That was why the Japanese were so scary: their willingness, their *eagerness* to die. We Americans saw life as something precious, worth holding on to. The Japs saw it as something inconsequential, something to give up for their emperor. That scared me."

"With all this going on at night, did you manage to get any sleep?" I asked.

"I tried, but it was always interrupted. Nobody could tell where and when a Jap would emerge from the ground. Sometimes a Jap would appear in the midst of our foxholes and find everyone sound asleep. Defenseless. Exhausted and totally unaware. This Jap could do anything he wanted to us, and we could do nothing to stop him." He paused for effect.

"What happened?" I asked urgently.

"He'd steal food! Rather than open up with his weapon, kill as many of us as possible, he would steal food. The Japanese were in dire straits. They were starving."

"Did they get away with it?"

"Some did, some didn't. One time a Marine not far from my foxhole woke up just as a Jap was crawling away with the supplies he'd pilfered. The Marine shot him."

"I understand you saw the flag-raising on Suribachi," I said reverently.

"Yes, I watched it from my foxhole," he said. "It was a good distance away, but I had a clear view as those Marines pushed the pole into the ground and lifted it up. When that American flag appeared on top of the mountain, a cheer went up along our line, as if we were at a football game and somebody had scored a touchdown. It was a great morale booster. But we still had a long way to go to say we owned the island. Even Suribachi itself still swarmed with Japs. Three of the soldiers who raised the flag got killed in just a few days. Nobody was immune. Clearing out all the Japs would take until March 26.

"But I wouldn't be there to see it happen. On March 6, as we fought for every inch of ground just outside one of the airfields, a Japanese mortar shell swooped in right behind me and exploded. A jagged shard of hot metal the size of a quarter tore through the flesh of my neck and burrowed in.

"The pain was indescribable, but I didn't lose consciousness. I could talk and move around, but I was losing blood and I was definitely out of the battle. A superior pointed back behind the line and told me the aid station was somewhere in that general direction, maybe a mile or two. He said, 'We can't send anyone with you. We need all the help we can get.' And that was that. So I left my BAR with another soldier because it was so heavy and took his M-1 and set off to find the aid station with a jagged piece of metal sticking out of my neck.

"That terrain was difficult enough to walk through uninjured, but in my condition it was excruciating. Every time I took a step the shrapnel tore at my neck. With every jolt it seemed to dig deeper into my flesh. The blood loss was draining my strength. And I had no idea where I was going.

"I moved farther and farther from the security of my company, supposedly behind the lines, but the truth was this battle didn't *have* lines. Japs could pop up anywhere at any time. I spotted figures moving around now and then, sometimes American, sometimes Japanese. I saw weapons fire and had no idea who did the shooting. I moved from shellhole to shellhole, trying to stay under cover and avoid blundering into Japs. Occasionally I came across groups of Americans and asked them for directions to the aid station. A lot of times they had no clue. Sometimes they pointed vaguely in the direction I was already headed.

"As I moved from one crater to another, bullets whizzed right past me. I whipped up the M-1 and fired several times right back at the source. The shooting stopped. I scrambled away from there, breathing hard, expecting more bullets to come after me. But none did.

"I finally found the aid station, a large crater dug out to make room for cots and covered with a tent to keep the sun off. Four or five corpsmen worked on the wounded. One of them gave me a cot and told me a doctor would be along to pull out the shrapnel. So I waited."

"How many wounded men were at this aid station?"

"I saw about thirty. A lot of gunshot wounds. Men shot in the arms and legs. One man got shot through his helmet, and the bullet ricocheted around the helmet and lodged in the back of his neck. I saw a lot of shrapnel wounds, metal sticking out of limbs and torsos. I was the only one with metal sticking out of his neck.

"The doctor finally got to me and put something in my hand. I looked down and realized I was holding a tennis ball."

"A tennis ball?" I echoed.

"That's right. I thought, 'That's odd. What in the hell is a tennis ball doing in this god-forsaken place?'"

"What was it for?"

"The doc said, 'Squeeze that as hard as you can, because this is gonna hurt.' And he pulled the shrapnel slowly out of my neck. And let me tell you, he was right. He knew exactly what he was talking about. It hurt like *hell*. I squeezed the tennis ball so hard I thought it would split in two."

"Did you have any anesthetic?" I asked.

"No anesthetic, and I didn't pass out either. Unfortunately. I had no choice but to take the pain. Afterwards the doctor told me to try to sleep. What a joke. Aside from the pain, we were in the middle of a battle. The fact that this was an aid station gave us no protection against the explosions right outside the tent! I thought, 'Don't the Japs know they aren't supposed to be shooting around here? This is a hospital!'"

"Did you talk to any of the other wounded men?"

"Yes, we talked to take our minds off our wounds and the gunfire outside. The men talked about being glad to be alive, and how they hoped they would be sent back to the States. A lot of them did go back, because they were wounded too badly to fight again.

"The next day the corpsmen put me onto a C-47 transport plane to be airlifted to Guam, which had better medical facilities. As we waited to take off from a recently captured airfield, we saw a B-29 Superfortress that got shot up over Japan come in for an emergency landing. That plane would have had to ditch in the ocean if we hadn't been there on Iwo. We hadn't even won the battle yet and already we were saving aircrews."

By the end of the war, 2,251 bombers made emergency landings on the island. A lot of lives saved.

"How did the flight go?"

"The C-47 was filled with wounded men on stretchers. The flight seemed to last an eternity; all I could see out the window was water. It was my first time on an airplane. I was in pain the whole flight because the wound had become infected and my neck swelled up to twice its normal width. But once we got to Guam I finally got a blood transfusion, which I needed badly."

"How much time had passed between the time you got hit and the blood transfusion?" I asked.

"Almost two days. I recuperated there on Guam for a while, and then they sent me back to Hawaii. I was waiting on Oahu at the Royal Hawaiian Hotel when the survivors of my company came back weeks later, with the battle won."

R.L. Lanier (left) poses with buddy John Kernen in Hawaii in June 1945.

Lanier had narrowly survived the bloodiest battle in the history of the U.S. Marine Corps. It took the lives of 6,821 Marines and wounded 19,030 more. Of the 22,000 Japanese defenders, a thousand were taken prisoner. The rest died in battle.

"Of my company of 250 men, only 26 of us were fit to remain in the division for its next planned invasion: mainland

Japan," he said. "The rest either died on Iwo Jima or got sent back to the States because of the severity of their wounds."

"You would have had to land on mainland Japan?"

"That's right. Iwo Jima and later, Okinawa, showed us how deadly an assault on mainland Japan would be. But that was what we were going to do. My unit even knew its destination: Sasebo. Fortunately, it didn't happen. The atomic bomb made sure of that. Iwo Jima was my one and only battle.

"I've kept in touch with some of the other men over the years. Phone calls, Christmas cards, occasional reunions. I'm one of the last ten living men from my company," he said with a solemn tone.

"I haven't talked about the battle a whole lot. And now that I am, a lot of details I'd forgotten long ago have come back to me. It's been a little hard to go to sleep at night.

"But, I'm glad to do it."

R.L. Lanier today

*Didn't they know they weren't
supposed to shoot at me?*

James McKernon
Jones
Corpus Christi

While many were called up whether they wanted to go to war or not, other men eager to join the fight had trouble getting accepted into the service, and when they succeeded, they found the military less glamorous—and less organized—than expected. James McKernon Jones told me about how the Army overlooked a few important details before shipping him off to England.

"I wanted to volunteer and get in on the action, but the military wouldn't have me," Jones said. "You see, my left eye is real bad, the vision's only correctable to about 20-70. I kept getting rejected in the physical exams. But I didn't give up. I thought about all the people who had to serve and didn't want to. Surely the Army could use somebody who *wanted* in. There must be a job I could do, even with a bad eye. I tried again and again, and finally a doctor took pity on me and let me 'pass' the eye test.

"My father, a doctor, wanted me in a medical unit and he had connections, so he pulled strings to get me assigned to a unit at Camp Blanning, Georgia I traveled there with orders to join them, still wearing civilian clothes, but by the time I got

James McKernon Jones poses on the grounds
of his high school before shipping off to war.

there they'd already shipped out overseas! It was just one of those unavoidable things that happens when everything is cloaked in tight secrecy.

"The Army had to do something with me, and I found myself in what's called a 'repple depple' at Camp Kilmer, New Jersey: A replacement depot packed with bored men waiting for assignment. I still had no basic training, no uniform, no equipment. I was supposed to get all that stuff from the outfit I'd missed. I scrounged around some empty barracks vacated by GIs who'd already left to go overseas, and picked up enough clothing to get by. I joined in the drills with the rest of the men and worked the regular duty roster, waiting. But I had a problem. The units coming through the depot to fill up their ranks didn't request people by name, they requested them by their MOS number, their military occupational specialty, whatever skill they were specially trained for. GIs got their specialty in training. I'd never gone through basic training, so I didn't *have* a specialty.

"I could have spent the entire war stuck at that depot, lost in the shuffle. But my father pulled strings again. An outfit called the 52nd General Hospital came through the depot. Major Gordon Hoople, an officer in that unit, knew my father and requested me by name. Next thing I knew I was being shipped out to England even though the Army never gave me any training!"

"The Army sent you overseas without basic training?" I asked in disbelief. I'd never heard a story like that before. "Was that a common situation?"

"I think it was rare. During the whole war I only met one other person who never went through basic."

"How did you react to that?"

"I survived. I had fired guns plenty as a kid, and I picked up the close order drill right quick, so I did OK."

"Where in England did they send you?"

"The hospital unit set up in a town called Kidderminster near Birmingham. I spent a lot of slow, dreary days pulling guard duty and grunt type work. That didn't hold my interest very long! I wanted some *action*. I requested a transfer to a military police outfit in Birmingham, the 769th MP Battalion. They made me a motorcycle patrolman and trained me in the use of firearms.

"Before long we loaded onto troopships and sailed over to France, landing at Omaha Beach on D+17. As combat MPs, we helped guide the flood of tanks, trucks, and Jeeps into Normandy, controlling intersections, patrolling streets, guarding occupied areas. I traveled through Cherbourg, St. Lo, all over Normandy. I don't know the names of all the towns. When you're a private you don't know where you are half the time. You don't get to see the maps, you just go where you're told.

"I had studied French in school and was able to get around with it OK. One day a lieutenant in CID, the criminal investigation department of our battalion, came up to me and said, 'I understand you speak French. I need to take you on a case with me.'

"I said, 'You may be overestimating me, my French isn't all that good.'

"'You're the only one we've got, so come on.'

"We got in a Jeep and drove out to a farmhouse. The lieutenant told me the case involved the farmer's daughter, who worked in the town and reported she'd been raped by four black American soldiers on her way home in the evening.

"'I need you to question these people and get the whole story from the daughter's viewpoint,' the officer said.

"I got her story as best I could. In that region tall hedgerows lined the country roads. She was walking home and passed through a crossroads, and around the corner of the hedgerows she saw four black guys sitting in a Jeep. They came after her, threw her down, and gang-banged her. The girl told

James McKernon Jones as a military policeman in Normandy.

me the men wore uniforms just like mine, but they wore red hats."

"Red hats?" I echoed, knowing this was not part of any GI uniform I had heard of.

"That's right. It didn't make any sense to me because our uniforms didn't have red hats. But that was what she said.

"I told the lieutenant and he said, 'Come on Jones, this can't be, what do you mean red hats? Was it a party or something?'

"I asked her again and told him, 'Sir, it's basic French. *Chapeau rouge* means red hat, you can't get away from it.'

"He said, 'OK, we'll put it in the report that way, but it's gonna make us look awful foolish.'

"When we drove back to the bivouac area, we found our battalion mounting up to move out. The headquarters battalion moved to Chartres and the lieutenant went with it. My platoon went to Alancon, a small town just down the road. A buddy and I struck out on foot to tour the town and familiarize ourselves with the streets we'd have to patrol. We walked down a street and here came four black guys in GI uniforms—wearing red hats!"

"No way," I said.

"Yeah! I hurried over, stopped them, and said in English, 'Guys, you're out of uniform. Show me your ID.' And they started jabbering back at us in French! I said, 'Cut the crap, will ya? Don't try to fool me. You're Americans.'

"Then I saw their IDs. And guess what? Those red hats were *fezzes*."

"Fezzes...?"

"You know, a round red hat with a tassel hanging off the top. These guys weren't Americans, they were Algerians!"

"But what about the GI uniforms and the American Jeep?"

"Lend-Lease, all of it."

"Aha!"

"The minute I realized the French girl was not assaulted by Americans, I ran back to my motorcycle, hopped on it, and rushed down to Chartres to let the lieutenant know I'd solved his case for him. As I wheeled into the courtyard of the head-quarters building, I saw him walking across and I zoomed up beside him and said with excitement, 'Guess what, Lieutenant? I solved your case!'

"And he glared at me and said, 'No, you didn't. I seen 'em around here too.' And that was the case of the red hat." He chuckled.

"I understand you went through V-1 'buzz bomb' attacks," I said.

"Right. We moved to Liege, Belgium, which was under con-stant attack by flying bombs. I saw those monsters come down as close as ten blocks away. We had all heard the rumors spreading about this thing, this rocket that carried a mighty warhead. People said the Germans launched it just like you'd launch a firecracker on the Fourth of July. It was not a pin-point-accurate weapon, but it could certainly find a city. The Germans pointed it in the right direction and measured the fuel so it would run out when the bomb flew over the target. What happened after the engine stopped was anybody's guess, because sometimes they turned around and went back the other way or turned off to one side or went straight down. It was a god-awful mess. Just one could destroy four or five town-houses. Those that didn't go off could be more dangerous than the ones that did because somebody had to get in there and dis-arm them, and they were pretty ticklish.

"Those things made a scary 'putt-putt-putt' noise as they approached. Sounded almost like an outboard motor. I could clearly see the fiery tail and just prayed the thing kept putt-putt-putting past me, because if the engine stopped making that noise, it meant the bomb was diving. One killed a couple of my buddies who took cover in a captured German pillbox on a street corner. The V-1 landed right on top of it and took 'em out. We learned to sit and wait and pray when we saw them because we had no safe place to go."

"Tell me about the one that hit ten blocks away?"

"Even at that distance it was plenty powerful. The concussion slammed through my body, and a frightening *kaboom* tore at my ears. The flames reached as high as a thirty-story building. I counted flying bombs every night, one, two, three, up to ten. A few came during the day too, but they scared me more at night because I could see that flame coming out of its tail."

"Was the V-1 what scared you the most during the war?" I asked.

"Only one thing scared me more: the Battle of the Bulge. After retreating for months, the Germans made a last-ditch effort to turn the tables on us. My unit stood right in the path of the Germans. They threw everything they had into that battle and almost reached us. For a time I expected to look up and see them heading right for me.

"About that time, I decided … you have to understand I was eighteen, overseas, and tantalizingly close to the front lines. You're immortal at that age, know what I mean? I wanted to get into the fighting. I requested a transfer to the 29th Infantry Division and became a rifleman and first scout. I carried an M-1 and sometimes I carried the BAR because I was the biggest guy in the platoon. By the time I was assigned to a unit, the Germans had lost the Battle of the Bulge and I sensed victory close at hand. I pressed forward with my new unit through northern Germany.

"One day my platoon got orders to 'march and fire' across a wide open field near Munchen-Gladbach. We spread out in a long line, eight to ten feet apart, and walked deliberately forward, firing straight ahead every few seconds. I kept firing even when I didn't see anyone to shoot at. The point was to pin down

James McKernon Jones

any remaining resistance and keep going, no matter what happened, even if somebody got hit.

"I walked between empty German foxholes. When the Germans dug foxholes they hauled away the dirt rather than leave it piled up around the edges. That way we couldn't see the holes from a distance. They dug them six or seven feet long and three or four feet wide, with a little riser in the middle a few feet wide, so two Germans could sit back to back on it, look out in both directions, and cover each other's back. I glanced down into foxholes as I passed, looking for Germans and seeing nothing.

"We couldn't see anybody up ahead of us. I don't know where the machine gun was. It could have been hidden in some brush at the end of the field or down in a foxhole, I don't know. But it opened up on us, and three bullets hit me. One knocked my helmet off. The second tore a buckle off my combat boot. The third cut through my right arm, shattering the bones above the elbow.

"It felt like somebody took a sledgehammer and swung it full force into my arm. I spun around. My rifle flew up into the air. I hit the ground on my back and yelled, *'Jesus Christ!'* and probably some other profanities. The rifle landed next to me, useless because I couldn't move my arm. It had gone completely numb. I couldn't feel a thing. I knew I'd been hit but didn't know how bad. I took out my bayonet and started cutting the sleeve off my field jacket, getting blood all over the blade. I wanted to get at the wound so I could use my first aid kit. Then I glanced over at the ground next to me and saw little geysers of dirt exploding up into the air around me, making *poof* sounds.

"One of my buddies yelled, 'He's still shootin' at ya! Get in that hole!' and pointed to a foxhole ten feet away. The other soldiers kept moving forward, firing their guns. The German machine gun didn't have tracer bullets so they couldn't tell where it was. But march and fire means you keep moving forward, regardless."

"What were you feeling at this point?" I asked.

"Fear and shock. Fear because I'd been hit once, was I about to get hit again? And shock because when you're eighteen years old in combat you're invincible! I couldn't believe they had the gall to shoot me. Didn't those fool Germans realize they weren't supposed to shoot *me*? I honestly didn't think it could happen to me, or I wouldn't have been so nonchalant about doing the march and fire. I would have been more scared. I wasn't scared at all! Up until the time I got hit.

"With difficulty I rolled over and crawled to this foxhole, hadn't even seen it before I got shot—and fell into it upside down with machine gun bullets slamming into the ground right outside the hole. My legs draped over the seat and my backpack sank into the deep part of the hole next to the seat. I looked down over my stomach and saw a German soldier sitting next to my feet."

"Uh-oh..." I said.

"He felt me land behind him and rose up, turning in my direction. He was about thirty years old, no taller than five-eight, unshaven and filthy, wearing a muddy gray winter coat. He had a burp gun, a light machine gun, in his right hand. Thank God he turned to the right instead of the left, because that meant it took longer for the gun to come around and point at me, and before he got the gun around he turned his head and looked at me. He saw me holding the bloody bayonet and froze. His face paled. He thought I had just killed one of his comrades. He immediately dropped the gun, threw his arms up, and surrendered!"

"No way!"

"When he stood up I thought the machine gun out there would get him, but the firing petered out. With my arm out of commission I was stuck there with my butt wedged in the hole, but some GIs pulled me out and took the German prisoner. He kept saying, 'Kamerad! Kamerad!' He had no fight left. The Germans knew they were beat, but their officers would be angry if they didn't keep shooting. I think a lot of Germans were thinking, 'Let me get a couple of these Americans before I have to give up. I'll keep firing until they get up here too close and are about to kill me, and then I'm gonna put my hands up and yell Kamerad!' If this German had turned to the left instead of the right, he would have gotten the gun pointed at me before he saw the bayonet and had time to think about it. I was lucky.

"The men helped me off the field and into an ambulance that took me to a hospital in Aachen. I had what they called the 'million-dollar wound,' bad enough to send you home but not bad enough to take your life. I spent several months in a hospital in England. I had no concussion or any injury from the bullet that knocked my helmet off. The bullet that knocked a buckle off my boot didn't even penetrate the leather, just skinned it. But my arm bones were shattered, and the doctors put me into a full body cast to keep the arm still. The cast went from my right shoulder down to my wrist, around my body down to my waist, and passed under my left arm so I could use it. I was in it for months. The best feeling in the world was the day they took it off and I could take a sitting bath with a washcloth. It itched like crazy under there, dirt and dry skin."

"Has the wound troubled you over the years?" I asked.

"The scar's there, you can see the holes where it went in and came out, but the medics did a nice job with it. It hasn't affected my life that much. I still have a pension with the Veterans Administration for 40 percent disability. Of course they're not going to drop any of those no matter how good your arm is because it would be politically inappropriate. I tell everybody this joke, that once when I went in for a medical exam, the VA guy asked me, 'Are you havin' any problems?' and I said, 'Yeah, I can't raise my arm any higher than this.' And I brought my arm up to shoulder height. He said, 'How high could you raise it before you got hit?' and I said, 'Like this!' and raised my arm straight up toward the sky!"

James McKernon Jones today

For Christ's sake, they're killing
people all over the place

Harry Haines
Houston

Harry Haines spoke with a clipped, energetic style and a high-pitched voice, but only after pausing for a long moment to contemplate each question I fired at him. I often found myself tempted to ask, "Are you still there?" only to realize he had been silently composing his answer.

"Being in armor, we learned a lot of skills men didn't get in other branches of the Army," Haines told me. "I think we mastered more different types of weapons than any other kind of soldier. In training I fired everything except a .45. I fired Springfields, light machine guns, mortars, cannons. I used hand grenades, rifle grenades, bangalore torpedoes. I was only ten points away from a perfect score with the M-1. I knew how to lay mines, how to blow trees down by wrapping primacord around them, how to blow craters in the ground by burying kegs of ammonium nitrate. I remember a demolitions class where the instructor taught us to crimp the fuse onto the primacord with a special non-sparking pair of pliers. He told us to hold it behind our back with our off hand, so if the cap exploded, the shrapnel would go into our back instead of our stomach, and if it blew off any fingers, at least it wouldn't be your writing hand." He chuckled. "I got kind of nervous."

"Ever see any accidents like that?" I asked.

Harry Haines poses in front of his Sherman tank.

"No, but I do remember in hand grenade training the instructor told us, 'You can't outrun a grenade. The only thing you can do if somebody throws one at you is to pick it up and throw it back.' He waved this grenade around as he spoke and suddenly dropped it, and the handle flew off and it started spewing. All the men sitting in the bleachers stampeded, just about stomped each other to death trying to get out of there. Not one person ran down to pick up the grenade and throw it.

"Of course it didn't have any explosives in it, just the fuse and the cap. That instructor chewed everybody's ass out for not following his instructions!" He laughed.

"We practiced driving tanks, firing the guns, firing the guns while the tanks were moving, and firing at moving tanks. We even dug foxholes and lay down in them while a tank drove right over us. They wanted to teach us it was safer to hide in foxholes when tanks came rather than try to run from them."

"When did you go over to Europe?" I asked.

"Right after the Battle of the Bulge," Haines said. "The Army was desperate for armored officers. We were supposed to get a two-week leave before going overseas, but all I got was a three-day pass, just enough time to go home for one day and turn around and come back. I put everything I had in my footlocker: my clothes, canteen, belt, all my field gear, and shipped it up to the port of embarkation at Ft. Meade, Maryland. I had nothing with me riding the train up there except the dress uniform I wore and a toilet kit in my hand. Of course my footlocker never got there. I worried that I might have to buy everything all over again at a cost of $200. I earned $125 a month.

"They put four of us armored officers in charge of 200 infantrymen for the trip across the ocean. Before we left, I inspected the men to make sure they had all the necessary clothes and equipment. This captain there at Fort Meade was a real nervous little guy, constantly afraid if he didn't get a good efficiency rating he'd be on the next boat to Europe. He kept bugging me, 'Lieutenant, if a man is missing a canteen or a spoon from his mess kit, I don't want you to mark it down. Just let me know and I'll send a runner over to supply and get what you need right back. That way you can mark each guy as having all his equipment.'

"I looked at him and thought about it and said, 'I guess I can do that for you, but I need a favor from you.'

"He said, 'What's that?' and I told him my sad story about losing all my gear and how I couldn't afford to buy everything again. He said, 'No sweat. I'll fix you up with everything you need and a duffel bag, too.' And he did, he outfitted me for free. He sure wanted that perfect score so he could stay on this side of the ocean. I've laughed about it many times; I'll never forget that scared little son of a bitch.

"From there we went to Camp Kilmer, right outside New York City. The great thing about Camp Kilmer was this place down on one corner of a field where a soldier could lift up the barbed wire and sneak through a depression in the ground without getting his uniform dirty and go spend the night in New York City! Everybody knew about it except the officers who ran the joint. I got into town and had a good time two nights before they put me on a ship."

"What ship?"

"The USS *Wakefield*, a troopship that carried about 7,000 men. We sailed out of the harbor one morning and on the eighth evening we reached Liverpool. The next morning we boarded a train for Southampton, where we got on an LST that took us across the English Channel. Another train carried us to the front. I was in the front line about fourteen days after I left New York."

"Wow," I said. "They didn't mess around."

"No, they were in a hurry to get replacements. I wish I could have kept a diary, but they ordered us not to do that because the information in them might fall into enemy hands. Of course all the generals kept diaries so they could write their memoirs after the war. But grunts couldn't do it. Who do you think would have more information that could help the enemy, a general or a grunt?" He sniffed. "You've heard of those forty-and-eight boxcars?"

"Yes," I said. "Forty men or eight horses."

"Right. That's what they used to get us to the front. Fifty-three men crowded into mine. It had straw on the floor and a potbellied stove in the center. We carried our own water in canteens, and we only got two K rations a day. I always wondered whether the transportation corps was selling one of our daily rations on the black market in France. Maybe they gave us all they had, but we had our suspicions.

"We rode the train three days. One of those days we stopped and took the men out and let them zero their rifles in. I felt sorry for some of the guys because the Army gave them reclaimed M-1s picked up here and there on the battlefield. Guns covered with rust and cobwebs. Men came up to me and said with tears in their eyes, 'Gee whiz, Lieutenant, I had a better rifle back in the States when I was training. Now I've got to shoot a German with this damn thing?'

"Moving from one repple depple to another, I climbed in the back of a two-and-a-half-ton truck and saw a classmate from the New Mexico Military Institute sitting there. We had men scattered everywhere; I kept running into them all through the war. I said, 'Hello, J.J.! Looks like we're going in there together.' He didn't say much, just sat there and stared into space. We got off at different stops. I've seen him at reunions since, and he doesn't remember seeing me at all! I think the poor guy was so damn scared he didn't know what was going on around him."

"Were *you* scared?" I asked.

"At first I was too ignorant to be scared. I didn't grasp what it was all about. I wasn't like that scared captain. I think most people didn't get truly frightened until they got their nose stuck in it. War is like manure, it doesn't smell bad at a distance. It only stinks when you get up close."

"When did it really hit you what war was all about?" I asked.

He thought for a long moment. "A couple of unnerving things happened. The first night I got up to battalion headquarters, I came across our battalion surgeon and some other men on a muddy ridge, next to an ambulance. I heard them talking about a company commander. They talked about what a good guy Mike was, good officer, good company commander. I finally put it together—this Mike was in the ambulance, dead. That was an eye-opener.

"Two days later I headed down a road in a column of tanks. I looked left and saw a message painted in white on the side of a building. It said, 'See the Rhine and Let Your Head.' The Kraut who wrote it didn't know how to say 'leave your head!'

"I laughed. Then I looked over to the right and noticed a Jeep upside down in the mud, surrounded by four or five dead GIs and a few dead Germans too. What had happened was, GIs were marching up the side of the road, and German prisoners were coming back in the other direction right next to them. The Jeep hit a mine that killed everybody close by. Some men dragged the American bodies off the road, but they didn't get all the Germans off. When I looked down over the side of my tank, I saw that the five tanks ahead of mine had run over a German's body. He was smashed pretty flat, I can tell you that. That's when it suddenly dawned on me: For Christ's sake, they're killing people all over the place out here!"

"The sight must have made you want to throw up," I said.

"Naw, I never got sick during the entire war. If I was going to get sick, it would have been on the USS *Wakefield*. The crew told the men not to throw cigarette butts in the john because the plumbing on the ships couldn't take that abuse. Of course those idiots didn't pay any attention, and the johns promptly plugged up. When we stepped over the firewall into the johns, we'd see turds floating around in four inches of water. Men waded into the stench and vomited, creating a mixture of vomit and turds floating around. This was five decks below with no air conditioning. If somebody is going to get sick, that's where it'll happen. I didn't even get sick on the Liberty ship coming back home. Sometimes that ship rose up high on a wave and the screw stuck clear out of the water, and when it churned in the air the entire ship vibrated. That was scary. I sat there thinking the damn ship was about to fall apart. A lot of Liberty ships broke in half. They built them at an extremely fast pace, so they weren't the sturdiest ships around, you know. And that was true of a lot of our equipment."

"What do you mean by that?" I asked.

Disdain tinged his voice. "Our equipment was built for quantity, not quality, and that goes for our tanks as well. The Germans destroyed something like four allied tanks for every German Tiger tank we destroyed. Four to one! Now the historians say we won because we outnumbered them." He laughed derisively. "That's some comfort to the guy who's sitting in an inferior tank! 'Oh boy, we've got 'em outnumbered!'"

"Inferior?" I asked. "Would most GIs have agreed with that assessment?"

"Oh, yes. We all felt our tanks were inferior across the board."

"What about them in particular was inferior?"

Another long pause. When he answered, I could hear anger over the quality of equipment he'd been given to fight with.

"When you've got three inches of steel on the front of your tank and the other guy's got six inches, you tell me what's inferior," Haines said stridently. "And when the other guy's got a gun on his tank that has a muzzle velocity faster than an M-1 bullet! That damn 88 will go through six inches of hardened steel at 1,000 yards at a 30-degree angle. Their Tiger tanks had about a 1,000-yard advantage on us. They could penetrate us at 2,000 yards. Tigers used the same gun and same optical sight that the Germans used to shoot at airplanes flying over at 40,000 feet, several hundred miles an hour. And here we were, moving in first gear at four miles an hour with infantry walking on each side of the tank.

"Our tank company supported the footsoldiers of the 2nd Regiment. This was old Army, a lot of history. George Washington signed their activation papers. They were everywhere: Philippine insurrection, San Juan Hill with Teddy Roosevelt, World War I. Each platoon has five tanks, so as leader of the 2nd Platoon, I was in the sixth tank to cross the Rhine. The books say Patton crossed it at Oppenheim, but that's not 100 percent correct. There's twin cities there, Oppenheim and Nierstein. Technically we crossed at Nierstein."

"Was this when you really got into the thick of the fighting?" I asked.

"Yes, I was right in the middle of it. But one thing worked to my advantage: I joined an outfit that already had been through hell, which meant its men had lots of experience in battle. This battalion earlier had a general who gave a stupid order back in France. He wanted this battalion to liberate a surrounded battalion of the 31st Infantry. That outfit was trapped up on a hill and held it for a week while the Germans kept trying to make a counterattack to push the Allies back to the beach. If they'd gotten past that hill, they would have succeeded. But this battalion held its position and called in artillery and air attacks every time German tanks approached. The Germans couldn't get down this road. Meanwhile the battalion on the hill grew desperately short on supplies.

"This general ordered our infantrymen to load up on the backs of our tanks, and he ordered the tanks not to leave the road as they went up to relieve the guys on the hill. That was a crazy order because it gave the tanks no chance to maneuver. The Germans lined that road with 88s and waited. We lost fourteen out of seventeen tanks at 2,000 yards, all because that general wouldn't listen to reason.

"I was fortunate to get into that company later because the guys who survived that mess were tough, battle-hardened guys. I listened to everything they said. If I started to give an order and my platoon sergeant said 'Aww, I don't think we ought to do that, Lieutenant,' then I reconsidered. I relied on the experience of the old-timers."

"I'll bet that was rare among officers," I said.

"Hell, yes. A lot of officers thought they knew everything and refused to listen to their men. Plenty of officers told themselves, 'I'm an officer and this guy is only an enlisted man, so obviously I know better.' Those officers came home in coffins. Not me; I listened to my men and often asked the guys in my tank if we should do this thing, and if they said 'Hell no!' we didn't do it! That simple. The experience of my enlisted men helped me stay alive."

"What did you think about the officers over you?" I asked.

"I didn't get along too well with my company commander at the time. Guts are sort of a perceived thing. The farther someone was behind the front, the less guts you thought he had. I thought my company commander was a little lacking in that area. But a year ago at a reunion, he made a comment to me that the only way our *battalion* commander could have gotten wounded was from shaving! See what I mean? I didn't think my company commander had much guts, and he thought our battalion commander had even less guts! The company commander stayed ten to fifteen miles behind the front, and the battalion commander stayed another ten to fifteen miles behind that. The farther back somebody was from the front, the less guts you thought he had."

"And why specifically did you think your company commander lacked guts?"

"He never came up to the front in his Jeep to see how we were doing. The only time we saw him was when everybody in the company pulled together behind the front. But when we were up on the line he never came to see us. He sent a sergeant and a clerk with mail and hot chow in his place. In A Company they lost one commander during the war. B Company lost four. D Company lost one. My company, C Company, had the same commander throughout the whole war. That tells you right there."

"Tell me about your combat experiences," I said.

He paused, mentally selecting the best from a vast collection of stories.

"A Messerschmitt 109 strafed my tank as I crossed the little pontoon bridge over the Rhine. All our people along the bank shot at this plane with everything they had, and nobody could hit him. The anti-aircraft guns were lined up on the bank, and he flew in parallel to the river, which put him at a right angle to all the guns. He flew in low, 100 feet off the water, and they couldn't traverse the guns fast enough to keep up with him. By the time the guns went from left to right, hell, he was gone, circling for another pass. He made several passes at me, but he kept missing. I guess he shot off all his ammo, because he gave up and disappeared.

"When we got down into Trebur, the second town across the Rhine, Patton had pushed us across too far and too fast because he wanted to get across before the British. After dark in that second town, I walked down to battalion headquarters to get an update on our situation. The officer in there had a couple of GIs guarding him with submachine guns while he burned all his records in the fireplace.

"I said, 'What's our situation?'

"He said, 'It's bad. A squad of Krauts is in the house right next door to us. So be careful when you go back out there to return to your tanks.'

"I said, 'I'm gonna put the tanks in the center of town and point the guns up the street, because I can hear German tanks rumbling around outside town.'

Tanks in the town square at Ortenburg, Germany.

Harry Haines in Ortenburg, Germany
with C Company, 737th Tank Battalion.

"He looked at me and said, 'Yes, that's right. We're cut off. The town is surrounded.'

"He told me we had two battalions in town, but he couldn't get a runner through to the other battalion headquarters, and his men were running low on ammo. I pulled the tanks into the marktplatz in the center of town, and we cut our .30-caliber machine gun belts into sections eight or ten inches long, maybe a dozen bullets each, and handed them out to the footsoldiers. A Jeep drove past me in first gear and didn't get more than 100 yards down the street before Germans hiding in doorways and second-story windows shot it to hell. The Krauts were that close to us, but they were too scared to come in and attack our tanks. The next morning we cleared them all out. Thanks to help from the air force, we broke out of Trebur and continued to the next town.

"I've been back to Trebur twice, trying to get the people there to show me where that marktplatz was. The people ignore me. Even when I go to the city hall, they won't help me, because we blew up that town so bad, to this day they still don't like us. They say they don't know, don't remember, give me all kinds of crap. They stall me. Once they told me the city historian, who had the maps of the old city, would be back in a couple of hours, but we didn't have time to wait. The next time I came with plenty of time to wait. That time the man was sick. So I don't know whether that old marketplace still exists or not."

"Well, how many marketplaces could there be?" I asked.

"Those old German towns only had one marketplace."

"So they couldn't help you find the only historic marketplace in the town?"

"That's right. That's it, exactly."

"But a lot of Germans don't have any hard feelings toward the GIs, isn't that right?"

"Absolutely. I go back to Europe twice a year and visit very good friends in Germany and Czechoslovakia both. I've kept in touch with a lot of people I met over there. There was a sixteen-year-old boy in Trebur who acted as an interpreter for us. He now lives in Arizona. I remember two young boys who did KP for us to get food. One has died, but the other now lives in Syracuse, New York."

I looked for a way to return the conversation to combat, feeling certain he hadn't scratched the surface. "Did your tank ever take any hits?" I asked.

"Yes, we took 40mm hits. It makes a deafening noise inside the tank, but 40mm couldn't penetrate. Anything bigger would have cut right through us."

"Tell me about the tactics you used to survive under fire."

"Survival depends on quick thinking and doing the right thing at the right time. Once we came down through a valley with a German 40mm up on a hill behind us. He had the sun behind him. In our training manuals it said the platoon leader should always be in the center of the platoon. But we didn't do it that way because our radios were unreliable. So we didn't bother with the radios. We put the platoon leader in the lead tank and ran around like a mother hen and her little chicks. Wherever the mother hen went, the little chicks followed.

"This 40mm opened up on the middle tank, which carried my platoon sergeant. I'm sure the Germans thought they were shooting at me. We needed to get out of there, but I saw a road-block made of huge logs up ahead of me. I told my gunner, 'Hit that thing as fast as you can, it might be mined.' I wanted to blow up any mines and weaken the logjam. Time was at a premium with the Krauts shooting at my platoon sergeant back there.

"My gunner and loader started shooting so fast, the loader came up with a shell as the gun was coming out of battery and it hit the fuse and smashed it. Next thing I knew he pulled on my left pants leg, and I looked down to see this three-inch round being shoved up under my nose. I saw that bent fuse on it, and my heart jumped into my throat. I threw it over the side and ducked."

He paused, letting me wait for the answer to the obvious question. "Fortunately," he said, "it didn't go off. We shot eight or ten shells into that roadblock and then rammed it with the tank, sending splintered logs flying away from the road, and got the hell out of there.

"We headed up a road following along an embankment, next to a row of houses that offered good cover. But then we reached a fifty-yard gap between houses. I was all set to make a run for it to the next house with infantry riding on the back of the tank, but they yelled at me not to go, saying, 'We don't have any armor back here!'

"So I got out on the back deck of the tank with them and used my hand mike to tell the driver to run for it. We made it across the gap, no problem. I looked back and saw my platoon sergeant trying to peek his tank around the side of the house to see what was out there, and smoke and sparks flew up from the side of the tank. The Germans had hit him with 20mm shells. Finally he made it across too. But my last tank didn't move. We waited and nothing happened. I climbed out and ran back, crouching behind that embankment for cover. I told the tank commander, 'Come on, you gotta move out.'

"He was trembling and pale. He told me, 'I can't do it. I just can't do it.' He'd lost all his nerve."

"Uh-oh," I said. "How do you handle it when that happens?"

"You have to do the right thing in a situation like that. To yell at a guy or threaten him with a court-martial won't help, because that's in the future. It's nothing compared to those guns waiting out there right now.

"I told him, 'I'm gonna have to go on with the infantry and leave you. You won't have any infantry protecting you. I hope the Germans don't stick a bazooka up your tailpipe in the middle of the night.' Next thing I knew I heard the motor turn over and that tank took off!

"You just have to scare the guy more than he's already scared. If I'd threatened that guy with a court-martial, that tank would still be sitting there a day later, except all burned out by a bazooka. Surviving the war required quick thinking. If you did the wrong thing, that was it."

"What was it like inside the tank when you got hit by enemy fire?" I asked.

"It was extremely loud and we shouted to each other, 'Let's get the hell out of here!' Actually, 40mm and 20mm guns were not anti-tank weapons. But the Germans were desperate. They fired anything they had at us, just hoping. When we went into Frankfurt, our infantry tried to cross a little concrete bridge, and the Germans would fire an 88 every time a man ran across the bridge. A big cannon like that, at *one man*.

"And we did it too. My gunner hit a running German soldier with a three-inch shell. Hit him right in the helmet with our main gun! The German was running to hide behind some haystacks, 600 feet away. I told Little Joe, our gunner, to get him. Joe swung the turret around and fired our cannon. I watched through binoculars and saw a bright flash. And then nothing. Another fella named Cecil, who was in the next tank, later claimed he saw the man's head and helmet fly 100 feet in the air. That's not what happened. The flash hit his helmet and the guy completely disappeared. It vaporized him. Think about it. How would a high explosive shell hit a guy's helmet and just blow off his head and helmet? It would blow the whole body apart. I still kid Cecil about that. It just goes to show you how two men can remember the same event. It also shows you we had some damn good gunners."

"How did you compensate when you went up against tanks that had superior range and armor?" I asked.

"There were only two ways to handle it. The first was to use cover. Northeast of Frankfurt we fought the 6th SS Mountain Division. We hid behind houses. We rolled out from one side of a house and shot at them, and then backed up behind the house real quick. The next time we'd roll out the same side again, and then next time we'd roll out the other side, so the Germans never knew which side we'd shoot from next. The tanks that rolled the same way each time, or rolled predictably from one side to the other, got hit.

"Other times the only thing we could do was rush them and close the distance. It wasn't easy for them to hit a moving tank, so we'd run in close where our guns could do some damage. We had a top speed of about 30 miles an hour."

"Did Tigers scare you?"

"Oh, yes. The Tiger was a terrible piece of machinery. The Panther was tough, too."

"Tell me what it's like inside a tank."

"We had five men in a Sherman. When I look at one of those little tanks now I think, 'My God, how did we get so many guys in that thing?' But at the time we got so used to it, it seemed like plenty of room. We practically lived in that darn thing. We slept in it at night, and some days we never got out of it. If we had to take a leak or a crap, we took an empty .50-caliber ammo box, crapped in it, put the lid on it, and threw it over the side. I spent so much time in it, it grew on me. Got to know it so well I could reach behind myself to flip toggle switches without even looking.

"Tank commanders had a policy of keeping half our body out of the tank at all times. It didn't do us any good to close the hatch and try to look through a periscope to see a camouflaged 88 hidden in the woods 800 yards away. I needed to have at least my head and shoulders sticking up out of the turret so I could see everywhere with my binoculars and spot the enemy. My left ear still rings because I always wore my headset with the left half of it above my ear. That way I could hear bullets that hit the side of the tank. But the cannon was on my left side, and all that firing with no protection over my left ear caused nerve damage. My left ear rings 24 hours a day."

"Would you say your tank crew was close-knit?" I asked.

"Yes. You didn't dare change a crew. One time my tank got hit by a 40mm, and about two miles later my track broke. I ran over to another tank and told its commander, 'I need to take your tank to keep up with the infantry, so you take my tank and wait until ordnance gets here.' Rather than just swapping tank commanders, the entire crews swapped tanks. I didn't want to get in there with four strange guys, and they didn't want me either, because everybody was so used to what the other guys

Harry Haines' tank crew in Ortenburg, Germany.

in his crew did, how they reacted. Everybody's life depended on the other guy.

"The assistant gunner in my tank had collected a cigar box full of Kraut wedding rings. We changed tanks so quick he didn't have time to take the box with him or ask the other crew to watch it for him. So of course the ordnance men stole the box when they came up to fix the tank."

"How many enemy tanks did your tank destroy during the war?" I asked.

"You know, I'm not sure. I think we took out three or four tanks, in addition to everything else we shot at. Our gunner was good. But we didn't really keep track. I think if you asked most tank crews, they wouldn't know exactly how many tanks they destroyed. We never painted symbols on our tank to show off our tally, like a few people did. Our attitude was, let's get through this thing in one piece, win it as soon as we can, and go home."

Harry Haines (right) in Volary, Czech Republic, with its mayor in 1996. Haines traveled to Europe to revisit many of the places he passed through during the war.

I interviewed Harry Haines on May 28, 2000. When I tried repeatedly to contact him again for some follow-up questions, no response came. Later his son informed me Haines passed away on June 12, only two weeks after telling me his story. I'm glad to have had the opportunity to talk with him—an opportunity I almost missed.

Bill Dallas

Austin

"I was watching *Sergeant York* at the Worth Theater in Fort Worth, and they interrupted the movie to announce that Japan had just attacked Pearl Harbor," Bill Dallas told me. "I don't think any of us knew what Pearl Harbor was! They went on to say we would probably declare war on Japan soon, and everybody started applauding. Of course they weren't in uniform like I was. I had been on active duty since November 1940. I thought, what the hell are they applauding for? We're going to *war*!

"I was in the Texas National Guard, 36th Division, 144th Infantry Regiment, Company B. Within a week we were on a train from Camp Bowie, Texas, bound for somewhere in the West. The officers didn't tell us our destination. After getting some new equipment and ammunition at Fort Lewis, Washington, we set up an observation post at Camp Clatsop, Oregon, where we watched the Pacific Ocean for enemy ships or submarines. Never did see anything. It was a very cold winter. Even the sand on the beach was frozen hard.

"Supposedly one night a Jap submarine came up and shelled the beach. But I don't think it was a Japanese sub."

"Why not?" I asked.

"Because they picked a spot that was completely void of human habitation. I suspect it was an American vessel waking the people up to the reality that we were at war. From where they shelled they could easily have seen the lights of a nearby town, and yet they shelled an empty stretch of beach.

"Then we moved to Longview, Washington, to guard a bridge over the Columbia River connecting Washington and Oregon. This was the only bridge west of Portland, Oregon, and would be strategically important if the Japanese landed nearby.

"We got to Longview just before Christmas. The people of that town were so nice to us. They kept inviting us to Christmas dinner, and they wouldn't take no for an answer. I ate three Christmas dinners that day! They'd give us a ride back to the city square, and we'd try to walk back to our barracks, and somebody else would come along and invite us to *their* dinner! I tried to get out of it the second time, but the man said, 'You're a growing boy, you can eat another dinner.' I didn't eat nearly as much the second and third as I did the first one! That was a fantastic Christmas.

"I understand the city of Longview, Washington, was originally settled by people from Longview, Texas, and once they heard we were Texans, we could do no wrong in their eyes. They rolled out the red carpet for us. One time we let it be known that we sure could use a washing machine, and we got five or six of them! Most of them didn't work, but we took the parts and built two or three working ones. Anything we asked for, those folks jumped to get it to us right away.

"In the spring we moved to Vancouver Barracks across the Columbia River from Portland, Oregon. It was still very cold up there. I was in charge of the quarters, and one of my duties was to start the fire in the morning. The building was heated by steam from the boiler down in the basement. I looked around and found some gasoline, some wood, and some coal. I put the wood in first, shoveled some coal on top, dumped gasoline on it, and threw a match in. It made a sound like *whooomp* and went out. I threw more wood in and poured more gasoline and tried again. *Whhooomp!* and it went out. This time I poured a *bunch* of gasoline, maybe a gallon. I threw a match in and boy, did it catch on! I nervously watched the needle on the pressure gauge as it climbed closer and closer to the red line. When it hit, I ran frantically to wake up the first sergeant and yelled, 'Evacuate! Evacuate! The damn thing's gonna blow!'

"The sergeant knew more about the furnace than I did. He went down and closed the vents. It cooled down and didn't blow up. They never asked me to build a fire again." He snickered.

"We moved to Fort Funston near San Francisco in a convoy of Jeeps and trucks. It was right on the Pacific, south of Seal Rock. We had the same job of watching the ocean. I found out the Army Air Corps was accepting anyone who could pass the examination for pilot training.

"I was a high school dropout. When I was first called up to active duty in 1940, you had to have a college degree to take that test. Then a while later after war was declared and they needed more people, they started to take people who'd had *any* college. Then they still couldn't get enough so they let high school graduates take the test.

"Then they started taking *anyone* who could pass the test. I took it and got lucky. It was a written test with multiple choice questions. On a lot of those questions I had absolutely no idea, and had to make a wild-ass guess. But I passed, and they transferred me out of the infantry into the Army Air Corps.

"I became a copilot on a B-17 crew, and in December we got orders to go overseas. We flew to Gander Lake, Newfoundland, and stayed there a week waiting for better weather. We needed favorable winds to make it across to England. In fact we lost planes flying over there. If the pilot didn't practice good cruise control, the plane would run out of fuel over the ocean.

Bill Dallas in August 1943, just after graduating from pilot training.

"I was on the first big raid to Berlin on March 6, 1944. By then we had more or less knocked the German air force out of the air, so we had few fighter attacks to contend with. The only time their fighters came up was when they saw a straggler flying along. Only one plane came at us over Berlin and he didn't do any damage, in fact he passed by our plane without shooting. He might have been out of ammunition.

"I flew ten missions. Attacked Berlin, Frankfurt, Cologne. My last mission was supposed to be a 'milk run,' only 26 minutes over enemy territory. Our target was a rocket site. Being a smart-ass 2nd lieutenant, I said, 'This is Sunday and the Krauts are in church, so they won't be shooting at us!'

"An instant later, flak hit us. It knocked out all our superchargers, and I looked out and saw the right wing burning. I tapped the pilot's shoulder and showed him, and he pointed to the left wing and it was on fire too. We decided the best move was to get the hell out of there.

"He hit the alarm bell and we yelled, 'Bail out! Bail out!' Almost everybody left immediately. The pilot was setting up the automatic pilot, and I said, 'Time for me to go,' and headed down for the nose hatch. I saw the navigator and bombardier sitting up front. It looked like they were sitting there talking to each other. I motioned to them to go out the nose hatch, because the normal route out the bomb bay was closed. I found out later shrapnel had hit the navigator in the side of the nose and the bombardier was trying to bandage it.

"Then I realized I didn't have my escape kit, which had a map, money, and a compass in it. I went back to my seat and grabbed it and zipped it up in my flying suit. The pilot was still fiddling with the automatic pilot. On the way out, I saw the navigator and bombardier were still sitting there, so I motioned to them to follow me again, and I jumped out of the plane.

"We bailed out at 20,000 feet. A couple of weeks earlier a paratrooper giving a lecture told us that around 10,000 feet, suddenly the ground looks like it's rushing up at you. That's how you can tell how high you are. Before that you don't have any sensation of falling, and even after that it seems more like the ground is moving up than you're falling. I figured out how to get into a stable position, head down slightly, stomach down.

Sure enough before long the ground started rushing up towards me, so I knew I was at 10,000."

"You were in freefall for more than 10,000 feet?"

"That's right. I knew it was time to pull the ripcord so I rolled over just like you would in bed, pulled the cord, and I swung just a few times and I was on the ground! I thought, 'God damn, how the hell did I get down here so fast?'

"I hit the ground, fell down, got up and looked around, and heard a popping noise. I saw the ground kicking up around me and thought, 'Oh hell, somebody's shooting at me!' I nose-dived into the ground and they quit shooting. But I had no chance to escape. A group of Germans came up, mostly young boys, fifteen to sixteen years old, and they got me.

"They took me into a house and asked a few questions. I didn't answer them; I was only supposed to give name, rank, and serial number. I had some shrapnel in my leg. A doctor put a bandage over it, apologizing that he couldn't do more with his limited medical supplies. I had a wound on the knuckles of my left hand, and he put a splint on it so I couldn't move it. He said, 'There's metal in there. If you move your hand you'll ruin it and will never be able to use it again.'"

"What happened to the other crewmembers?" I asked.

"We all made it out. The bombardier evaded the Germans and got back to England six months later. The pilot took too long setting up the autopilot and just as he was leaving the escape hatch the plane blew up, and the flames burned off most of his hair. But we all survived.

"The Germans put us together in an underground cell. The ball turret gunner had landed in a bomb crater in a military compound and stayed there all day long watching Germans go by on a walkway. As soon as it got dark he started walking through the fields, but it was rough going so he decided to walk along a road, and they caught him. He rejoined us the next day.

"A funny thing happened, they put twelve to fifteen prisoners in the back of a pickup truck. There wasn't enough room for the guards, so they had to walk along behind. The officer sitting in the front seat had a Belgian driver who would very gradually increase his speed. The guards would fall behind and start running, and holler at the officer, who would chew out the driver and tell him to stop it. The Belgian would look around at us and grin and give us a V for victory sign. And then he did the same damn thing all over again! He did it three or four times before we reached a jail.

"We got on a train for our destination in Frankfurt, a place they called Gulag Luft, an interrogation center. We spent several nights on the train. They always stopped us at a railroad station for the night. We figured they did it so if the Allies bombed it we'd be killed, and they wouldn't have to worry about us any more.

"My leg started bothering me. Every time I stood up I felt intense pressure on the wound, and then it would go away. But I'd sit down and it would hurt again. I took the bandage off and found the wound covered with pus.

"I put my hands on both sides of the wound and pushed down real hard and pus blew out. I saw a shiny object in there. Nobody had a knife, of course, but one guy had a fingernail file. We burned the tip of it clean and I dug out a little piece of steel, L-shaped, about the size of a .30-caliber bullet."

"That must have hurt."

"No, it didn't hurt at all. My leg had gone completely numb. Once I got the metal out, it healed up right away.

"One time I looked up and down the train and realized there was no guard anywhere to be seen! So I ran back to my railcar. All the wounded were in one car. None of us were wounded very badly, but we acted like we were. I grabbed the navigator and said, 'Let's get off this damn thing!' and he got up and we ran to the door. But by the time we got there a guard came in from the next railcar. We'd probably have gotten shot if we'd jumped off, so maybe the good Lord was keeping track of us.

"Frankfurt was in a shambles. The railroad station was nothing but twisted steel. When we got off the train a little old German woman was waving a walking stick at us and shouting, 'God damn son of a bitch! God damn son of a bitch!'"

He laughed. "Aw hell, I think we probably deserved it. That place was a mess. We'd been told we would not bomb indiscriminately in the occupied countries, France, Belgium, Holland. But in Germany it was different. We had orders that if our primary target was covered over with clouds, we would drop our bombs on the center of town. That's what we'd done there at Frankfurt, just demolished the place."

"They interrogated us at the Gulag Luft for several days. They put us into separate rooms with windows they could control automatically. They'd leave those windows open at night. This was in March, and it was still pretty cold. They didn't give us blankets. After the room became extremely cold, they'd close the windows and turn on the heat. The heat came up through the floor, so hot you couldn't stand on it because they made us leave our shoes outside the room. It would get boiling hot in there and then they'd turn the heat off again and open the windows. I guess they were trying to wear us down. But I really didn't know anything to tell them, so they didn't get anything.

"We rode a train to a camp at Barth in northern Germany, on the Baltic coast. The Germans left us on the train in rail yards at night, and we heard the British dropping bombs nearby, but fortunately they never bombed the rail yard we were in. We knew they were British because the Americans bombed in the daytime and the British bombed at night.

"At Barth they separated the officers and enlisted men into different camps. The camp commander, a Wehrmacht officer, 'welcomed' us into the camp. To him, the military was an honorable profession, and under him our treatment improved. He told us, 'It is your duty to escape, and it is my duty to keep you here. I will win.' And he did. None of us ever got away.

"They put me and my navigator into a room with fourteen others. We had top bunks side by side. At first, people didn't talk to us much. I guess they were suspicious. But people came around to meet us after recognizing my name. It turned out several of my flight school classmates were in the camp, and that provided proof to the others that I was who I said I was. After that we started getting a little friendlier, talking more openly."

"How well did the Germans feed you?" I asked.

"For a while we got Red Cross parcels once a week. That was pretty good fare. We probably ate better than a lot of Germans did. But in 1945 the parcels stopped coming. We got one meal a day of boiled dehydrated vegetables, plus a small potato. Then the dining hall burned down, and they didn't have any way to cook, so they started giving us Red Cross parcels again."

"You must have lost a lot of weight," I said.

"I started at 160 and went down to 120." He laughed ruefully and said, "I have a 69-inch waist now. I'm not even recognizable as that guy now. He's changed a lot over the years."

"How was your health?"

"I was extremely thin. I started getting bald, and I lost all my back teeth. We didn't have toothpaste or toothbrushes. We tried to clean our teeth by putting salt on our fingers and rubbing our teeth. We finally got toothpaste that was like pumice."

"What about hygiene?"

"Once a month we got a hot shower. Several years ago my wife and I went to the camp at Auschwitz in Poland, and we saw the 'shower room' where the Nazis gassed the Jews to death. And do you know, that shower room was identical to our shower room in Barth. If I'd known at the time..." his voice trailed off.

"I grew a beard for a while, but then the Germans made us shave them off because it changed our appearance too much. The Germans had issued us little numbered tags that we had to show at roll call. Some of the bearded prisoners traded tags with each other at roll call just to see if they could get away with it. The Germans caught on and made us all shave. I kept my mustache. But one day I came out of the latrine and a couple of my buddies grabbed me and shaved half my mustache off. I was so infuriated I refused to shave the other half off for a week!"

"How did prisoners pass the time?" I asked.

"Well, one thing we did was play pranks on the Germans," Dallas said with mischief in his voice. "One man dirtied the soles of his shoes real good and walked them up one wall, across the ceiling and down the other wall. A German guard came in, saw the tracks and said, '*Was ist los?*' which means, roughly, 'What the *hell* is going on here?'

"And we'd tell him, 'Oh, that's just Joe over there. He walks in his sleep at night.' Most of the Germans got the joke, but I think a few of the dumb ones believed it!

"If it rained we went outside and made little sailboats to sail in the water. Anything to pass the time. Someone made a crystal radio set. The mess hall had steel beams inside the walls, and if we drove a nail through the wall until it touched a steel beam, we had an antenna! We were able to pick up the BBC and find out how the war was progressing. A prisoner would take notes and write up a newsletter, one copy for each building."

"How did you get enough paper to do that?"

"We bribed a guard. One man would stand watch while the rest of us read it. If a German happened by, our man hollered 'Goon up!' and we hid the newsletter.

"One time the men bribed a guard and had him sign a receipt for the cigarettes they gave him! And then they had him by the balls. They told him, 'If you don't do what we want, we'll turn this over to the camp commandant.' They had him, man. They got all kinds of things from him, even a camera and film.

"We played a lot of bridge. Sometimes at night the guys would lay their cards down ready to pick up right next to their bunks and go to sleep. When the Germans popped a surprise nighttime inspection on us, which they did quite often, these guys jumped up in the dark, picked up their cards and got into position. When the guards came into their room with flash-lights, they'd shine the lights in our guys' faces and see them sitting there playing cards in pitch black darkness. They asked what in the world we were doing, and we'd say, 'Just playin' cards. We can see just as well in the dark as we can during the day. Can't you?'

"That really startled some of them. They fell for it! We did a lot of little things like that to irritate them, since we couldn't escape."

"Did you try?"

"A group did make it out of camp once. We had roll call twice a day. On this day, our ranking officer ordered us not to fall in when the Germans told us to, unless *he* said to fall in. The idea was to delay the roll call to give the men a chance to get as far away as possible.

"The Germans called for us to fall in and we ignored them, just kind of milling around. They brought in a bunch of armed men and dogs and said, 'If you don't fall in within ten seconds, we'll turn the dogs loose and start shooting.' We decided discretion was the better part of valor, so we fell in. Those guys got caught anyway. We didn't help them much.

"We dug a number of tunnels, none successful. They always caved in, or the Germans found them. I couldn't get down in the hole to dig, it was only two foot square. So instead I helped get rid of the dirt. I wore pajamas with drawstrings in the legs under my pants, filled with dirt. Whenever a ball game or some activity was drawing a crowd, I'd go mingle among the people and pull the strings to release the dirt. Then I'd walk on it, milling around as casually as I could, and spread the dirt around on the ground."

"You managed to do this without being noticed?" I asked skeptically.

"That's right. We concealed it by standing in the middle of a bunch of prisoners. I'll bet we raised the level of the whole compound three or four inches! But it was all to no avail. Nobody ever got away.

"We liked to go out and cheer when we saw an air raid nearby, but then the Germans ordered us to stay inside and be quiet. We thought the Allies knew where we were, but they didn't. A fighter pilot got shot down right outside the camp and became a prisoner with us. He told us he had mentally flipped a coin to strafe either a nearby airfield or the nearby compound, which he thought was army barracks. *We* were the 'barracks!' But he decided to strafe the airfield instead. Lucky for us.

"We knew the war was coming to a close because of our radio. The dining room had a huge map. The Germans gave us a newspaper that told their version of what was happening in the war, but we knew the actual lines were a lot closer to us than the Germans admitted. We put a string up on the map to show the lines according to what the Germans said. But if you looked real close you'd see these subtle little smudges on the map three or four inches in front of the string. That showed where the BBC said the lines were. Soon we could hear the fighting getting closer to us, big guns going off.

"Then one day we woke up, and guess what?"

"The Germans were all gone?"

"Exactly. Just disappeared in the night. The Russians came through the area the next day. We were left to our own devices in the camp, so some of the guys went into town and looked around and said it was deserted. One of the fellas in my room was gonna take off, but I told him, 'Bill, don't do that. Stay here with us.' Then we heard over the radio that General Eisenhower would have a personal message for us, so we should stay near the radio for his instructions. We waited until the next day for this big message to come in. And here's what we heard on the radio: 'General Eisenhower's personal message is, *Stand by.*' Unquote."

I groaned. "You're kidding me. That was it?"

"That was it. I got disgusted and told my buddy Bill, 'Let's get outta this damn place.' A bunch of us grabbed cigarettes and chocolate bars and ventured out from the compound. We came up to a large lake and found a boat. Six of us got in it, and I think some of them had never been in a small boat before, because they rocked that boat so bad I thought it was gonna sink. We crossed about 400 yards of water and then cut cards to see who would take the boat back to pick up more guys. Bill and I got away from there, and the first night we knocked on the door of a German farmhouse and asked for a place to sleep. The family gave us a room and we went to bed."

"The Germans let you in their house?"

"Yes. Of course they could have come in the room and killed us that night. But they didn't show any animosity at all. They were nice to us. The next night we stopped at a farmhouse and there was a young lady there. We thought she was a beauty, but after a year without seeing any women...I don't know if she was pretty or not.

"She told us the Russians came there at night and raped all the women. Bill talked mighty big. He said, 'You come and get us tonight, and we'll protect you.'

"Later that night she woke us up and said frantically, 'The Russians are here, please help us!' We went downstairs and as we walked into the living room we saw three Russian officers sitting on one side. Not so bad. Then as we walked farther in we saw three Russian enlisted men on the other side, pointing submachine guns right at us.

"I said, 'Bill, we'd better get our butts out of here.' So we left. We felt bad about it, but we had no weapons.

"We kept walking. One of the prisoners back at the camp had said he could write and speak Russian, and he drew the American flag on the backs of our jackets and wrote what he thought was the word *America* across the top. That was supposed to keep the Russians from accidentally shooting us. But then we heard rumors the Russians were taking American POWs back into Russia. So we were sneaking around this town to avoid being spotted by the Russians. Walking down a side road, we looked back and saw somebody was following us. A Russian soldier. We picked up our pace, but he caught up with us and greeted us in good English.

"We said, 'I guess you knew we were Americans by what we have written on our jackets.' He said, 'I don't know what that is you've got written there, but I recognize Old Glory!' He'd gone to school in the States, and was a teacher in Moscow. We told him we were looking for a ride out of there, and he stopped a tractor coming down the road. We all got on the back and rode it for a while. But it was heading into town and we didn't want to go that way, so we got off and said goodbye to him.

"We came across some Russians driving a herd of captured horses, and they let us take two. So we each jumped on one, but I couldn't make the one I got do a damn thing. Bill said 'You don't know anything about riding a horse!' and I said, 'I may not be an expert horseman but I know how to steer the damn thing. I tell you, he won't cooperate.' Bill was sure he could control it so we traded mounts and went through some woods. I lost track of him in there and came out the other side looking for him. Finally I saw him walking out of the woods alone! I was so startled I jumped off my horse to run up to him and see what was the matter. He said that damn horse was blind and had just been following the other horses. But once he took it in the woods it had no idea where it was and headed off in the wrong direction, and he got knocked off by a tree limb. The horse I'd been riding took off as soon as I jumped off it, so that was the end of our horse riding.

"We walked a little farther and came upon a Russian guard. We asked him for something to eat and gave him a pack of cigarettes as payment. He took us up to an apartment, screamed something in Russian to the family inside, and kicked the door in. They told him they didn't have anything to eat. He grabbed his submachine gun off his shoulder and was about to shoot them, but I grabbed him and said, 'Don't do it! Don't do it!' So he took us to another apartment, and the Germans there gave us some soup.

"Afterwards we asked him to get us a ride. A truck came up the road and he motioned to it to stop. The truck didn't look like it was going to stop, so he jerked his submachine gun off his shoulder again, and the driver stopped immediately. The Russian motioned for us to jump on the back while he talked to the driver, and we tossed him another pack of cigarettes. We rode that truck all the way to the British lines. The Russians questioned us for some time but finally let us go.

"That's my story," he said. "What else can I tell you about?"

"How would you characterize the treatment you got from the Germans?" I asked.

"Considering the circumstances, I'd call it reasonable."

"Really?"

"Sure. I remember back in '45 or '46 the U.S. government was going to give all the former POWs a dollar for every day we got substandard treatment. When I filled out the form I only put down the time between my capture and my arrival at prison camp as substandard treatment. I left off the whole period of time I spent in the camp. The government sent the form back to me, thinking I didn't understand it. But you see, we were *prisoners of war.* You can't expect them to roll out the red carpet for you. Our treatment wasn't as good as German prisoners got over here, but it wasn't cruel."

"Did you witness any brutality?" I asked.

"No, I never did. There was one incident that came close. The camp had a double barbed wire fence, twelve to fifteen feet high with a six foot space in between. Fifteen feet inside the fence was a warning wire. We were not supposed to cross that wire unless we signaled a guard that we needed to cross. For example, if we were playing ball and the ball rolled across the wire, a prisoner would wave to the guard and point to the ball, and the guard would give you the OK to cross.

"One time a fella got the OK from one guard to go get the ball, but then another guard walked up outside the fence, saw him, and instinctively shot at him. Fortunately he missed.

"Some of the other prisoners were so angry they made little makeshift hangman's nooses and waved them at this guard as he walked back and forth. He never did react. That was the only incident like that I ever saw, and that was a mistake.

"Even if they found a tunnel, they wouldn't do anything to us unless they actually caught us in the tunnel. They didn't punish anybody else even though it was obvious we must have helped. And the guys they did catch in the tunnel, they'd just stick 'em in the hole for a while. These were German army guards, mostly old fellas, and they didn't have any personal animosity toward us.

"One guard, we called him Alfie, was actually a United States citizen. He'd grown up in the States, but in the thirties his grandmother back in Germany had fallen ill, and he came over to visit her. And while he was there the German army drafted him.

"He had a very American sense of humor, and we joked with him a lot. Once when he tried to count the prisoners we kept horsing around, and he'd laugh so hard he'd lose count. We did it to him three or four times. He begged, 'Please don't do that again. The commandant will get mad at me and put me in the cooler.' But they had no mercy on him.

"Don't misunderstand me," Dallas said. "Some Germans were very cruel. I think once they started killing, it got easier and easier, and after a while it didn't bother them at all to shoot someone. The Jews were less than human to them. I have the highest regard for our Jewish airmen. They had Js on their dogtags, and they had a lot of guts to leave those Js on their dogtags as they flew over Germany."

"How did the Germans treat the American Jewish POWs?"

"At first the Jewish fellas were mixed with the rest of us, but toward the end of the war the Germans moved them into another building all by themselves. We just kept going over and visiting them like nothing had ever happened.

"See, the Germans thought if they separated us, we'd segregate ourselves and ostracize the Jews. In other words, they thought we'd act like *them*.

"Well," Dallas said, "They were wrong."

Bill Dallas with his wife, Allyne, on a trip
to England in the summer of 2000.

They're not gonna get me,
it's gonna be somebody else

Manuel Palmer
Houston

"**A**n officer came into the room and said to me, 'You're just the man we need. You've got a Quartermaster 3rd Class rating, and you don't have any family. We're an all-volunteer crew and our quartermaster chickened out. Will you serve?'

"And that's how I ended up on an LCC, a Landing Craft Control," Manuel Palmer told me.

"I'm not familiar with that kind of craft," I said. "What was it?"

"It was a fifty-six-foot boat loaded with all kinds of special, top-secret equipment. Our job was to guide an invasion force toward shore and make sure they landed in the right spot. Before they started using LCCs, our landing craft were going off track, getting caught on those traps the Germans made out of railroad ties and concrete, and the men aboard were getting killed. But with LCCs guiding them in, our landing craft could be certain of hitting the lanes we cleared through those traps."

"How did you guide them?"

"First, PT boats went along the beaches and took radar images of the shore. It was sort of like today's radar weather maps, with the borders superimposed on the radar image. That image was placed over our radar screen for comparison, and we used that to guide the boats in. We had radar, three between-

Manuel Palmer at Corsica

An LCC, Landing Craft Control, moving at its full speed of 10 knots.

ship radios, two depth finders, even sonar. We had a radio that would go all the way up to UHF that we could use for a homing device. And we had three twin .50-caliber machine guns.

"An LCT, a Landing Craft Tank, would tow us around to save fuel. We had a crew of two officers and twelve men, including a radarman, an electronic technician, three radio men, three gunner's mates, and the motor machinists who ran the engines. And there was me, the quartermaster. I was an assistant to the officers, did whatever needed to be done. For a while that included being a radarman. We had this boy, a baker from Arkansas"—Palmer laughed derisively—"and until he caught on, it was up to me to do his job.

"Our commanding officer, Ensign Bob Williams, was a high school football coach from Duluth, Minnesota. One night we were on maneuvers off Italy and another boat bumped into ours, and the next thing I knew a fraternity brother of mine, Milton Kessel of Dallas, was sitting right next to me! He became the executive officer under Williams. Right after Kessel came aboard I found in my desk a bottle of whiskey with a note that said 'For medicinal purposes only!' Together, Kessel and I kept the boat running.

"We crossed over to Salerno, Italy, a small town that had taken quite a beating during the landing there. It had been a really nice town before all the destruction. Apartment buildings had been blown apart on one side, and we'd look up and see people sitting on the furniture in their living room on the sixth floor with no wall! To make matters worse Mount Vesuvius had erupted just before we got there, covering everything in nine inches of ash.

"We did what we could to help the people out. We had two garbage cans at the end of our chow line. As we ate, we hid a chicken wing or two. When we left, at the end of the line we threw the trash into one can and the food that was still good to eat into the other can. The kids of Salerno came around, picked up the good bag, and ate all the food in it."

"Were the Germans still close by?"

"Oh, yes. Not far from our tents were some tracks leading up out of the water, where they pulled up ships for repairs. That place was under 24-hour guard. We threw compression grenades into the water at odd intervals to keep German swimmers from sneaking up under the tracks to place explosives. Just to be sure, before they put a ship back in the water, our divers inspected the rails and always brought back five or six bombs that had been placed on one side of the rails to dump the ship sideways when they exploded. We stood there dropping those grenades every half hour and never once got a German swimmer. They always made it through.

"We listened to Axis Sally on the radio. This German woman always ended her show with an American-sounding train whistle to make us homesick. She would say, 'Ensign Pierpoint, we know all about your boat. Ensign Pierpoint, what is your wife doing tonight?' Well, Ensign Pierpoint was on the boat next to ours. He had a prominent wife, a Dupont, and that was how they knew his name. Every night she would taunt him about how they knew all about him and his boat. But they didn't know anything. Their spies couldn't get on a Landing Craft Control. Even if an American officer tried to get on our boat without clearance, we told him no, and if he insisted, he got a .45 poked into his stomach. Some officers thought they could go anywhere. But not our boat. Those boats had so much sensitive equipment, they cost half a million dollars in 1942 money.

"We explored an abandoned Italian torpedo factory near our camp and found the steel plates they rolled to make the torpedo bodies, and we realized they'd make perfect floors for our tents. So we swiped them and set them up on bricks, and that got us out of the mud. We had a little hole under there we called our wine cellar. A tiny little Italian man came by our tents selling cherry brandy, the best thing available to drink. He took our orders and brought it the next day. This was in the middle of a tightly secured camp with guards everywhere. I have no idea how he slipped through.

"An Army supply depot was nearby, surrounded by a chain link fence, and we found a huge roll of wire sitting just inside the fence. We reached through the fence, grabbed the end of the wire and hid behind some cover as a guard walked by. When the guard was gone, we started pulling the wire off that roll, always stopping just before the guard passed. Before long we had all that wire, and we used it to set up electric lights in every tent. We found a knife switch and set it up so whenever the base went to general quarters we could cut out all the lights in an instant."

"Clever," I said.

"We were just trying to improve our living conditions," he said. "Our section of the camp was constantly being inspected. The executive officer of the base was never on the same wavelength with the boat crews. He didn't like us because we were a secret, independent unit always off doing our own thing. Once a captain came through and inspected our tent, and he asked me, 'Where'd you get all this deck plate?' I told him, 'We liberated it from the abandoned torpedo factory.'

"The executive officer said, 'I will have everything returned immediately, sir.'" Palmer imitated the man with a nasal, high-pitched voice laced with contempt.

"The captain told him, 'If you touch one thing in any of these tents, *you'll* be disciplined.' He said, 'Look at how your own officers are living, with their cots in the mud. If these men want to take the initiative to improve their conditions, don't you interfere.'

"We had some fine officers over there. Once a captain inspected our boat, and we had a deck plate missing back toward the stern. Nobody had bothered to put it back into place like it was supposed to be. Our poor Ensign Williams just about died of a heart attack when he led the captain back there and saw the deck wide open. The captain looked at the opening, saw Williams' obvious discomfort, and said, 'Now wasn't that smart, letting me see how clean the bilges are!' He walked around the ship talking to every single one of us, asking where we were from, and when he met Tommy Thomas from Charleston, he said, 'Why, *I'm* from Charleston!' and he sat down with this enlisted man for half an hour to chat about their hometown. Just as nice as could be.

"Our officers got a truck and took us into Rome, and we drove right by the beach at Anzio. What a terrible smell ... Dead guys lying around under a thin layer of sand. They'd been buried, but only in very shallow graves. It stunk terrible.

"Went into Rome, which was largely undamaged, and looked around. I was outside the Vatican when a Swiss Guard walked up to me and said, 'You're invited to a private audience with the Pope.'

"I said, 'I'm Jewish.'

"He said, 'He won't hurt you.'

"They took forty-five Allied soldiers they'd picked into an audience chamber, where we admired the tapestries and the red rug. They told us to stand in the center to be blessed by the Pope. A door opened and they carried Pius XII in on his throne. He reached down to cup his hand over our hands and bless each of us. He spoke for fifteen or twenty minutes, first in English, then several European languages, everything except German.

"I explored the Coliseum from top to bottom. You can't do that anymore. They've got everything cordoned off. But back then, you could go anywhere in Rome you wanted. I looked around down at the bottom where they kept the gladiators under the floor. I climbed all the way up among the seats where the spectators sat and into the box where the emperor sat.

"I also got to see Pompeii, the Roman town destroyed by Vesuvius. The caretaker of the place walked me through houses 2,000 years old. I saw paintings on the walls of men on top of concubines. It took us a whole day to go through that town. Now they only let you see 10 percent of it. I got to see a lot of unique and fascinating things during my time over there. I hear friends telling about how they had such a terrible time. They're talking about combat, but they're not talking about the rest of the time. Even the ones that did should be able to remember the great experiences they had in their free time.

"I remember when my crew got liberty in North Africa and we drove around those little towns. In Africa, every single town had a Joe's American Bar, and inside there would always be a woman sweeping up the cigarette butts. That seemed to be the popular name. They probably still have them there.

"Our commander liberated an Army Jeep he found sitting unattended somewhere, and we drove up to the beach to see Carthage. At that time the site was nothing but sand. The ancient city's location hadn't been discovered yet. But we knew it was under there somewhere. We just rode around the beach for a while, hoping to see something. Then we took that Jeep with us back to Italy! Several of us packed onto that thing and rode up to the top of Vesuvius and looked down in the crater.

"Then that damned executive officer of the base discovered the Jeep and made us give it back to the Army. So we lost our transportation. We had it two or three weeks before he realized something was odd about a bunch of Navy guys driving around in an Army Jeep.

"After that an LCT towed us to join Operation Dragoon on August 15, 1944."

"What part did you play in the invasion?" I asked.

"We were part of Alpha Attack Force, on the western edge of the invasion. Our landing zone in Cavalaire Bay, southwest of St. Tropez, was codenamed Red Beach. Before dawn the morning of the invasion, I saw the battleship *Texas* and some other ships make a pass along the beach, shelling inland. A battleship fires a huge projectile, so I figured I should be able to see that shell cross the sky. I watched the *Texas* fire over us from about five miles away, and strained my eyes, but I could not see one of those things. I could only see the tremendous red flare from the gun and then a big puff of black smoke.

"Fifty minutes before the landing craft hit the beach, we sent in drones full of explosives to take care of those traps made of crisscrossed railroad ties that I mentioned earlier. An LCC guided those drones right up to the traps and set them off, blowing paths through them. That was where my boat came in: to guide the landing craft precisely through those gaps.

"Something went wrong with one of the drones. LCC-40, the boat in charge of controlling the drones, passed over the top of it and it exploded, obliterating the LCC.

"The landing boats circled and then started following the leader, meaning us. On the way toward the beach, we passed the Isle de Levant, which was said to be a nudist island, on our left. We had been told the island would be left alone because they didn't think the Germans were on it. But what really

Off the southern coast of France during Dragoon, around 9 A.M. on August 15, 1944. The beach is still active an hour after the landing.

happened was, some Rangers landed on it and climbed up a cliff, expecting to find big guns the Germans were supposed to have there. They didn't find any Germans or any guns. They found garbage cans carefully lined up to look like guns from the air.

"The boats hit the beach and dropped their bows and the soldiers rushed out the front and looked for cover from the German machine guns and artillery. My boat's next job was to check behind the landing craft for debris or obstacles and help them back out safely, so the next wave could come in. Already a lot of debris from the explosions was floating around, and I could hear *bump bump bump* as the boat moved through the water. So we helped the landing craft get through all that on the way out. Every move was carefully orchestrated and timed. From the moment the first men hit the beach to the moment the last men hit was only fifteen minutes."

"You must have had a front-seat view of the fighting," I said.

"Yes. At first I was down below, ready to take the place of one of the radarmen or radiomen if they got put out of commission. But then I went up and watched the battle. The LCT that towed us carried a tank, and that tank started its engine and tried to get ashore, but the minute its tracks hit the waterline a German 90mm gun above the beach knocked it out and killed the entire crew. I would have expected our bombers to get rid of a gun that big in advance. We had good intelligence on their defenses, knew where everything was, but that gun didn't get taken out.

"The British had some LCTs equipped with rocket launchers and were supposed to go up to a precise distance from shore and fire the rockets up on the beach. But they miscalculated the distance and the rockets landed among our boats. Fifteen or twenty feet away from me, right alongside us, was an LCVP carrying fifty men. Those rockets blew that thing to bits, and when the smoke cleared, the only thing left floating was a life preserver with a chest in it.

An LST, Landing Ship Tank, reaches the beach in southern France during Operation Dragoon. The photo was taken from a gun turret on LCC-97.

"During the battle I had to decode a secret message. It was from an Air Force general: 'I will withdraw air support if you do not cease firing at my aircraft!' I don't understand why our troops would have been firing at our own planes because *all* the planes up there were ours. By that stage of the war, the Germans had no airplanes left in that area. So I just don't know what to think about whoever it was that shot at those planes.

"It was a fierce fight, but it didn't last long. The German line was thin. When our troops broke through and made it inland, they found the Germans defending with old men and children."

"Did your boat survive the battle without a scratch?"

"You know, in the middle of it, you think, they're not gonna get me, it's gonna be somebody else. But after the invasion an LCT was towing us back, and we noticed the bow was down. We found out the front end of our boat had been ripped open during the battle, and we never knew it! The damage was below the deck where we couldn't see it. We had no idea how it happened. In the excitement, the terrible noise, chaos, smoke, explosions, splashing water, we never felt or heard the explosion that got us. The bow had been drinking water ever since. We secured the hatch over the compartment where the water was coming in and pumped it out. If we hadn't discovered the damage, we would have sunk.

"Dragoon was a major invasion, but it isn't prominent in history. You never hear about it. But we landed all across southern France and took the bottom half of the country. People don't realize it."

"Why do you think that is?" I asked.

"Because on June 6 they had already invaded Normandy, and that got all the attention. Nobody ever heard about this one. People seem to think Normandy meant the war was over. They don't realize how strong the Germans still were and how many more battles had to be fought."

A view of Palmer's craft, LCC-97, at Nisida, Italy.

"What did you do after the invasion?"

"My crew got to go to Marseilles on liberty right after that, even though it was still a war zone. One of our officers got an open-bed truck with seats on it to go touring around in. I remember the first day we went into town a good bottle of champagne cost two dollars. Two days later, it was fifteen dollars. The Americans were in town, you see.

"That first day, one of our crewmembers wanted to visit a whorehouse. Our officer spoke French and asked a policeman where we could find one. The policeman was very helpful; he climbed up into the truck with the officer and guided us through town to a whorehouse! It was a little narrow building next door to a hotel. The sign on the hotel next door said in French, 'Rooms for the Night for Lovers.'

"The madam said the place was closed, and the policeman asked her why. Our officer interpreted for us. The madam said the police had shut them down because there were rumors that the fleeing Germans were sending infected men to all the whorehouses as a vengeful parting shot. The Germans were still very close by, you see.

"The policeman said, 'I am the police!' and she said, 'You're not the police *chief.*' About that time another police officer came by and gave the all clear. So our buddy got to go in while we waited outside.

"We drove around looking for souvenirs and went into a German barracks. Next thing we knew we heard gunfire close by. Our troops were still taking the damn building! Germans were still defending it at the other end! We got out of there real quick."

"Did you like serving on an LCC?" I asked.

"Yes, I did. Like I said, we were a very independent unit, insulated from a lot of the military nonsense unless something big was going on. Of course we weren't *completely* insulated. After the invasion our boat got classified as a patrol craft, and we got orders to go out and patrol. That same night a gale hit us. We kept telling them our boat wasn't designed to operate in those conditions, but they made us go out. So we took her out into the storm and had a ride like you wouldn't believe. That boat rolled a full 90 degrees, hung literally straight up and down on a wave, stayed there a moment, and then rolled back onto its bottom, thank goodness."

"In November of '44 I got orders to rotate back to the States on a Liberty ship. Funny thing was, when we took on soldiers at Naples, the ship would just be sitting there at anchor and half the soldiers turned green! We took them over to a gun platform and hosed it off when they were through being sick. But after we cleared Gibraltar and entered the Atlantic, where the seas were higher than the ship for nineteen days and the bow would come down and the screws and propellers would stick up out of the water, not a single soldier got sick the entire time. They were too excited about going home to be seasick!

"Our food supply was under a tarp on the deck: C rations, nothing but C rations. A C ration was a can with a little meat in it, a biscuit, and some coffee that was terrible. There just wasn't much to it.

"The officers on the ship had a big argument about whether Thanksgiving fell on the third or fourth Thursday of November. We ended up celebrating two Thanksgivings. We had the first one on the ship on the third Thursday. We found enough canned chili on the ship for everybody, and had chili for Thanksgiving. Then when we docked at Pier 92 at New York, we found out Thanksgiving is on the fourth Thursday! So we had another one in a big dining room after we got off the ship. They had a rule that you had to eat what you took, and an officer stood guard by the trash cans to make sure. I took two bites out of a drumstick and couldn't eat any more. None of us could. After nothing but C rations for so long, our stomachs had shrunk and we couldn't handle real food. But a rule is a rule. We had to get an officer to excuse us from the table."

Manuel Palmer in April 1998.

Charles Clinton Green
Granbury

My next interview was with a man who became a Texan after the war and enjoyed an illustrious career in business and government. He became president and CEO of the Bonanza restaurant chain before serving as a regional director of the Department of Health, Education and Welfare. He got his first crack at handling large sums of money as an Army grunt during the war.

I realized quickly the interview with Charles Green would be different. Often the grim details of war must be coaxed out of a veteran. This is understandable considering the distance in time, not to mention the ordeal of reliving long-faded horrors. Green, on the other hand, pulled no punches when he described life as an enlisted man in the Army. Words like "degradation," "misery," and "bullshit" flew like bullets from his mouth. I frequently asked him to repeat himself, sometimes because he spoke so rapidly, sometimes because I couldn't believe he said what he just said.

"I've got all kinds of stories I can tell you about the crap we went through. We just weren't ready for war. Guys who hadn't been in the service long enough got shipped overseas. I'd been

Charles Green in his winter uniform before shipping out in 1942.

in thirty-five days and found myself on a boat heading over to land on a hostile shore! None of the guys I went in with were prepared, and our officers were a sorry bunch. Arrogance, incompetence..." his voice trailed off.

"After the Japs attacked Pearl Harbor, I tried to join the Aviation Cadet Corps but couldn't pass the eye test. I also have a crooked arm from falling off a horse as a child. I got an appointment to Annapolis, but thanks to my arm, I couldn't pass the physical for that either. So despite being married, employed at a defense plant, and attending Kansas State Teachers College in Pittsburg, Kansas, I got drafted in July of '42. I had to fold up my tent and quit everything. I took my exams early to get my summer school credits and took my wife, Margaret Ann, back home to Neodesha, Kansas. I fixed her up a room to live in, said my goodbyes, and caught a train to the induction center at Leavenworth.

"I endured the indignity of the induction process, along with all the other fresh meat. I quickly lost the pair of white coveralls I had worn. They ordered me to strip. I stood in a long line of naked men, holding a bag to carry the clothes and equipment they issued me. I got fitted for a pair of boots by standing with a bucket full of sand in each hand. That's how they could tell the boots would fit when I wore a full field pack. For the physical I had to open my mouth wide, skin my penis back, show them my balls, turn around and spread my cheeks. When they saw my crooked arm they pulled me out of line and sent me to a different doctor, who said he'd have to classify me 1B. But I really wanted in as 1A."

"What does that mean?" I asked.

"1B means you don't get called unless they really get desperate for men. But hell, they'd already messed up my college and my job! I told the doctor, 'I've gone this far, I might as well just go on.'

"He said, 'You'd have to sign a waiver.' I said, 'Where is it?' and signed it. But then of course they wouldn't take me into Officer Candidate School because of my crooked arm. Because of this damned arm I couldn't ever get anything.

"The first time they took us out to the grinder and tried to teach us to march, most of us didn't know a thing about the military. They lined us up and we attempted to march a ways. A buddy of mine from high school was right in front of me.

"I said, 'Swede, one of us is out of step.'

"The old sergeant yelled, 'HALT!' and demanded, 'Who said that?'

"And I spoke right up like a dummy and said, 'I did!' I didn't know any better, but I learned quickly you don't do that.

"He said, 'Fall out!', pointed at a spot on the ground, and said, 'Stand right there!' He said, 'See that gate?' I looked and there it was, way far over on the horizon. He said, 'Up there and back on the double!'

"Little did he know I lettered in track in college as a distance runner. I hoofed it up there to that gate and back, sprinted the whole way, and pulled up to him with a smile. He said, 'How'd you like that?'

"I said, 'No sweat!'" Green snickered at the memory of his own impertinence.

"The sergeant said, 'Well then, try it again.' By the time I got back I decided the best thing to do was keep my mouth shut and look serious.

"For my first job I had the privilege to serve as latrine orderly. I made my way through school cleaning toilets and sweeping floors, so I was well prepared for this. I got the latrine sparkling clean and disinfected and turned the lids up for inspection. An officer marched in with a sergeant, who yelled 'Attention!' and I stood at attention and dutifully said my line: 'The latrine is ready for inspection, sir.' And the officer looked around and marched out of there like he was God Almighty. The sergeant said, 'As you were' and followed him."

Green snorted. His contempt for officers was palpable.

"They sent me to Fort Benjamin Harrison, Indiana, an Army finance training center. One out of every 1,000 soldiers became a finance specialist; we handled payments and deposits. I didn't get any training at Fort Ben, just stood around waiting to do something. Suddenly I got orders to go overseas with half a dozen other raw recruits. On the way to the port of embarkation we got stuck for a short time in Fort Dix, New Jersey, the asshole of creation. A swampy, miserable place miles from anything where the officers treated enlisted men like dogs. You could get in trouble there for no reason at all. Before long they shipped me overseas. Hell, I never did get any training."

"Say again?" I asked.

"I said, I never got any training."

"Did that happen often?" I asked, thinking about James McKernon Jones of Corpus Christi. The same thing happened to him, but Jones thought it was a rare occurrence. But here already was another veteran who got sent over to the war in Europe without going through basic.

"It happened *lots* of times," Green said, "even though you don't hear about it. Hell, we were totally unprepared for anything. Our leaders could just as well have slaughtered us with shotguns, for all the preparation they gave us before they threw us into the war.

"One night they drove me and the other half-dozen finance guys to a port of embarkation near New York City to ship us across the Atlantic. We had no officers. No basic training, no firearms training, no combat training. Just a bunch of bodies, nothing more. There was Donald Uher from Iowa, we called him Stinky, a small guy who smoked constantly. Marty Conners, from Boston, was older than the rest of us, maybe thirty-five. He drank constantly and didn't much care for the Army. Marty

Kaufman was a Jewish kid from Brooklyn. Leonard Kent was a real bright guy from Philadelphia.

"A colonel named Neilson met us. He was a short little guy with a mustache who carried a riding crop and thought he was God Himself. Apparently God worked at Chase National Bank of Manhattan before the war.

"He told us he was our commanding officer, ordered us to board the *Queen Elizabeth*, and disappeared. We crowded onto the *QE* with its blackened windows in the dead of night. I hoped I'd get to see the harbor, especially the Statue of Liberty, but we steamed out in the dark. We were on our way and didn't know where."

"They never told you where you were going?" I asked innocently.

"No!" he said emphatically. "They jammed 16,000 troops aboard the *QE*, and she ran blacked out and alone. Nobody could light a cigarette at night."

"Alone? Didn't you have any escort?"

"No, because she could run faster than any other ship. German submarines would have to be lucky enough to catch her from out in front to torpedo her. To prevent that she changed course every three minutes, zigzagging all the way to Scotland. The men got to eat only once every twelve hours. The whole voyage I lived on the promenade, an open-air deck with a roof. It was like living on a porch. We crowded into rows of bunks five high, and the deck turned into one huge craps game.

"We unloaded in Scotland, again at night, so I never got to see the damn boat I sailed over on. As we assembled to board trains in Glasgow for some unknown destination, our colonel reappeared. We hadn't seen him once during the trip because he spent the whole time in officers' quarters while we lived like dogs. A Scottish enlisted man strode up to him, snapped to attention, and told him, 'Sir, you can put your men on this train here.' Somehow the colonel took offense at this and said,

'Young man, I've been here before. I've been traveling here longer than you've been alive, and I can quite competently take care of my men.'

"So the Scottish soldier snapped his heels and walked off. Guess what? That was the last time we ever saw the colonel!"

"You're kidding," I said.

"No, I'm not! And he was our commanding officer...."

"I rode a train all night, my mind long on questions and short on answers. When the sun rose we unloaded and hid in barracks, out of sight of German aircraft. Night fell and we rode the train the rest of the way to Salisbury, where we holed up. We waited there several days for information. None came. Hell, I got so bored I volunteered for KP!

"German bombers flew over from time to time, and I had lots of fun jumping in a trench full of icy water. I could hear the engines from a long way off. The German bombers didn't have synchronized engines like ours, and they made a kind of throbbing sound, so you could tell them apart from ours. We lived in a blacked out Nissen hut that had a maze at the entrance to keep light from escaping at night. When the air raid sirens sounded a sergeant ran in and shouted, 'Everybody out!' and we ran outside and jumped in a slit trench behind the hut. Of course it rained all the time, filling the trench with water, and this was in the middle of winter. We got tired of that *real* quick. So when the sergeant came and shouted 'Everybody out!' we started to get up, but the minute he left we all went straight back to bed!

"Once I walked with an older soldier back from the mess along some trees, and he looked up and said, 'Jesus Christ, that's a German bomber!' A Ju-88 flew straight toward us, 200 feet off the ground. I stood there and watched it, fascinated, and I heard my buddy shout, 'Get over here, you shithead!' from his hiding place behind the trees. I stared the pilot in the face and then ran for cover as the bomber flew over me. I guess boredom does strange things to your judgment.

"A lieutenant finally paid us some attention; he ordered us to lay out our gear and prepare to move. I asked him, 'Where we goin'?' and he looked at me like I must be out of my mind. If he knew, no way would he tell *me*. We had a problem: Our gear had stayed behind somewhere in Scotland, presumably with our missing colonel. We didn't even have an NCO. Nobody was in charge.

"The lieutenant came back and started eatin' on my butt because we hadn't laid our gear out, and I started asking questions. I said, 'We don't have our gear with us and we don't belong to this outfit. Where are you going, and what are we doing here?'

"So he asked, 'Who's your officer?'

"'We don't have one.'

"'Who's your NCO?'

"'We don't have one.'

"'Where are your records?'

"'Don't have any.'

"Finally he said, 'Well, I can't just leave you here.' He got us restocked with clothing and equipment, took us to Liverpool, and loaded us onto a boat, the SS *Brazil*, with the other men. Still nobody knew a damn thing about anything."

"Let me get this straight," I interrupted, perplexed. "You traveled halfway around the world without ever hearing your orders? Your commanding officer just disappeared without a trace? You didn't even know what unit you were supposed to join up with or where you would be stationed?"

"Hell, we didn't even know who this unit was that we were staying with. Nobody told us a thing. The colonel never came back. We found out later he realized our destination and had no intention of going there. So he didn't."

"Did you even have a gun at this point?" I asked.

"Hell no, but what if I did? Nobody ever trained me how to shoot it."

I let out a deep breath, trying to imagine how I would react to this situation at the age of twenty: unarmed, untrained, and lost in the swirl of humanity.

"When daylight came we looked out from our boat and saw the damnedest armada you ever saw afloat. As far as you could see, nothing but ships." Even now the memory struck awe into Green's voice.

"Officers passed out M-1 rifles and ammunition. My group of finance guys had no idea how to use this weapon. We started figuring out how to take it apart and put it back together. We blindfolded ourselves with socks and mixed up a pile of parts and tried to build rifles in the dark."

"Did officers help you with this?" I asked hopefully.

"Are you kidding? No officers helped us, we just did it on our own initiative. No officer would be caught dead coming down into that mess where we lived, down in the bowels of a Liberty ship full of 5,000 men stacked five high, 18 to 24 inches apart.

"Then they passed out a little book. It said we were about to make a landing in North Africa and went on to tell us all about the climate, the Arab customs, and the diseases. And it had a little warning. Listen to this: 'Your present journey will be taking you to new parts of the world where the people, their customs and manner of living, and the geography of the country will be, for the majority of us, completely strange and foreign. Furthermore, our welcome by the inhabitants of Morocco, Algeria and Tunis is not known at this time.'" He chuckled ruefully.

"And this was the first time you heard where you were going?" I asked.

"That's right. My ship landed November 11, 1942, at Mers-el-Kebir, the place where the British earlier sank part of the

French fleet to keep it away from German hands. None of us knew what to expect. This was D+3, so the beach was already secured. We unloaded our gear and headed off down the road to Oran like a bunch of idiots, loaded down with equipment: gas masks, respirators, first aid kits, canteens, extra pairs of shoes, blankets, clothing, bandoleers of ammunition, and rifles. We burned up under the sun, wearing woolens impregnated with oil against gas attack, terribly hot and greasy. It's the same latitude as Texas."

"My God," I said.

"That's right. Men melted down, passed out, and fell into ditches. Medics scrambled to take care of them. Soldiers started throwing equipment away. My little group hired an Arab with a two-wheeled cart to carry our stuff. That was great while it lasted.

"We tromped toward Oran out in the open like we owned the place. But we didn't. German snipers started shooting at us from hiding places. GIs ran likes quail in every direction. Men got hit as they ran and fell. Our Arab abandoned us. The road offered very little cover.

"Germans shot at me many times, but I never fired my M-1 back at them because hell, I never could see anybody. I never once got a glimpse of a German soldier while we were in combat. North Africa was one confused mess. Half the time we didn't know who we were up against: Vichy French, French Foreign Legion, and Germans were all out there. And a lot of Arabs didn't like us much either.

"We straggled into Oran and holed up for the night in a huge old elevator, where sniper fire couldn't reach us. Rats scurried around the place. Guys screamed and yelled all night, waking up with rats running over them. Outside some huge barrels full of wine sat on the dock. German snipers shot holes in them and GIs zigzagged out there, hid behind the barrels, held their helmets under the stream, and came back with wine."

"You've got to be kidding me," I said. I uttered that phrase a lot during this interview.

"No. Some people will do anything for a drink."

"What did you do next?"

"We followed a bunch of soldiers around without knowing who they were or where they were going. I learned later it was II Corps, and we had participated in Operation Torch."

"How did you find out?" I asked.

"History books."

"Excuse me?"

"Look, people may not believe it can be this dumb, but it is! We had no idea what unit we were with. I found out in history books."

"Wow," I said. Green shattered myths I cherished with every new revelation. I could imagine a dapper officer telling his gung-ho soldiers, "Men, we're going on a top-secret mission, but I can't tell you where. Load up and let's go." But the Army gave Green and his buddies less than that. Not only did they lack information, they lacked the luxury of an officer who refused to share it with them. They had nothing.

"We holed up in a parking garage that ran several stories down a hill. Our commanders expected the Germans to drop paratroopers on us, so we sandbagged the whole place, put up gun emplacements, and waited. Even at this point, none of us had ever fired a damn gun.

"It rained for days, covering the town with mud. The food got contaminated and 200 to 300 men became desperately ill. Some drank themselves into oblivion. With the Germans gone the town quieted down, and we started getting organized. Officers arrived to set up a finance unit. Somehow they found us, even though *we* didn't know where the hell we were. We started doing our job, handling money. We became the 132nd Finance Disbursing Section. We never had an officer for long. We kept getting new ones because the old ones got sent back to

Leavenworth for stealing or losing money. Corruption was everywhere. Lousy leadership, poor morale...." Disgust laced his words.

"We worked day in and out, living in tents, eating out of mess kits while sitting on the floor the whole damn time I was over there. The Germans hit us with air raids from time to time, just enough to keep us on our toes, but by that time they didn't have many planes in the air. We spent our time guarding money and counting money. Besides the soldiers' pay, we handled Lend-Lease money and prisoner-of-war pay. Of course most criminal activity eventually ends up in money, so we worked with the criminal investigation department catching crooks and thieves. We reported every time the criminals came and went, and CID put a tail on them."

"What kind of criminal activity?" I asked.

"Prostitution rings depositing their money, that sort of thing. GIs would take entire caravans of trucks loaded with contraband out into the desert to sell to Arabs on the black market. Officers would set up dummy payrolls with fictitious names, knowing years would pass before anybody checked any of this. One group came in every month with payroll records full of different signatures of all kinds, smudged like payrolls would be after being carried around in the weather. A captain, a lieutenant, a master sergeant, and a buck sergeant. I don't remember what tipped us off, but we grew leery of them and reported them to CID. It turned out they were deserters who had set themselves up as a bogus company. The investigators found these four men living high on the hog in town with a bunch of women and bringing in a whole company's pay!

"One of our officers, a lieutenant named Jones, got done in by his own stupidity. Roosevelt and Churchill met in Casablanca and changed the franc rate from fifty to seventy-five francs a dollar. At the time Lieutenant Jones, the man personally responsible for the cash, was covering up all kinds of shortages in his accounts, and he had just disbursed a million dollars worth of payroll. Then the troops started depositing their money back to send home to their wives and families. The money had gone out at one exchange rate and it came back in at a different rate! For every dollar worth of francs a soldier got paid the day before, he now had $1.50. This Lieutenant Jones got so confused he didn't know what to do, it was too complicated for him. He panicked and said, 'Just shut her down, close the doors, and we'll figure out where we are.'

"But his superior, Colonel Rovin, a big, fat Jewish man, very likable, found out about it and stormed in and demanded, 'What's going on?' Lieutenant Jones told him, and the colonel said, 'By God, this is war! We never shut down! This is war!'

"So he opened the windows back up and we went about our business. But at the end of the month when we tallied everything up and accounted for the change in the exchange rate, Lieutenant Jones had gone from being short to having *too much* money. The confusion had exposed his slipshod practices or worse. Two sergeants, good men named Kunkle and Gervitz, had the goods on him and blew the whistle. Of course they ended up getting court-martialed for the discrepancies themselves."

"You're kidding," I said. "What were their first names?"

Green thought a moment. "Don't know," he said. "Sergeants didn't have first names."

"OK. What happened to the officers involved?"

"The Army sent Colonel Rovin home and dismissed him from service. Lieutenant Jones ended up in a repple depple and never got another assignment. No unit would take him. He showed up once at our office drunker than a hoot owl, wanting something, but he was so damn drunk we couldn't understand him. Being in that depot was like being in Siberia. A man could get lost forever in there. As far as I know he spent the rest of the war there.

"So he disappeared, and two or three other officers followed him for similar reasons, until we finally got a colonel who came from the Mercantile National Bank in Dallas, Texas, a diehard Aggie by the name of A.O. Nicholson. I never knew his first name, but we came to call him 'Nick.' He became our permanent officer, and we started handling all the money from the North African theater of operations. Nicholson sat down with us and said, 'You take care of the money and the procedures, and I'll see that you're taken care of.' That was the first time I'd ever heard an officer say anything like that. Thank God we had him for the rest of the war.

"A lot of the previous officers got done in by their own incompetence. Their subordinates stole from right under their noses and they came up short. Once Nicholson arrived we never had that problem again. After the war he settled with the General Accounting Office, which found his total loss to be $20 out of $76 million."

"You mentioned the lieutenant being drunk," I said. "How often did you see officers in that condition?"

"Alcoholism ran wild," Green said. "One evening a buddy of mine and I walked back to camp and noticed an officer stumbling along a wall, holding it for support. We got closer and by God it was Nicholson, our own colonel! An enlisted man who got caught with a drunken officer would find himself in deep trouble. That's considered fraternization, very bad news. So we said, 'Colonel, we'll stay behind you and point you in the right direction.' From a distance we guided him toward the hotel where he was staying. I shouted across the street to the guard in front of the hotel, 'We're gonna point him in your direction! You got him?' The guard knew the drill well by now and said, 'Send him over, I got him. But you guys better get out of here before somebody sees you.' Nicholson never said a word about it to any of us. But my relationship with him improved after

Major A.O. Nicholson in Rome.

that. Until then it had been very strained because of the way he treated me when he first got there.

"We enlisted men couldn't get hard liquor, but the officers could. Enlisted men drank whatever they could get, meaning native wines and cognac, which we weren't used to and could make somebody crazy. Some men just couldn't handle being stuck out there and turned to drinking. I woke up one night and found one man in the DTs, trying to crawl the wall, screaming and yelling. I called the medics and never saw him again. Another man came into the tent at night so drunk he thought he was in the latrine and pissed all over another guy.

"Then there was this fellow in my unit named Jim Graves, an extremely bright lawyer from Florida. Knew jujitsu. He wouldn't take a promotion, didn't want any responsibility, and he didn't intend to fool around with the damned Army. This man was an operator, let me tell you. Somehow he managed to come and go as he pleased, just like a civilian. He never lived in camp with us. With money, negotiation, and his own smarts, he held the Army at arm's length that whole time, never let it run his life. When he came into the finance unit under my supervision, I told him what I needed him to do for me. I found him reading magazines and told him I couldn't let him do that, he had work to do. He just smiled at me and said, 'You know, Charlie, I'm not very good at this, and I'll make lots of errors if you push me.' And that was the way he was with the whole Army. Nobody could get him to do anything he didn't want to do.

"I thought, 'What the hell am I going to do with this guy? I need people who'll do the job.' A position opened for a finance specialist at Gibraltar to refinance pilots who'd been shot down over Europe and brought out by the Spanish underground. I recommended him for that position to get rid of him. I'll be damned if I didn't read about him in the Stars and Stripes. He started up a nightclub right there by the Rock of Gibraltar! He changed into civilian clothes and crossed into Spain to get stuff to sell: leather goods, clothing, souvenirs. People came to his club to buy and sell and drink. He had a sign on the door that said 'Hang your rank when you come in.'

"The Army ordered him back to Oran. He came back with only half a barracks bag of belongings. I said, 'Don't worry, I'll get you fixed up in camp, get you some quarters arranged.' He said, 'No, don't bother, Charlie, I'm not going up there.' Here I'd been living in a tent all this time, and he never did live in camp with the other soldiers! And that half-full bag he brought with him? Turned out to be half full of Swiss watches.

"One night, walking back to camp through Oran with another soldier, I heard something in an alley, looked back there, and saw a soldier down. I ran to help and it was Jim Graves, absolutely poison drunk, lying in his own vomit. We couldn't leave him there; the locals would rob him and quite possibly kill him for his clothes. We took him back up to our office building, with him still vomiting, and cleaned him up and left him to sleep on the floor where he'd be safe. He never said a word about it—no thank you or kiss my butt or anything. But later I would be very glad I had helped him.

"It's understandable why the men drank," Green said thoughtfully. "It was a long hard dreary damn tour of duty in a hot, dusty place, sleeping in tents and getting mail maybe every two months. All this time I was in my sexual prime, and I was confined to camp every night in the middle of a society where if you mess with the women, you get your balls cut off."

"Pardon me?" I asked.

"That's right, the Arabs will cut your balls off if you come around their women."

"And did...?"

"Yes, it happened to one guy I knew about. The tent city I lived in stood on an old flea market, next to a high cemetery wall. All the time I heard them holding funerals over there on the other side. You know they pay their mourners, who carry

The tent city where Charles Green lived in North Africa.

on something awful until a bell rings and then everybody shuts up and goes home. Anyway, our officers warned us to stay away from Arab women. I got up one morning and walked to the john and saw one of our guys naked, draped over the cemetery wall with his penis stuffed in his mouth."

The words caught me off guard. "Uh ... dead?"

"What do you think? We lost a lot of guys over there to causes other than combat with actual Germans. The Military Police authorized certain streets and protected us only on those streets. GIs got drunk and wandered off limits into rough districts, thinking they could flirt with Arab women the way they could with American women. You can't do it."

"Did the Army ever retaliate when the locals killed American soldiers?" I asked.

"Not that I know of. Our officers told us where we could go, and they kept certain streets safe. But if a GI went outside of those areas, that was his problem. I don't know how to run an army, frankly, but … you wouldn't believe the things military people do sometimes, in the name of following the rules. One night we didn't get off work until 9 o'clock and had to walk two miles to our camp through Arab districts. The damned MPs picked us up for violating curfew and hauled our asses down to the police station. It took us 45 minutes to get hold of our colonel, who ordered them to release us. The bastards threw us out on the streets farther away from camp than we were in the first place and in a worse district! They just said, 'Get on out of here,' and I said, 'God damn, guys, can't you get us some transportation?' And they said 'No way!' They said the rules forbade them from providing transportation. The whole point of the curfew was for our safety, and these idiots picked us up, ran us through the mill, and then dumped us out on the street in a dangerous neighborhood with no protection! In the Army, a rule's a rule even when it doesn't make sense.

"Later when we moved the operation to Casablanca, we ran the currency control office at the port. Sailors off incoming ships were supposed to convert their American money into local currency. If they didn't, they'd spend their dollars in town where foreign spies could get their hands on it and use it to get into America. We tried to warn these sailors to watch themselves and stay on approved streets. But these young nuts said 'We've been in ports around the world, we can take care of ourselves.' Many mornings when we came back to work we saw two or three stiffs lying on the floor of the shore patrol office next door. Guys who didn't heed our advice. Clothing gone, money gone, stabbed to death."

He paused to take a breath, seemingly for the first time. I thought about everything he'd told me so far and observed, "What you are describing to me is chaos. Drunkenness, lack of communication, soldiers getting murdered by the locals…."

"The army *was* in chaos in North Africa," he said firmly. "We just weren't ready for war, plain and simple. We lost a lot of men due to accidents, drunken fights. Rommel would have beat the hell out of us if he hadn't run out of fuel and supplies."

"Tell me more about the officers you served under," I said. "You didn't think much of most of them."

"The officers I knew were a real sorry bunch. Now this Colonel Nicholson would stand up and look after his men, and that was the first thing an officer was supposed to do, so he was all right, but even he got horsey sometimes. Every letter I ever wrote for two and a half years, an officer read it before sending it on. Nick had just come over and his first job was to read the mail. The rule stated if a soldier said something objectionable, the officer could cut it out or send the letter back, but he couldn't punish a guy for what he wrote. Despite that rule, Nick brought me in to chew my ass because he didn't like what I said about the outfit. I had been cussing the Army about the lack of promotions and the kind of officers I served under. We'd never even met before, that's how new he was. We had words and I asked him if I could talk to him man to man. He said yes.

"I told him, 'You just got here and you haven't the slightest idea what we've been through. We've been in this damn hole eighteen months, working our asses off and getting the job done, and here you come with all this bullshit, *blah blah blah*.' I blasted him until he'd had enough. He jumped up, shouted, 'Ten *hut*!' to shut me up and put me on company punishment."

"What does company punishment mean?" I asked.

"It's disciplinary action that doesn't require a court-martial. In my case it meant I 'walked the line' in full field gear, backpack, and rifle, back and forth for three hours that night. Another time I got punished I had to paint the mess hall... black, for some reason."

"What about other officers?" I asked.

"We got it from both ends. Nicholson didn't have anything to do with us after we left work at the end of the day and returned to camp. Another group of officers ran that. We had one there named Lieutenant Smith, from East Orange, New Jersey. I'll never forget the bastard." Venom tainted Green's voice.

"Know his first name?"

"Nope. Lieutenants didn't have first names. The men had been getting up from their tents every day to get cleaned up, get some breakfast, and then get dressed for work. We'd go to breakfast looking any way we wanted to, you know. Then one day at four in the morning this Lieutenant Smith jerked us all out of bed and lined us up and told us what a sorry bunch we were. He said we had it easy back here behind the lines and by God he'd been to war, and by God all this nonsense was gonna end. He put us on butt detail. Here we were old pros, and we had to go around the camp and pick up cigarette butts like raw recruits. He made us do it two or three mornings.

"Then one morning I stepped out front and asked for permission to speak. I said, 'Lieutenant, we do the job we're supposed to do. We handle enormous responsibilities with huge amounts of money, walking two miles to work and back; we've been doing this a long time just fine, and now you're coming in here and all you're accomplishing is to destroy our morale.'

"God damn, that made him mad! When I came back from work that night he took me down to headquarters for a hearing. I saw enough brass in that room to make a tuba.

"The lieutenant told these officers a bunch of lies, including that I had cussed him, which I had not. The colonel in charge said, 'Sergeant, let's hear your story.'

"I said, 'That's his language, not mine. I didn't cuss him.' The lieutenant tried to interrupt me but the colonel silenced him.

"I said, 'We're getting our job done, and if any of you resent us for not being on the front, well then send us up front, we'll go fight. But this is where you assigned us, and we're doing what we've been told to do, and we're doing it well.'

"This old colonel listened to me and said, 'OK, thank you.'

"Before long Lieutenant Smith got fined $100 for conduct unbecoming an officer and they transferred him out!" Green cackled with glee.

"How about that," I said.

"The money kept piling up. We ended up with $76 million in cash. We counted it over and over again and moved it around in field safes. When our unit moved from Oran to Casablanca in '44, I drew the job of shepherding about $30 million of that in two of those 'forty and eight' boxcars, so called because they carried forty men or eight mules. My superior, a constantly drunk lieutenant, showed up after the POWs loaded the field safes onto the train. He brought a satchel full of cognac and said, 'Where's my bunk?' I said, 'There's no bunk. We're sleeping on these field safes, and yours is over here.' This man was responsible for $30 million, and he stayed drunk the whole trip through the Atlas Mountains into Casablanca. That's what I mean when I say officers were a sorry lot."

"Describe a field safe for me."

"A three-foot-square metal box with a locking lid. Each one held $1 million. We counted a million bucks, mostly in twenties, had somebody recount it, filled up the safe, and Colonel Nicholson poured wax all over it, in the keyholes and around the seams. Then he pressed his Aggie ring into the wax. That was his seal.

"Some general found out we had $76 million. An Army regulation stated no unit will have more than $30,000 in cash, so he sent people over to raise hell. Finally he thought about it and said he could keep track of one man with $76 million a hell of a lot easier than he could 76 men with $1 million, so he told the colonel to keep it."

"How did you accumulate $76 million?" I asked.

"Well, just imagine. Hundreds of thousands of troops keep coming over, bringing money with them. What are you gonna do with it on the front? You deposit it to send home. We didn't ship cash home, we sent paperwork. So our pile of cash just kept growing. The regulations require that the amount be verified by actual count every thirty days, so headquarters always sent two 'disinterested officers' down to count the money. When they came down Nicholson always took them into his office and had a drink with them. They just signed the report and left. No damn way could they actually count that much money!

"Then one month two men came down who refused to sign unless Nicholson changed the order so it didn't specify 'actual count.' Otherwise they insisted on counting. Nicholson didn't trust them without one of his own men watching, so he sent them with me. They sat down and started to count while I watched. Another enlisted man relieved me from time to time. Remember, this pile of money consisted of small bills, nothing bigger than a twenty. Well, hell, they counted and counted and counted, and the pile didn't seem to get any smaller. Before they knew it the month passed and they hadn't even made a dent in it! So headquarters did away with that procedure.

"When I escorted the $30 million through the mountains to Casablanca, I had orders to arrange quarters for our group at a certain camp and then come back to the train to get everybody. A sergeant let me in to see the commanding officer, and who did I see but this same damn Lieutenant Smith!"

"Uh-oh," I said.

"He got this evil look in his eye and said, 'Well, well, Sergeant Green!' I told him my group needed accommodations, and he said, 'We don't have any room for you.'

"I said, 'All right, sir, I'll report that back.' I flipped him a salute and returned to the train. Colonel Nicholson drove up and demanded to know why the hell we were still at the train instead of in quarters. I told him. God damn, I thought he was gonna blow up.

"He said, 'Come with me!' and we drove in a staff car to the camp. He marched in there and had a piece of that guy like you wouldn't believe. And guess what? The lieutenant got fined $100 *again* and was cashiered out!"

"What does that mean, cashiered out?" I asked.

"It means he's gone, booted out of the unit." Green could not contain his delight.

"This man had been with the 36th Division when they got slaughtered in Salerno, and he was one of the screwups in that disaster. I guess he thought he'd make himself feel better by kicking us around a while. Let me tell you, lotsa sorry officers. A lot of them got dismissed from the service and sent home. Enlisted men go to jail, but officers get sent home."

"I understand you went on a top secret mission while you were based there at Casablanca," I said.

"That's right. In December of '44, Colonel Nicholson ordered me to fly to Naples, Italy, to accompany $3 million in Canadian gold. The crate was so damn heavy I made some prisoners of war load it on the C-47. Standard procedure called for the pilot to look at his weight and balance book before takeoff to find out what he had aboard, how much it weighed, and whether the weight was properly distributed on the plane. But he didn't do that, because when he glanced back into the cargo compartment he didn't see much, just one big crate. He taxied out and tried to take off and the plane just kept rolling down the runway, groaning. The pilot struggled to get her off the ground, and finally pulled up way down at the end. He walked back later and asked, 'What the hell we got on here?'

"I said, 'I can't tell you.'

"He asked, 'Can you tell me after we get there?' and I said, 'I don't know, we'll see.'

"I had boarded the plane wearing khakis, we took off in Africa after all, and just about froze to death on the twelve-hour flight to Italy. A general took the flight, escorting a civilian who turned out to be the new ambassador to Italy.

"After a while we all started getting hungry, but the pilot only had enough food for his two special passengers, not us dogfaces. But the general and the ambassador shared their food with us! I've always said the higher the rank, the easier he is to talk to. It's the 2nd lieutenants who are chicken shit.

"We landed in Italy and the pilot asked me again about the cargo.

"'We just hauled a fortune in gold,' I told him.

"'It's a damn good thing you didn't tell me before,' he said, 'because I would have junked the whole damn plane and you with it and kept the gold and buried it!'

"It was just talk...probably. Most of the guys over there were straight shooters. But you never know. Crooks gather around money like flies to honey.

"After I delivered the gold I still had these papers marked 'Top Secret,' and a light bulb went off in my head. I thought, 'Hell, I'm in Italy. I'll never be here again. I'm going to use

Visiting friends in Naples in 1944. Charles Green is crouching in front.

these orders and go see Rome!' So I went to the transportation office and requested transportation to Rome. At that time the fighting was going on just north of Rome, so the soldier said he'd have to see my orders. He was just doing his job."

Delight at the memory of mischief lifted Green's voice.

"I told him with a dead serious face, 'I can't show you the orders, they're top secret, but I can show you the heading.'

"He took one look at the words 'top secret' marked on the paper and nodded. 'I've got a truck going up to Rome in the morning and I'll put you on it,' he said. It shouldn't have worked but it did. I got a frosty ride in the back of a truck covered by nothing more than a tarp with fifteen guys. Somebody loaned me an overcoat because it was so cold. The coastline between Naples and Rome had been blown to bits. Buildings stood with half of them missing, exposing the furniture in the rooms. Women washed clothes in ditches, and children huddled around little fires. I had intended to go sightseeing in Rome, but I began to wonder what would be left for me to look at.

"What a relief to discover that Rome was largely untouched! I spent a fantastic week exploring it. I had to find room and board with civilians; I couldn't get quarters with the Army since I wasn't supposed to be there in the first place. An Italian lawyer I met gave me a tour of the city. I bought a cameo broach, a doll, a bracelet, and earrings and sent them home to Ann. My granddaughter Amy has all those treasures now.

"I hitchhiked back to Naples. My orders said for me to return to Casablanca by boat, but I didn't want to do that. I'd had enough of boats. So I pulled the same trick with the top-secret orders and finagled a plane ride back! I returned to Casablanca ahead of schedule, and nobody ever knew I had gone to Rome." Green sounded very pleased with himself. "At Casablanca I found out the gold's purpose: bribery of Italian officials to help ease their minds about capitulating.

"The Army's rotation system sent soldiers home for thirty days when they accumulated enough points. After two and a half years I had a battle star and plenty of points. You'd think they'd just put me on a plane back to the States from Casablanca, but no, they flew me back in the other direction to Naples and stuck me on a god damned Liberty ship. They piled 300 of us in a compartment below the waterline in the bow. We spent twenty-one days on the ship without a bath, and hadn't had a bath for fifteen days before. Men got sick as hell. If you've never been in the North Atlantic in February, that's some of the roughest water in the world. Men vomited and heaved down there for twenty-one days. A lot of these men were older guys from the 36th and 34th Divisions, shot-up guys full of holes."

Green's rapid-fire speech suddenly slowed. He collected his thoughts.

"Let me warn you," he said cautiously, "Every time I try to tell this story I go to crying. The ship approached New York City, and everybody wanted to see the harbor. Men crowded like rats all over the deck that evening, covering everything they could climb or stand on. As we passed the Statue of Liberty, a ferryboat came alongside carrying a Red Cross band that played the 'Star-Spangled Banner.'"

He struggled to force the words out.

"Everybody cried like babies. We'd been through three years of degradation and human bullshit...."

I waited, a little embarrassed, while he wrestled for control of his voice.

"I couldn't wait to get off that ship. It takes a long time to unload 6,000 men. By the time I got off it was four in the morning, colder than a well-digger's ass. And then on the dock... Give me a minute...."

"Take your time," I said.

"When I came down the gangplank I saw gray ladies ... Shit, I still can't tell this story after all this time."

He coughed and cleared his throat.

"They served us hot chocolate and doughnuts ... We hadn't been treated with any kindness for so long! It got the best of us all. It still gets me."

Green took a moment to recompose himself.

"After more than thirty days without a bath, we stank like goats. My clothing was slick with filth. The guys coming back from artillery positions in Italy had it even worse. But they took us to a camp for the night, and in the morning we bathed and went down to chow and couldn't believe our eyes. They treated us to a feast. We got to eat out of real plates. People served us like we were kings. 'How would you like your eggs, sir? What kind of cereal would you like?'" His voice trembled again.

"The next day I got on a train and headed west. By this stage of the war they had the movement of men so organized, the train just dropped railcars off at every stop, getting shorter the farther it traveled. I was among the last on that train. I got off at Kansas City and rode a bus to Leavenworth and went home to my wife. It was strange, being close to her again after so long. We were glad to see each other, but there was an awkwardness between us.

"The war ended in Europe, and the Army notified me it had extended my leave fifteen days and then it was gonna send me to the South Pacific! Jesus Christ, I'd already given them three years, and now this!

"First they sent me to San Antonio for reclassification, and after I sat on my ass there two weeks they determined I was most useful in ... Whattaya know? *Finance!*"

We laughed.

"On the way back to the finance training center at Fort Benjamin Harrison, I rode the train by my wife's house. It sits right next to the Frisco railroad track. I passed right by the damn house and I couldn't even stop.

"The Army decided rather than sending me to the Pacific, they wanted me to return to Africa. I didn't want to go. I walked into Fort Benjamin Harrison for the last time before my departure and ran into who else but Jim Graves! He asked me what I was up to, and I told him I was about to ship out. I said, 'When you get off let's go get some coffee.'

"He said, 'Hell, I don't need to get off. Let's go have some coffee now." So we did, and we talked about my problem, being shipped back to that hellhole. He asked me, 'Where would you like to be?'

"I told him the nearest thing to my hometown of Neodesha, Kansas, would suit me just fine.

"'No problem,' he said. 'I owe you one for saving my life in Africa.'

"'But how you gonna do that?' I asked.

"He said, 'None of your damn business.'"

I thought about those Swiss watches and laughed.

"The next day I got orders to Camp Chaffee at Ft. Smith, Arkansas, just down the railroad track 100 miles from Neodesha! Can you believe it? I couldn't wait to go home, so close by. But they wouldn't let me out of the Army because I had a critical specialty. They needed finance specialists to discharge other soldiers and pay them. I specialized in officers' pay and had 1,500 officers to take care of. I got so damn pissed off about being stuck in the service so these lousy officers could get their pay, I raised hell until they finally let me go home. I went home with only $60 in my pocket and nothing but the Army uniform on my back. And that was my miserable three years of crap all over the Mediterranean theater, living like a dog.

"One disappointing thing, there is no mention on my discharge papers of having served with the 132nd FDS, where I spent two and a half years and had all those experiences! So I wrote the Army to see that my record reflects where I served, and I got a letter back stating all records for several million men burned in a huge fire at a records center in St. Louis."

I nodded sympathetically. "Right, in 1973. I've heard about that."

"So the only record of what I've done is my own memory! Except my discharge paper, but a soldier's discharge paper only shows the very last unit he was stationed with, and that was some damn service battalion in Fort Smith, Arkansas, where I spent all of two months! I look back over all that hell we went through, and now there's no damn record? As far as the record is concerned, we didn't even go!"

"Amazing that one fire could destroy all that information," I said.

"But the worst thing," Green said, "was to come back from all that depression and struggle for two and a half years to find out I had been cuckolded."

"You're kidding," I said.

"No. Back when I was a sophomore in college, I had married my neighborhood girl, Margaret Ann, who lived across the alfalfa field. While I was off to war she had an affair with Gene Cram, a local businessman. That nearly destroyed me. I'm telling the honest to God truth, I sat in those tents all that time, the time of my highest virility in my entire life, and I came home clean. And she broke my heart."

"What did you do?"

"I didn't find out about it until after she became pregnant with our only child, so I decided to stick with her and try to rebuild the marriage. I had to put up with a hell of a lot of stuff. The marriage was never the same. But she had diabetes and needed care. Preserving the marriage was the right thing to do. So I did it. We were married thirty-five years until she died in 1975."

"Did you remarry?"

"Oh yes," he said, brightening. "I've been married twenty-five years now to a wonderful woman, Louise Schaffer."

"What happened to the local businessman?"

"I carried him out to the edge of town fully intending to kill him. But I decided I was doing something stupid, so we had a lot of words and then I took him back to town. I told myself, 'This is crazy, I'm gonna get myself in trouble over something I didn't do. I didn't do it, *they* did it. They're gonna have to live with it.'

"And anyway," he said smugly, "he died young."

Charles Green
today

Ninety percent of what I know
I learned aboard submarines

Rufus Roark
Graham

"I had tried to get into the Air Force but I was six feet tall and weighed 118 pounds, and they wouldn't take me because they said I was underweight," Rufus Roark told me. "So I went home and waited to be drafted, and before long I was in the Navy.

"I didn't much care for boot camp there at San Diego and was looking for a way out. So when they came around looking for men to join the submarine fleet, I jumped at the chance. The Silent Service was an all-volunteer force.

"I figured they'd send me to sub school in New London, Connecticut. But I was wrong. They immediately put me on a Navy ammunition ship on its way to Pearl Harbor, and in three weeks I found myself on the submarine USS *Barb*, SS-220. This was the first time I'd even seen a submarine, let alone been on one. She had just come around from the Atlantic to join the war against Japan.

"I went down into that sub, six feet tall and 118 pounds, and the chief of the boat saw me, pointed at me with a gleam in his eye, and said, 'You're just the guy we're looking for!' He had a special job for me. He took me to a semicircular hatch, about 21 inches across and told me to crawl inside. I got down in there by going in with one arm down my side and one arm up over my head. He said, 'Great! You're in the aft freshwater tank. Your job is to clean it and repaint it.' They gave me a wire brush and I scraped the scale off the bulkheads, dried them off with rags, and then painted the whole tank with barely enough room to turn around. I just got into whatever position I could get in to reach all the nooks and crannies, crouching, standing, on my knees, using a drop light to see what I was doing. It was pretty tight, but I was OK. I don't have claustrophobia. I just don't like heights. Put me on a six-foot ladder and I get a nosebleed.

"I spent three days in that musty-smelling tank, and when I got out the chief of the boat said, 'I've got another one just like it up forward for you!' So I spent the next three days cleaning and painting the forward freshwater tank. That was my introduction to submarines."

"How nice," I said, and he chuckled.

"You could try for any job you wanted on the sub, and I thought it would be exciting to be a torpedoman, so I started studying to make my rating. Training was hands-on, under the supervision of petty officers. They gave me all kinds of diagrams and books to study the workings of the torpedo, how it was made, how to maintain it."

"Did you find it difficult adjusting to life on a submarine?" I asked.

"Life aboard a sub was whatever you made it. It could be considered confining, but you had all the room you really needed, and you weren't going anywhere anyway. Bunk space was very tight. In the mess hall we had only four tables, and only a third of the crew could eat at a time. Everywhere I went I had to go through watertight doors with hatches about four feet high. I've still got ridges on the top of my head from smacking the tops of those things all the time.

"Must have been tricky getting around, being six feet tall," I said.

"Yes, and by the time I got out I was six foot one and a half. I was still growing, like all the other boys."

"Can you describe what it looked and sounded like inside the sub when you were submerged?" I asked.

"Condensation on the inside of the hull was common," he said. "Especially in cold climates like northern Japan, the Kurile Islands. The air inside the sub became quite cold in winter. Icicles hung from the bulkheads. Water started dripping off everything. Especially if we were submerged and our oxygen supply got depleted, things got really sweaty.

"As far as sounds, I actually felt more than I heard. I always felt the vibration of the ship. We could hear sounds from outside coming to us through the water, like porpoises and whales."

"You heard them?" I was fascinated. "What did they sound like?"

"I could hear grunts. Whales made a long moaning sound. Sometimes a porpoise would bump the side of the boat. The sub made a lot of creaking noises when we dove, and if we dove really deep, the sub made peculiar groaning noises. That was kind of an eerie sensation, hearing that. It made me wish we were back on the surface. Eventually I got used to it, but the first trip out was quite an experience."

"Did any of the men have trouble making the adjustment?"

"Yes, some of the guys did. When the sub reached its patrol station and stayed submerged for a long time, it really got to some guys. But I handled it OK.

"My first few weeks there, they put me to work helping the cooks, taking out the trash. But before long I got to do topside watch. I'd stand watch four hours, hit the bunk four hours, then had four hours to eat and do whatever I wanted to do. We could read books in the submarine's library or play dominoes. I also had a lot of studying to do. Every crew member had to be able to operate any system on the boat in a pinch. I didn't have to be an expert, but I had to be ready to take somebody's place if he got put out of commission. I had to learn how to maneuver the sub and how to start the engines.

"Ninety percent of what I know today I learned aboard submarines. It's not like that on a surface ship. On a surface ship the sailor has his job to do and that's it, and they don't train him in all the other stuff. On a submarine, you're in a sealed tube with sixty-five other men, and you have to learn how to get along with other people. Whether you like them or not, they're part of the crew. It's like a big family. Serving on a submarine is a study in people. Right now, I feel closer to some of the guys I served with back in the war than I feel to people I associate with every day."

"Tell me about your duties as a torpedoman."

"The biggest part of the job is maintenance. We had to keep the fish in tiptop shape at all times. We had both steam and electric torpedoes. We spent a lot of time maintaining the tubes. We had to keep the rollers and the door hinges greased. Everything had to be polished and shiny. We used a high-pressure grease gun to lubricate the hinges on the outer doors that led to the water.

"When we went to battle stations each man had a specific job to do, either setting the gyros, opening and closing the doors, or loading the torpedoes. It was a fast-paced, demanding job. Six men worked around the tubes and six more loaded the torpedoes, so we had a dozen men crowded in each torpedo room. Our sub had six tubes forward and four aft.

"When we got the order 'Make ready the tube,' we vented the water out into the bilges. Then we opened the inner door. The reload crew, who might be cooks or electricians when we weren't at battle stations, used a block and tackle to lift the torpedo off the rack, line it up with the tube, and slide it in. Once the torpedo got to the stopping point, we removed the locks from the blades of the screw and closed the door. We flooded the tube with water and equalized the pressure with the water outside. We had to crank the outer doors open, they didn't have hydraulics. When the order came to fire we pushed the torpedo out with a blast of high-pressure air, and by the time it left the tube the screw was spinning at full speed. The torpedo had a trigger on its top that tripped on the inside of the tube and started the motor. When we fired one we heard a loud *swish* and felt the room jolt.

"The officers fired the torpedo electrically from the bridge, but we also had a firing switch on the tube. When we heard the order, 'Fire!' one of us would hit the switch in case the electric system failed. Once the torpedo was gone, we closed the outer doors, blew out the water and reloaded. We could turn it around and be ready to launch another fish in 90 seconds."

"Which part of this did you perform?" I asked.

"I did all of it at one time or another. My station was on the starboard side of the aft torpedo room, tubes seven and nine."

"What was the difference between a steam torpedo and an electric one?"

"Steam torpedoes were faster but left a huge wake behind them, and the enemy could see the wake coming long before the torpedo got there, which meant they had time to take evasive action. Electric torpedoes didn't leave such a wake."

"Where did your sub patrol?"

"We operated all over the place. North of Japan, China Sea, Philippines, Singapore. Never went down by Australia, though. Most of those runs were in wolfpacks, three subs working together."

"Tell me about the runs you went on."

"The first one was a dry run, and we didn't ever see anything. Our skipper at that time was old school. He believed the best thing was to stay submerged all day and come up at night and find something to shoot at. We didn't find anything that way. On the next run we had a much younger fellow in charge, Commander Eugene B. Fluckey. He was only thirty-two. He believed a submarine should get out there and hunt. We stayed on the surface most of the time unless enemy vessels or aircraft attacked us and forced us to dive.

"We had better luck that time. We sank one ship and bombarded a shore installation with our deck gun while the Japs were trying to unload some ships. From then on we never sank fewer than five ships on a patrol run. The *Barb* sank twenty-eight or thirty large ships and all kinds of small craft. *Barb* was first in number of ships sunk and second in tonnage sunk during the whole war. We were the only submarine that blew up a train! We sent a landing party ashore to do it.

"Not only that, but *Barb* was an early missile submarine! On our last patrol they outfitted us with a rocket launcher on the forward deck and loaded us up with seventy or eighty rockets, each one about five feet long. We blew up factories and petroleum refineries with those rockets. The launcher was a stationary mount at a certain elevation, and we knew how far the rockets would fly, and we had to place ourselves at precisely the right distance from shore to hit the target. We'd sneak in and fire five at a time and we'd hear *swish-swish-swish-swish-swish*. I would like to have seen that, but I was always in the aft torpedo room taking care of my job."

"What was it like going into combat in a sub?" I asked. "It must have been frightening, being inside that thing and not being able to see what was going on out there."

"I was nervous the first time I went into combat, when they sighted our first convoy and called for torpedo action. But I was so doggone busy I didn't have time to think about the consequences. Only when it was over did I have time to reflect on what had happened, and then I felt relief at surviving and exhilaration, knowing I had done my job well and helped us accomplish our mission."

"What kinds of ships did you sink?"

Torpedoman's Mate Second Class Rufus Roark receives the Bronze Star Medal for heroic service on the USS *Barb* during its 11th patrol, December 1944 to February 1945. The citation reads: "Skilled in the performance of duty, Roark contributed materially to the success of the *Barb* in delivering attacks to sink 60,000 tons of enemy shipping and to inflict damage on over 26,000 tons despite severe enemy countermeasures."

"Lots of cargo ships. Troopships. Tankers. We sank an aircraft carrier off the Philippines. Standing there in the aft torpedo room I could hear ships breaking up in the water after we torpedoed them. It sounded just like tearing down a building. Popping. Explosions. Metal ripping apart.

"One of our ships torpedoed a Japanese freighter carrying a bunch of Allied prisoners of war. The Japs didn't put any markers on the ship to let us know it had POWs. They had 1,500, some of whom had already been prisoners for three years. Men from Bataan, Corregidor, Burma, British guys who'd been forced to build railroads for the Japanese. The Japs were taking them back to Japan to work in coal mines.

"One of the boats involved in the sinking of the ship went looking for Japanese survivors and they picked up an Australian! They realized what had happened and called for help searching for survivors. It took us three days just to get there. We picked up fourteen men, surfaced next to them and threw out a lifeline. They were too weak to help themselves, so our guys dived into the water to pull them aboard. They'd been in the water five days. Out of the 1,500, about 150 were rescued."

Roark sounded disgusted. "The Japanese deliberately left it unmarked and just loaded them up like cattle. They could have put a red cross on that ship."

"Was your sub ever in danger of being sunk?" I asked.

"The Japs fired torpedoes at us several times, and their destroyers dropped lots and lots of depth charges on us. We even had some of their planes try to bomb us."

"What's it like being depth-charged?"

"Visualize yourself sitting in a metal can with somebody banging on it with a sledgehammer!" Roark said, and he laughed wryly. "The Japs would set the charges to go off at a certain depth. Inside the sub we could hear that *click-click* when a detonator went off. If it sounded close, I'd grab onto something to keep from being thrown against a bulkhead.

"We had many close calls. The depth charge explosions warped our deck plates. Planes were really dangerous because they flew in low and we didn't see them until they were right on us. It took 45 seconds to get the sub to periscope depth. We needed to dive about 150 feet to be safe from aerial bombs, but that took a minute and a half. If our guys didn't spot the plane in time, we wouldn't be able to get any water over us. Some of those planes dropped bombs pretty close to us. But we got lucky. The pilots missed us, dropped their bombs short or to the side. They shook us up pretty good, though."

"What was it like inside the boat at times like that?"

"We were taking on water in the ballast tanks, blowing vents, all kinds of noise going on. Exhaust flaps were flapping, the diesel engines rumbled, and men were running from one place to another. It wasn't exactly chaos, because everybody knew what to do. We just had to stay out of each other's way. I never got thrown clear off my feet by one of those explosions, but I got knocked around pretty good. Light bulbs shattered. Chunks of cork flew off the bulkheads.

"Yeah," he said, remembering, "we had some pretty close calls."

"What was your crew's biggest day?" I asked. "Your best mission?"

"That would be our adventure at Namkwan harbor on the China coast. Commander Fluckey had been observing ships heading down a coastline, entering a bay, and not coming out. He decided we'd just go in there and see what was going on. The sub snuck into the harbor behind the fishing fleet late that evening. They opened the submarine net across the mouth of the harbor to let the fishing boats back in, and we followed along behind them."

"Submerged, right?" I asked.

"On the surface."

My mouth dropped.

"On the *surface*?"

"Right. It was nighttime, so they couldn't see us," he said nonchalant. "We penetrated into the harbor, looked around, and saw nothing but targets all around us, all kinds of ships at anchor everywhere. So we lined up and fired six fish forward and four fish aft. We sure woke the Japs up that night! As their ships exploded and burned, we made our getaway by a different route. The way we went was uncharted, full of rocks, and too shallow to dive in. The Japs hadn't mined that area because they knew it was too shallow for submarines to come in submerged. But they hadn't figured on a sub coming through on the surface! We had to run about an hour at top speed to reach water deep enough to dive."

"How in the world did you get away?"

"The harbor was in such chaos they didn't know what hit them. At first they thought aircraft had bombed them. It took them a while to figure out it was a submarine. When they detected us, I guess they couldn't believe their eyes. A couple of patrol boats headed out toward us, but then they turned around and went back. I don't know whether they were afraid of us, or they figured there was no way we'd get through that rocky water.

"They say it looked like the Fourth of July there. We sank about five ships, including an ammunition ship. That was our high point. Our skipper got the Medal of Honor for it."

"What did you like least about serving on a sub?" I asked.

Roark took some time to think up an answer. Apparently he had little negative to say about his experiences.

"We were isolated from the rest of the world," he said finally. "The sub was out there on its own. It was a lonely feeling, out there in the middle of the ocean all by yourself.

"I never felt as confined as you might expect. But sometimes I would have liked to get out into the sunshine. We had a couple of weeks on the beach every time we got back, and we were so pale after sixty-five days without any sun that we blistered up real fast. The worst part was not being able to take a bath. When the sub left port, they closed the showers, and the next time they opened them was a few days before the sub came back in. I'd go sixty-five days without a bath. Of course, everybody else did too so we all smelled the same."

He brightened. "But they fed us well. In fact we had the best food in the Navy. I guess they just felt sorry for us, being down in those subs. We had steak, chicken, fish, frozen vegetables. When we came back into port, the surface sailors and even men stationed on the base would come down to eat with us! Our food was so much better than theirs.

"I liked being who I was, there's no other duty like it. I liked the camaraderie of the crew. Wherever we went, people treated us with the utmost respect. When we went on shore leave, and people saw the insignia on our uniform, you could see the respect in their eyes.

"When we went into port I'd see these guys come off a surface ship, some of them with arms or legs missing, and I just thanked the good Lord, because I knew I'd either come back whole or I wouldn't come back at all."

Rufus Roark in August 2000.

I woke up to see a rifle
muzzle pointed in my face

Ira Simpson
Dallas

I spotted Ira Simpson's house as I drove down the street; it was the one with the best-kept yard on the block. A couple of tough-looking young men standing in front of another house eyed me suspiciously as I parked and walked up to Mr. Simpson's front door, notebook in hand. I smiled at them, but they did not smile back. Maybe they thought I was selling insurance.

A tall, white-haired man with a friendly face opened the security door and greeted me. He took me into a living room that proudly boasted polished antique furniture. It was warm and I loosened my collar.

After a bit of conversation I positioned the tape recorder on a coffee table between us and turned it on.

"I understand you were a navigator on a B-24," I said.

"That's right. I was with the 389th Bomb Group, based in Hethel, England."

"How many missions did you fly?"

"Twenty," he said. "We flew a lot of missions over northern Germany. We bombed airfields, railroad yards, oil refineries. It was a big push to knock out the Germans' ability to transport men and supplies. Our plane got pretty beat up by ground fire on those runs."

Ira Simpson

"How about German fighter planes?"

"No, they never hit us, though our gunners shot one down. They attacked our group but never picked out our airplane. By the way, we saw one of the first jets the Germans put in the air."

"You saw one?" I asked enthusiastically.

"That's right. Our gunners shot at it, but it was so fast they didn't have a chance of hitting it. It streaked through our formation and sped away. We didn't know what it was! It *looked* like an airplane, but no airplane moved that fast. Our commanders didn't tell us until quite a while later what it was."

"Tell me about your final mission," I said.

"On our twentieth run we bombed a railroad yard at Magdeburg, Germany, with flak bursting all around us. We took a hit over the target, and one engine caught fire. We managed to put the fire out by cutting off the fuel to that engine. A few minutes later they shot out our control system, but the flight engineer managed to repair it so the pilot could keep the plane flying. "Then they knocked out a second engine."

"Uh-oh," I said.

"Our airspeed dropped down to about 80 knots, barely enough to stay in the air. That plane would just swerve through the air, stall out, lose a little altitude and gain a little speed, stall out again, until we reached the Dutch coast. The Germans kept shooting at us the whole way.

"We flew out over the North Sea and then realized we didn't have enough fuel to make it to England. Our commanders had always warned us not to bail out into the North Sea in the winter; we wouldn't survive. This was February 14. So we had no choice but to turn back. We bailed out over an island south of Rotterdam right on the coastline."

"Did everybody make it out of the plane?"

"All except one man, the tail gunner. The Germans say his parachute didn't open. But I'm not sure they didn't shoot him on the way down."

"Why do you say that?"

"Because they were shooting at *us* the whole time *we* were coming down."

"Oh."

"We bailed out at about 2,000 feet. I looked down and saw I was heading straight for some power lines. I slipped my parachute to the side, trying to steer it, and ended up dumping the air out of it. I fell 40 feet to the ground and knocked myself out.

"I woke up to see a rifle muzzle pointed in my face. A German soldier stood over me. My face was wet. I've since talked to some Dutch people who were there, and they say he poured a bucket of water over my head to wake me up.

"I spent that first night alone in a cell. The next day they reunited me with the rest of my crew. I saw the body of the tail gunner. The German commander assured me they'd take care of him, give him a proper burial. And they did, my Dutch friends confirmed that."

"What kind of condition were you in after bailing out and hitting the ground so hard?" I asked.

"I had a severe concussion, with double vision for three or four days. I also discovered I had a piece of shrapnel in my leg. The pilot broke his ankle when he landed."

"Did the Germans give you medical attention?"

"No."

"Where did they take you?"

"They put us on a train to Frankfurt. We only traveled at night because Allied planes attacked their trains during the day. When we stopped at Dusseldorf, the British had just finished bombing there. The train had to stop outside the city and we had to walk through all that wreckage. We walked between burning buildings, heard delayed action bombs going off down the street. They marched us to a train station on the other side of town, where we encountered a group of German civilians waiting for a train. They saw us, recognized our uniforms, and became extremely angry. They called us names and headed toward us, shouting in German that they should hang us. But our guards got us onto the train and stood at the doors, holding them at bay with their rifles, and threatened to shoot them if they came any closer. And you know, I think they would have. They looked like they meant business.

"They took us to an interrogation center in Frankfurt. A German major demanded information from me, and when I refused, he started giving *me* information about myself that they already had on file! They knew my hometown, when I graduated from navigation school, when I came overseas, when I was assigned to the bomb group. He showed me a big book full of information about our bomber crews.

"I ended up in a camp at Nuremberg, with sixteen men in a room about fifteen foot square that had one window, three-tiered bunks, and mattresses made of straw. In the mornings the Germans gave us hot water, and at noon they gave us two tiny slices of bread"—he held his fingers a few inches apart—"with a little jam. The bread was made of sawdust. At first we refused to eat it, but as we grew hungrier we gave in. It was very sour, but edible. At night they gave us soup made with potato peels.

"Occasionally they passed out Red Cross parcels; I think I got two the whole time I was there.

"They had coffee, powdered milk, cheese, a chocolate bar, a can of Spam, some hard bread, crackers, and cigarettes.

"Around the first of April we could hear the German artillery shooting at the approaching Americans, so we knew the end was near. The Germans told us to prepare to move out—not that we had anything to prepare! All we had was the clothes on our backs. They issued us Red Cross parcels to sustain us on the journey. But then they kept us in the camp another week, so we'd eaten most of that food before we left.

"A little while earlier the Germans had brought in a bunch of Yugoslavian prisoners. Generals and colonels. They spoke some English, and they told us about the war's progress in Yugoslavia, and we told them what was going on up here. When the Germans marched us Americans out of camp, they kept those people there, and they took them out and shot them.

"We walked all night through the rain. The next day around noon, a group of American B-17s flew over and opened their bomb doors right over us. They were heading to Nuremberg, where we'd just been. We stood and watched them approach their target. That was exactly why the Germans had hustled us out of town: They didn't want us to see what our forces were doing to them!

"We walked about 100 miles. On that march, which lasted about two weeks, we slept in barns, once we slept in a church. They gave us almost no food the entire time. The German guards were fed by local farmers. We did get some potatoes one day.

"After three days, we'd covered half the distance, and we decided we weren't gonna move any farther. We were exhausted and decided we were going to rest, no matter what. The Germans became exasperated and walked around hitting us with rifle butts, but it didn't do them any good. We sat there two days, while the guards tried to figure out what to do. Finally they called the SS in to get us moving or shoot us and warned us they were coming. So we moved." He laughed, shaking his head. "We knew the SS was executing people left and right. We were long gone before they got there.

"One day we marched alongside a railroad track and passed a train sitting there. I glanced up and saw two P-47s coming right straight down!"

"Oh, no," I said.

"All the Air Force people knew what was about to happen, so they ran away from the train. The others did exactly the wrong thing: They hid *under* the train. They didn't realize the train was the target. The bombs killed one man. I had climbed under a pile of lumber. I got stuck under there and had to have somebody pull me out.

"We had a radio with us that we managed to keep hidden from the Germans, and our commanding POW contacted the Americans and let them know where we were. They sent P-38s out to fly cover for us as we marched. They'd fly along parallel to keep other pilots from thinking we were Germans and attacking us."

"Did you have any contact with civilians?" I asked.

"From time to time. I traded cigarettes for eggs with a farmer's wife."

"So they were friendly?"

"I wouldn't say they were *overly* friendly. If they had been, other Germans might have gotten angry at them. But they certainly weren't antagonistic toward us. They were just farmers, trying to make a living like anyone else. Most of the people we saw were old. All their young people had been taken into the army."

"Did any of you try to escape during the march?"

"Yes, we had some try, even though the guards warned us not to because if the SS caught us, they'd shoot us. Some of them made it, but others did get caught and killed. Most of us just stayed put. Out there in the countryside, a lot of times we didn't have guards right there with us. And most of the guards with us were old men, barely up to the task of walking these distances with those big packs they had to carry."

"What kind of shape were you in?"

"A lot of us got ill. No medical treatment was available. I had diarrhea, vomiting, fever. This was in April, and it's still quite cool in Europe at that time of year. It rained all the time, and we had no rain gear. We tried to keep the water off by draping blankets over our shoulders.

"After two weeks we reached Moosburg. The camp there was packed with more than 100,000 POWs: English, American, Russian, Polish, French. The Germans were gathering us all together. I was fortunate: They put me in a building and I had a bunk. A lot of men slept on the ground in tents."

"What was hygiene like at this camp?" I asked.

"Staying clean was one of our biggest problems. I had two showers the entire time I was there. Our section of the camp had one water faucet. I don't know how pure that water was, but we used it for drinking and bathing. We did our best to keep clean to avoid disease. But some of the men became infected with lice. The Germans deloused us two or three times."

"How do they do that?"

"They had us run naked across a little area where they dusted us down with powder, sprayed it all over us until we were completely white. It was almost impossible to get it off."

"What do you have to say about the treatment you got from the Germans?" I asked.

"I was fortunate not to be subjected to particularly cruel treatment," Simpson said. "But they were cruel to some. Friends of mine got beaten. I did get hit by a rifle butt now and then."

"For what?"

"Not moving fast enough. They beat some of my friends pretty severely for moving slowly or talking back. We had very little food, no medical care, and they constantly threatened to shoot us for any little thing. The treatment was inhumane in that they did not provide properly for us. They just threw us in there like caged animals, counted us every day, and whether we lived or died didn't matter, as long as we didn't *escape*.

"When we woke up the morning of Sunday, April 29, after two weeks in the camp, we heard the rumble of tanks outside.

Next thing we knew the Americans and the German SS got into a tank battle only half a mile away. We heard the cannon fire and then machine gun bullets cut through the camp, and a ricochet hit a prisoner. We were told to stay inside or we might get killed. The prisoners were all trying to see what was going on. Then it got quiet. We waited.

"Suddenly an American tank rolled up into the camp! It was completely mobbed by all the prisoners. They brought in an American flag and raised it...that was my most emotional moment of the whole war. I didn't see a dry eye anywhere.

"They told us to stay put while they got some food for us. The next day Patton came in and talked to us, all dressed up with his ivory-handled pistols and polished helmet."

"What did he say?"

"He joked around with us. He said, 'I've been out there fightin' a war while you boys were just sittin' around in here!' He told us they'd get us home as fast as they could."

"How much longer were you in the camp?"

"Another week. We had some trouble with the Russians, who took off from camp, went into town, and broke into a brewery, got drunk, and started fighting each other. We had to set up a formation of POWs to block them from entering the camp, because they were literally fighting everybody they saw. They were drunk out of their minds, didn't know what they were doing. We wouldn't let them back in until the next day when they sobered up. They'd been severely mistreated by the Germans, so I couldn't blame them for letting off some steam. It was just a drunken brawl.

"They drove us in trucks to an airfield at Landshut, Germany, and we waited for airplanes to pick us up. C-47s would land, fill up with men, and take off, one right after the other. We spent the night waiting our turn. A German plane flew over, and all the GIs started shooting at it. But it landed, and it turned out to be a German colonel with his family, wanting to surrender. Our guys almost shot them before they got out of the airplane.

"To pass the time I rode through the little town of Landshut with another fellow and didn't see a soul. The Germans had deserted the town. I don't know where they went. Then we heard some firing and figured we'd better get out of there. Looked like the fighting wasn't entirely finished there.

"Several weeks later I was on a Liberty ship entering New York Harbor having another emotional moment. We saw the Statue of Liberty, and all the guys ran to the rail to get a look at her. The first thing they did after we landed was take us to a big mess hall where we could order anything we wanted and they would fix it for us."

"What did you have?"

"I got a steak, cooked medium, potatoes, apple pie. They had lots of ice cream, too. Everybody ate too much and got sick."

"What did you do after the war?" I asked.

"In 1946 I decided to stay in the military. I stayed twenty years. I flew B-29s for a time and flew over to Korea to fight in the Korean War but got grounded because of ulcers. Later I worked in the recovery of nuclear weapons from crashed planes. I retired in 1963 as a major."

"There's one thing I've got to ask you," I said. "After being shot down and captured and spending time in a German prison camp, I think a lot of people would say, 'Enough is enough!' What made you decide to become a lifer?"

He seemed genuinely surprised by the question.

"Well," he said, "I wanted to keep flying. And I liked the military."

Ira Simpson today

John T. Ferguson
Fort Worth

We sat on the front porch of John Ferguson's house on a warm September morning. He relaxed in a rocking chair, waving to the occasional passerby. His wife, Arlene, came out to listen from time to time.

"I joined the Army in 1936," he said. "Back then there wasn't no war and there wasn't hardly anybody in the military. I decided to volunteer because there was nothing else to do in Dallas. Only work they had was picking cotton, stuff like that. I wanted to move up out of that category.

"Basic training was tough. When I joined up they didn't have training centers, they only set those up when the war started. They just put a corporal and a sergeant in charge of ten or twelve of us and ran us through six weeks of drill training, rifle training, chemical training with gas masks, everything. There wasn't no discrimination as far as the training we got, we got all the same training the white folks did. It was segregated, though. We were eighteen-year-old kids, and all our NCOs were in their forties, and they had no patience for us youngsters.

"I served three years and then decided not to re-enlist. A sergeant said to me, 'I know you all are starving out there. You goin' back to that starvation?' I said, 'Yes, sir, I'm going back.' And I didn't re-up."

"Why?" I asked.

"I got tired of fighting forest fires in the mountains of Arizona. Whenever they had a forest fire they called the Army. It was hot walking up and down those hills.

"I came back home and got a job with the American Red Cross. I lived over there in Dallas, but I married a Fort Worth girl named Mildred. She was my first wife, we were married fifty-three years. I always liked Fort Worth better than Dallas. Fort Worth is a much nicer place to live."

"Why's that?"

"Segregation was like this in Dallas." He balled his fist tightly and waved it at me. "We were treated a lot better here in Fort Worth. Cops were a lot better in Fort Worth. In Dallas you could hardly walk down the street without the cops stopping you and doing something to you.

"I was working at the American Red Cross when the Army recalled me in 1941. They called me back on my birthday, February 11. They called me up again in '50 for Korea, you know. I ended up staying in the service until 1963."

"What changed your mind about staying in?"

"I got to liking the military life. I only had a seventh grade education, and the Army promoted me a few times, so I decided, this is my best bet."

"How were you and the other black soldiers treated by your white officers?"

"Most of the white officers were good men," Ferguson said, "but we always had one or two bad ones. They didn't want to be in a black outfit. We had several who abused their rank, abused the men, called them 'nigger' and all that. One guy was so mean, some of the men in another battery backed over him with a tractor."

"...and killed him?" I asked, startled.

"Oh, yeah. He stood behind a tractor. They saw they had a good chance to get rid of him and they took it. The Army never

did figure out what really happened. But we had some fine officers, too."

"Did you have any racist incidents targeted at you personally?" I asked.

"Not too much," he said, shaking his head. "I tried to stay
away from all that by taking care of my business. We had a job
to do, the white boys had a job to do, and that was what it was
all about.

"When they called me up in '41, I went to Fort Sill,
Oklahoma, and joined the 349th Field Artillery Battalion. We
shipped out to England and crossed over the Channel to Le
Havre, France. We traveled up to the Rhine River, and what
looked like the entire U.S. Army was gathered right there, pre-
paring to cross the river. It seemed like a line of troops and
tanks and trucks 2,000 miles long. That's where we joined the
fighting. We shelled the Germans across the river day and
night, and they shelled us.

"We had some old guns they got out of a museum; 155mm
howitzers."

"Did you have any accidents, using guns that old?" I asked.

"One battery had a gun barrel blow up, but nobody got hurt.
My battery fired thousands and thousands of rounds and never
had an accident. We kept our equipment in the best condition
we could.

"I was chief of the firing battery. The forward artillery spotters called in the coordinates to me, and I passed them on to the
gunners and gave the order to fire. We fired at targets more
than twenty miles away with 155mm guns. We were very good
at what we did."

"How so?"

"We could manipulate our artillery better than the Germans
could. One day we had a pretty close call. If the Germans had
dropped their elevation two millimeters, they would have
destroyed us all. But they shelled a spot less than a hundred

yards behind us for an hour and a half. They blew up a haystack and a fence pretty good. I was pretty nervous the whole time, I thought for sure they'd adjust their aim and blow us to pieces.

"By that stage of the war, the Germans were in no condition to fight us one on one. They'd hide in little pockets of forest and watch the American columns go by, and then they'd attack the last battalion to come through. When that happened, we'd turn our 240mm guns, our heavy artillery, on them and tear up an entire forest with them in it. German snipers on the other side of the river took shots at us too."

"What was the scariest part of the war for you?"

"The scariest part was the Battle of the Bulge," he said emphatically. "We thought for sure the Germans would reach us. But the worst thing was, Germans who could speak English put on American uniforms and came behind the lines to disrupt us. They couldn't do it to my unit, because they didn't have any black men, but they caused a lot of trouble among the white troops, giving orders to go to the wrong place or shoot in the wrong direction. But then Patton turned his attention to the German forces that were breaking through and tore them up.

"After that we took a lot of prisoners and sent them up to headquarters. A lot of Germans just walked up to us and surrendered. But the rest, we captured. That was the tail end of the war and they wanted to be captured anyway. They knew they'd lost.

"I came back in October of '45, and found a job five days later. Went to work at Carnival Trailways."

"Not much of a rest," I said.

"No, it wasn't."

"What was your daily life like when you were in combat?" I asked.

"Life in the Army wasn't too bad. A lot of guys will run it down, but if you just took care of your business, you did all right. We always had good food. Of course we ate a lot of field rations, but we had a good mess sergeant who tried to keep us fed with real food as much as possible. He almost always had breakfast food, coffee, eggs. I ate better than I do now, because now they won't let me have no salt. I can't taste a thing without salt!

"We slept in slit trenches that we covered with logs and dirt. About eight men could fit in one. We just slept in our clothes. A few times I did get to sleep in some fine German castles over there.

"There were always those guys who would try anything to get out. Hated it so bad they'd pull all kinds of tricks. One guy hid on top of a house hoping we'd leave him there. I saw a guy drop a breech block on his foot and break five or six bones. Did it on purpose to get out. They call that malfeasance. I could have reported him for it. But I didn't, because I knew he was gonna get to be forty years old and look back on what he'd done and regret it. He'd have to live with himself.

"A lot of people just don't like to be regimented. But it's not so bad. You just have to get used to it.

"You know," he said, turning thoughtful, "I think a lot of people who didn't go wished later they had gone. Those who avoided service never did anything with their lives, never proved themselves. They're old now. Too late. Ballgame's over.

"I'm proud, very proud, of my service. I learned a whole lot of things I never would have learned out here. Went to many places I never would have gone. I think it's good for young people to serve in the military. You've got to have an education to get a good job. If you're not going to go to school and get you an education, go into the military and get one. Do your job and pay attention."

"Do you think this country could do it again?" I asked. "If another war like that broke out?"

He let out a deep breath, looking grim. "I don't know about that," he said, shaking his head. "We came through that

Depression and it made us stronger. We were so poor, but people didn't go crazy and rob and kill each other like they do now. The way they raise these children today is a hell of a lot different from when I come up. People don't have control of their children. Most people let their children control them. All the things going on out there today, when I was growing up, we never would have thought of. Things have changed quite a bit."

John T. Ferguson with his first wife, Mildred, in 1966.

Robert and Virginia Gibeson
San Antonio

Glynis Sakowicz sent me an e-mail. "You've got to talk to my parents," she wrote. "They're both World War II veterans. Ask my dad about the time the Marines stole a train. And don't forget to ask my mom about the bleeding suitcase."

A pitch like that could not be resisted. I called.

"There weren't any jobs back then, and I had to decide what I was going to do with myself," Robert Gibeson told me. "This was during the Depression. I saw a picture in a history book of a bunch of men raising a flag on Guam. The caption said the men were Marines, and it said Marines got to travel all around the world because it was their job to protect our embassies. I thought, 'Man, that sounds like a good chance to go see something!' and I made up my mind.

"The morning after I graduated from high school I went to see the recruiter, and by four o'clock in the afternoon I was in the Marine Corps and on my way to California. Everything was fine until we got to San Diego, and right there I told myself, 'Man, you screwed up *de*-luxe.'"

I laughed. "Why's that?"

"Two men met us there at the train station. They looked like something out of a Popeye cartoon, know what I mean? They didn't talk very good English. Every other word was a cussword. And they weren't a bit bashful about using a No. 12 boot in the butt if we didn't move fast enough. That was when I found out what the Marine Corps was really like.

"After six weeks of boot camp we immediately got on a train to San Francisco, never got any liberty. But they paid us $20 and gave us the day off in San Francisco. Another old boy and I got three blocks into town and that's as far as we got. We stopped at the first burlesque show we saw, at Third and Market, and both blew our $20 there.

"The next day they loaded us aboard an old merchantman. Nobody told us where we were going. All we knew was a code name, Cactus. This was early 1942.

"We sailed to Aitutaki in the Cook Islands in the South Pacific and unloaded a bunch of crap. Then we went over to Port Vila on Éfaté in the New Hebrides. We got there the same day the U.S. landed on Guadalcanal.

"We formed the 4th Anti-Aircraft Artillery Battalion, 3rd Division. We had no idea what we were doing. Never had any combat training. There were only 600 of us, armed with a bunch of old Navy field artillery, some anti-aircraft guns, and machine guns. The newest equipment we had was from 1916. They put me on a 37mm anti-aircraft gun. First time I'd ever seen one. We would learn how to operate it through on the job training. Meanwhile we built an airstrip, helped do maintenance work on airplanes, whatever needed to be done. A lot of the wounded from Guadalcanal flew in to the little hospital we had there.

"A fleet of Army B-26s landed there, each carrying a torpedo. The torpedoes wouldn't fit inside the plane, so they hung them underneath. We didn't have enough planes out there that could carry a torpedo, so they were improvising.

"Some idiot we had with us said to the old man, 'Look here, we can get all the torpedo juice we want!'

"'What's that'; the old man asked. The other guy told him, 'It's 190-proof alcohol!' The torpedoes ran on steam, you see. The alcohol was mixed with hot water and compressed air to produce the steam that drove the turbine around. This fella proceeded to show us how to drain the alcohol out of those darn torpedoes. Everybody got drunker 'n Cootie Brown."

I wanted to hear what happened next, so I didn't ask who Cootie Brown was.

"Then those planes went out to battle. But nobody told anybody they drained all the alcohol out of the torpedoes. And those planes got themselves all shot to hell, dropping dud torpedoes. Wasn't a damn one of 'em worked. If they'd ever found out what happened, they'd have shot us all. But hell, we didn't know any better."

"What were your living conditions like on that island?"

"Ever eat any hardtack?" he asked.

"No."

"Hardtack is like a cracker, about four inches square and a quarter of an inch thick. We put that sucker in a sock and took a hammer or a rifle butt and smashed it. There was no way we could just eat it, nobody had teeth that good. We busted them up, dumped the crumbs in a canteen cup, mixed some bouillon cubes with it and heated it over a fire, and made a cup of soup. That's the kind of crap we were living on.

"We had one vehicle to go around, an antique Ford truck. We ended up having to carry almost everything by hand."

"Did you have contact with the Japanese?"

"Oh, yes. They came in close at night with submarines. One night we hit the sack, and another old boy and I were lying there yapping, and I looked out to sea and said, 'What do you know, it's gonna rain.'

"He said, 'How do you know?' and I said, 'I can see lightning flashing.'

"He said, 'You're nuttier than hell, because there ain't no clouds.'

"About that time we heard the first artillery shells swoosh in. A submarine was out there shooting at us with its deck gun. They never did hit anything, but they scared the devil out of us.

"Our first air raid got several people killed. At first it was just a big show, planes diving around and shooting at each other. Then we saw planes falling out of the sky and realized, hell, that was our people! A Jap plane cut loose on our beach and shot the hell out of us, and right then we woke up that this was real and we'd better dig a hole. Seemed like five minutes later, we all had foxholes dug!

"We burned up all kinds of ammo, got credit for eighty-six planes in ninety days. I shot at a lot of them but it's hard to tell whether you got them because of all the smoke, and everybody's shooting at the same time. But somebody got them. One battery got fourteen planes with only eighty-seven rounds."

"Did they ever come close to getting you?"

"Better believe it! At low tide you could walk out onto a coral reef, and we used to look for seashells to pass the time. We weren't supposed to go out there but we did. One day we were out there, me and a boy named Jones, and we heard a plane. I didn't even look up, just said, 'What are they, Jones?' and he looked up and saw the wheels hanging down from the planes and said, 'Oh, they're fixin' to land.'

"All of a sudden we both realized there was no place to land. We hadn't built the airstrip yet! And I looked up and realized they were those damn Japanese dive bombers, Vals, the kind whose wheels weren't retractable. Four of them dove down, and bullets hit the water around us. We ran for the shore and dove into a hole, and they passed right over our heads.

"Two days later at the same place more Jap planes came in while an LST was unloading right off the shore. We were sitting there on top of our machine gun bunker fooling around with an old BAR we were trying to fix. Here came the Jap planes, and I looked up and saw three bombs coming down. I yelled at Jones to duck and that was the last thing I remember. The bombs hit fifty feet from us, in the middle of trucks loaded with explosives.

"I don't know how long we were there, but when I woke up I was in a hole with water lapping at my armpits. I couldn't hear anything. Little black pieces of soot floated down in the air.

"The bombs had blown off the front of that LST and killed a whole company of men. I couldn't hear for two days.

"After several months they shipped us up to Wellington, New Zealand. From there we were supposed to drive a fleet of trucks eighty or ninety miles inland to a little town called Masterton. In port they gave us each a truck full of supplies, sent us on our way, and never bothered to tell us that in New Zealand, you're supposed to drive on the other side of the road! My goodness, I thought those New Zealanders were the craziest damn people in the world. Everybody was driving on the wrong side of the road. We didn't know any better.

"We got to Masterton without killing anybody and formed an artillery battalion. We ended up with one truck per man, and we had a four-acre patch of gasoline drums. A lot of the men bought themselves old cars. But the problem was, gas rations were only two gallons a year. A buddy named Will and I bought a '36 Chrysler for about $40, a beautiful old car, big enough to put a gasoline barrel in the back seat. We took a grand tour of the north island. Of course that big car was a good woman trap too.

"Our company commander, a major, was raising hell about people stealing all their gas. Of course we didn't know nothin' about it. He sent me and my buddy out there on guard duty with loaded weapons and ordered us to catch somebody stealing gas, he didn't care who it was. About midnight we decided it was time to go get somebody, so we walked out there and saw somebody in the dark. He was passing five-gallon cans over the fence to two cars out there, and we grabbed him. By god, it was our battalion commander the colonel and two of his lady friends. Oh, man. I didn't know what to do. I told my buddy, 'I ain't seen *nothin'*. Have you?' He said, 'Nope.'

"The next morning the first sergeant asked if we caught anybody, and we said absolutely not. He said, 'But there's a whole bunch more gasoline missing.' I said, 'Those barrels got holes in them. They're leaking.' He said, 'That sounds good to me.'

"The next day we got two weeks of liberty.

"Later they sent us to Wellington to help unload ships. The whole bay was full of ships sitting there with no way to unload because the stevedores all went on strike. General Smith ran them off with an infantry regiment and told them if they showed their faces again he'd shoot their butts off. He put us to work unloading ships 24 hours a day. I found out my cousin, Roger Crome, was stationed in a little town called Paekakariki north of Wellington, only forty or fifty miles away. He came down to see me when I had a half day off. A whole bunch of us Marines had a wing-ding going in some small town, and we had to leave town at 11 o'clock to get back by 12. We arrived at the railroad station all stewed up. The train just sat there ready to go. We were supposed to leave at 11 o'clock, and at 11:30 we were still sitting there. We asked what the devil was going on, and the conductor told us the crew was in the station having their tea and crumpets, and we would leave when they were ready.

"Some drunk idiot said, 'Well, I'm an engineer. Can I get a fireman up there with me?' And another drunk idiot said, 'I think I can be a fireman!' They took over the locomotive and we pulled out of the station, just left the crew sitting there! We went across some mountains, through a tunnel, and then rolled downhill toward Paekakariki.

"Now, this was an electric train," Gibeson explained. "The wires ended at Paekakariki, so electric trains couldn't go any farther down the line. Normally we had to get off at Paekakariki and walk the rest of the way to our camp at McCay's Crossing, three to four miles.

"Well," he said wryly, "Nobody wanted to walk. So we decided we were going all the way. Coming down the side of the mountain those old boys just let that engine go. The electric wires stopped at Paekakariki, but we didn't. They got that train going so fast, it coasted all the way to McCay's Crossing before coming to a halt. The next thing I knew, 500 Marines scattered in every direction. The guards at the gate had no idea what was going on, and by the time they figured it out, everybody was gone. The New Zealanders had to send steam locomotives to pull the train back to town. Our officers restricted the whole damn outfit.

"We ended up on a crappy little island called Vella Lavella right across from Kolombangara in the New Georgia Islands. The Navy kicked us off their ship and told us to build an airstrip. That's where the 214th Marine Corps Fighter Squadron came in. You've heard of the Black Sheep? They were exactly what you've heard: a bunch of misfits who fit in nowhere else, and they put them in high-powered planes and made a fighter squadron out of them.

"We set up on the side of a hill and we could use our artillery sights to watch across the channel as the Japs built a fighter base on Kolombangara. And whenever they were about finished, we'd get on the horn and get B-24s and B-17s from Guadalcanal to go blow the place up.

"When the Black Sheep pilots returned from their missions they flew in over the beach, and right off the beach near our position were some wrecked Japanese ships and barges. The

Black Sheep passed right over us and emptied their guns into those wrecks for target practice. A bushel basket full of metal cases flew out of the aircraft and rained down on us. If you get hit with one of those things, it could kill you. We asked them repeatedly not to do that, and they didn't pay us no mind. One day we told them, 'You do that again and we'll shoot at you.'

"Of course they didn't believe us, so the next time we put a bunch of holes into two of their planes. That was the end of that.

"Those guys were crazy. They'd sit there drinking the hooch they made. They'd go down to Australia and come back with extra fuel tanks hanging below the planes, filled with beer. They'd open it up and all of us would take a helmet or a bucket and fill up. That's where we got our beer from, otherwise we had to make it. We were on that god-awful island for two years.

"We could also see the island of Gizo. You've heard about Kennedy's PT boat getting run over?"

"Yep."

"That happened out there between Gizo and Kolombangara. Part of his squadron was stationed with us on Vella Lavella. The Navy commander in charge was so mad he could have died of a heart attack because Kennedy lost his torpedo boat out there. He said, 'How in the hell can anybody in a 40-knot boat get run over by a 30-knot destroyer? I'll never believe it!' He said the radar on that boat was working fine when they went out there.

"I remember people speculating Kennedy would be court-martialed for losing his boat and getting three men killed. But next thing you know, the government gave him a medal and made him a hero! I guess he was the only man in the Navy who ever got a medal for losing his boat and members of his crew. Most awful thing I ever heard of.

"Just like Purple Hearts. Back then we used to call them forgot-to-duck medals. If we had to go to the hospital for anything, they'd come around wanting to give us a Purple Heart, no matter what we were in there for. A lot of guys wouldn't take them unless they really got shot up. I was in a hospital for a while after I opened a gas barrel and it blew up on me and burned my hands. It scared the hell out of me and blistered my hands, and they tried to give me a Purple Heart for that!"

"What did you tell them?"

"I said, 'Hell no, I don't want that thing!' They said, 'But you got hurt.'

"I said, 'It wasn't from enemy action.' They tried to tell me it was from enemy action because we were fighting a war.

"I said, 'Enemy action means *they're shooting at you.*'"

"What did you think of your officers?" I asked. This question had been fertile ground in previous interviews.

"The officers had a beautiful head there at the camp; 'head' means outhouse you know. It was a beautiful four-holer with screens around it and all the latest magazines and a couple of lanterns so they could sit in there, smoke, and read. Of course the enlisted men had to build it.

"Early one morning an officer walked into the mess hall to eat breakfast, and somebody said, 'Cap'n, yer shithouse is on fahr.'

"'Oh, it couldn't be,' the captain said. The soldier insisted, 'Yes it is, there's smoke coming out of it.'

"About that time the camp was rocked by the damnedest explosion you ever heard. Somebody had put a big stick of dynamite in there and blowed that sucker all over the countryside. And that was the end of that."

"One of your own people did that?"

"Absolutely right."

"Why?"

"Those officers got all kinds of beer and whiskey and flew nurses in at night and partied! We enlisted men could go to a movie once in a while if we wanted to walk eight miles and sit on a coconut log. And that's all we had. The officers had Jeeps to ride around in, and we had to walk everywhere. And we had to clean that shithouse every day. It made the guys pretty unhappy with the officers.

"It was a bad place. I hated every minute of it. We had about 180 air raids. Japs were everywhere. We were only 100 miles from the huge Jap base at Rabaul.

"I wouldn't take a million dollars to do it again. I guess there were some fun times, except when they were shooting at me. You go to the movies today and see people get shot, and they just get up and keep going like it didn't hardly hurt! Well the first guy you see get killed for real, you think, 'Oh my God, these people are playing for keeps. That could be *me!*'

"After two and a half years overseas, I finally got rotated back to the States in January of 1945. I ended up guarding the gate at Ward Island by Corpus Christi. And that's where I met Mama."

"What happened?"

"The most scroungy lookin' Wave I'd ever seen tried to get out of the gate. She hadn't shined her shoes. She hadn't pressed her slacks or her coat. I didn't know Virginia was our kid sister, and I didn't realize she'd been working twelve hours. I told her she couldn't go anywhere looking like that. She told me in no uncertain terms she could and would, and I thought I'd have to club her on the spot!

"All the other guys were saying frantically behind me, 'Don't do that! Don't do that! She always brings us goodies from the galley!'"

"But somehow you ended up going on a date with her," I said.

"That was after Roosevelt died. Everything shut down for a day of mourning. I'd had the gate watch that night at Ward Island, and I was shaking down the sailors when they came in the gate, had confiscated a full fifth of Old Granddad. I was supposed to destroy it, but I kept it.

"I'd just gotten off work and I saw her. I told her I had a day off but everything was closed and I didn't know what to do. She said, 'I know a place that's open.' I said, 'You mean that?' She said, 'Absolutely.' She took me to an old café where she used to work, the only place in town that was open. I brought the bottle with me and we had a party."

"And you decided you liked her after all."

"Oh, yeah. She was good people. We've been married fifty-five years now."

His wife, Virginia, told me her side of the story. Her voice was bright and warm, perpetually on the brink of laughter.

"I was always somewhere between a Sad Sack and a Beetle Bailey," she said. "I never did anything really bad, but I was always out of uniform in some way. We had to wear rayon stockings with garter belts. There were no panty hose. I couldn't bear those stockings. They all had a seam up the back, so I took a light brown eyebrow pencil and drew lines up the backs of my legs. I always passed inspection, nobody ever noticed!

"I didn't like wearing my cap on the right side of my head, so I always wore it on the left side. Officers would look at me and I could tell they were thinking, 'She's out of uniform. Something's not right.' I'd just salute like nothing was wrong and they'd salute me back, looking at me out of the corner of their eyes. But they could never figure out what it was.

"I met Bob Hope in New York. He and Betty Hutton made a movie, *Here Come the Waves*, and they picked about eighty-five of us with the best voices to sing in the background. We had to stand in our blues out in the hot summer sun. We sang a couple of very jazzy songs by Johnny Mercer about the Navy. Women started collapsing because of the heat. Johnny Mercer didn't give us a moment to go get a drink of water. Back then we didn't have the little plastic water bottles you can carry with you.

"I told that Johnny Mercer what I thought of the way he was working us to death out there. I didn't hold my tongue at all. I said, 'You never make someone stand at attention in the sun all day in a full wool uniform. When you're standing at attention, you're rigid and your shoulders are back, it's an unnatural position for the body to be in, and before long you go numb and fall over. Your body can't do that forever.' He just said, 'I'll have to learn, won't I?' That was his only answer, and he went about his business."

"But he didn't do anything about it, did he?"

"No. Not only that, we had to go out two days later and redo the whole thing because he wasn't satisfied!"

"So you're visible in the movie?"

"You can see me in the background standing with all the other Waves. I'm the short one. Bob Hope had a program for the sailors there, and I got to sit up on the stage behind him with a group of Waves, and he'd turn around and ad lib with us. We never knew what he was gonna say, we couldn't prepare. We just had to sass back as well as we could.

"The Navy put me in cook, baker, and butcher school and then gave me a choice of three places to go. One was in California, the second was somewhere up north, and the third was Corpus Christi. A good friend of mine told me, 'Ginger, you should tell them you want to go to Corpus Christi, so you can be close to your folks!'

"I told the Navy, 'Send me anywhere except Corpus Christi.'

"Guess where they sent me?

"They put me on a troop train at 2330. I had an upper bunk. Everybody else was already in theirs, so I just crawled up into my bunk and fell asleep. The next morning at 0600 I got up, put my robe on over my pajamas, and started climbing down from the bunk to go to the head, and ohhhh, whistles, whistles, whistles! I looked around and almost fell off the ladder. I was surrounded by men, the only woman on that whole car! Embarrassing.

"I was stationed at Ward Island near Corpus. The Marine Guard liked me so much they voted me their mascot, their 'Kid Sis.' I took a lot of privileges I shouldn't have, you know. My parents lived in Robston, right outside of Corpus, and I went home every weekend to stay with them. Never bothered to take my ID or my pass. The guards always let me do whatever I wanted. They called me Tex.

"But one day I walked up to the gate to go see my parents, and there was this strange Marine there; he'd just come down from Memphis. He was a real gung-ho type, spit-and-polish. I walked past and said hello to him, and he stopped me and demanded, 'Where's your ID?'

"Like an idiot, I shot back at him, 'Oh, I always leave my pass and ID back in the barracks. I might *lose* them if I carried them around!' I was always being a smart aleck.

"He gave me such a frown. If only you could have seen it... his whole Norwegian forehead comes down when he frowns. He said, 'You're not passing until you shine your shoes and bring your ID with you!' Needless to say, it was *not* love at first sight.

"I walked back, furious, stomping every step of the way, and sat down by the flagpole near the Marine barracks, fuming and thinking, 'What am I gonna do?' And Gunny, the gunnery sergeant in charge of the Marine guards, ran out to the gate and shouted, 'Bob! I told you, anything Tex wants, she gets, and anytime she wants to come through here, you let her!'

"Robert said, 'I thought Tex was your mascot. That's what you told me.'

"'Yeah, that's her!'

"Robert said, 'I thought you meant a *dog!*'

"I waited half an hour to cool down and then went through the gate. And by the way, I did *not* shine my shoes. I've told my kids, he made me so mad that day, I swore I'd get even with him. And I did. I married him."

"Your daughter mentioned something about a bleeding suitcase?"

She gasped. "Oh, my ... she *told* you about that?"

"I'm afraid so."

"I was working in the chiefs and officers' mess and kept an unused half of a tenderloin. It was already thawed out so I was supposed to throw it in the trash. But I kept it. It was something everybody did, because everything was rationed. No butter, no this, no that. We couldn't afford to let things go to waste. We took turns taking the leftovers.

"The cooks wrapped it in wax paper for me. We didn't have aluminum foil then. I wrapped that in some towels, and put it in my suitcase for the weekend trip to my parents' house.

"I knew my name was dirt if the guard told me to open that suitcase. I was supposed to have a little chit made out authorizing me to take the meat. But the Marines had never stopped me before. They knew I frequently took leftover butter to my mom and dad. My dad had been hurt in a work accident, and there was no such thing as workmen's compensation back then. So I'd take leftovers to help my parents out.

"I couldn't see anything wrong with it, but it's against the law as far as the military is concerned. And there I was when Robert stopped me, holding a light-colored suitcase, and the blood from the meat was causing brown spots to show up on it. If he asked me to open it, I was dead."

"Did he notice it?"

"He didn't say a word about it. I guess he was too flustered to notice, because I had dared to quip back at him.

"You know, I could have gotten a chit, the chief would have given it to me, but I just didn't think of it. I wasn't thinking of anything but, 'How *dare* he?' I was a privileged person, you know. See, I had brought a little grill and an iron skillet I weaseled out of a friend of mine. At that time it was impossible to buy cooking utensils, but I knew the right kind of people to go to for that. I got somebody who was shipping out to donate his refrigerator to us, and I fixed those Marines up with a kitchen. I fixed meals for them so they didn't have to eat baloney every day. So naturally, they thought I was special, and I didn't like the idea of this one Marine *not* thinking I was special. I wanted to have the same effect on Robert Gibeson that I had on everyone else."

"Tell me about your first date."

"On the day of mourning for President Roosevelt, all the businesses closed. But being from there, I knew one cafe in town that would definitely be open. The owner, Lou, a friend of mine, had never voted for Roosevelt, and he wasn't about to close up shop for him! He got all the trade that day.

"Robert was looking for a place to eat, and he told me he'd buy me lunch if I knew a place that was open. So I took him to Lou's. We hit it off and became real good friends and later decided, this might work.

"We didn't date very long before we got engaged. He got his orders to ship out to the Pacific again. We sat in a little park in Corpus waiting for the bus to return to the base, and he told me, 'I'd ask you to marry me, but you're engaged to so many guys I don't want to be just one of the bunch.'"

Without warning Virginia Gibeson turned on her most alluring and velvety voice, and it threatened to melt the phone line. "I said, 'Well, you might ask me and find out.'"

Despite the passage of time, I knew, hearing that voice, that the young Robert Gibeson had landed himself a prize.

"So he asked me! I said, 'I'm gonna get you good, I'm gonna *marry* you!' We were inseparable friends. Of course back then there was no hanky panky. We didn't sleep around.

"We got married less than a month later on June 23. The owner of a local drive-in theater shut it down for the night and let us hold a reception in a big party room he had there. We had so many people there, most of them in uniform. We wore our uniforms for the ceremony. We had a two-day honeymoon and

Robert and Virginia Gibeson's wedding photo.
They wore their uniforms to the wedding.

then he shipped out. He was supposed to be in the invasion of mainland Japan.

"His ship was just about to leave port when the Japanese threw up the white flag. He didn't have to go."

Fifty-five years later, her relief was still loud and clear.

Robert and Virginia Gibeson's 50th
wedding anniversary photo in 1995.

201

Ron Vaughn
Eastland

"**M**y twin brother Don and I were reading the Sunday comics on the floor of our dining room on Dec. 7, 1941," Ron Vaughn told me. "We lived with my mother at my grandparents' house. A neighbor called my grandfather and told him to turn on the radio, and we heard the shocking news that the Japanese had bombed Pearl Harbor.

"My brother and I wanted to join up right away, at the age of fifteen. We tried to talk my mother into signing us up for the Navy, but she wouldn't have any of it. She said we were too young and would have to wait. At the very least, she insisted, we must finish high school. We tried the classic argument, 'But all the other kids are doing it!' After all, a classmate of mine got his dad to sign him up at fifteen; he brought the papers home and his dad said, 'Son, if you really want to go I'll sign the paper.' So he did. I guess he lied about his age. A lot of boys did that. Another classmate of mine joined at fourteen and went into submarines. Can you imagine, being in one of those things at fourteen? I thought if he could do that, surely I could pitch in and help!

"I couldn't grow up fast enough. I thought the war would pass me by. But Mom remained firm. High school first. As it turned out, we didn't wait quite that long. We quit high school at midterm of our senior year and joined up, because at that time if you waited until you were eighteen you couldn't volunteer, you had to wait to be drafted. We couldn't wait.

Ron Vaughn

"Don and I got sworn into the Navy side by side at Lubbock two days before our eighteenth birthday. Then we got on the train for San Diego for eight weeks of boot camp. The first night there the drill sergeant told us when we went to bed to be sure and put our money in our pillowcases and sleep on it so it wouldn't get stolen during the night. We had a strict daily routine: get up at 4:30 every morning, shower and shave, make up our bunks, and go to chow. After breakfast we did calisthenics and then we watched patriotic orientation movies. Physical drill included jumping jacks, squat-stand routines, pushups. We double-timed around the grinder, the parade ground, five or six times a day. Everywhere we went we marched in formation, and we ran about five miles a day. The drill sergeants treated us a lot rougher than they treat recruits these days. If you missed a step they'd throw some pretty foul language at you.

"Up until we finished basic my brother and I were together all the time. His bunk was right above mine. They assigned the bunks alphabetically, and his name was Donald and mine was Ronald so he got the top bunk. He went to radio school after boot camp, and they transferred me and about 300 other men aboard ship. Four small carriers had come in after completing their shakedowns and they needed men to bring their crews up to full strength. I joined the USS *Kitkun Bay*, CVE-71. You could fit three of these 'baby flattops' in one of the big aircraft carriers. We had thirty-seven aircraft aboard: twelve torpedo bombers and twenty-five fighters.

"Right after I went aboard, the ship entered dry-dock and we had to scrape and repaint the bottom of the hull. They gave us scrapers with sixteen-foot wooden handles, so big it took three men to hold one, and we stood on the floor of the dry-dock and scraped barnacles and old paint off the ship. It was hard work, and dirty. Paint fell down on us. My hands blistered and my muscles ached. We did that for two weeks. We put on 'red lead,' a waterproof coating, and battleship gray on top of that. Three hundred men at a time worked under the ship. We worked eight hours, and sometimes we got liberty in the evening.

"We loaded up aircraft and passengers and carried them to Pearl Harbor, leaving the States on May 9, 1944. The trip took almost a week because we zigzagged the whole way to make it harder for Jap submarines to target us. We traveled with three other baby flattops, *Gambier Bay, Fanshaw Bay,* and *Kalinin Bay,* and five or six destroyers. We went to battle stations every morning thirty minutes before sunrise until thirty minutes after sunrise, and we did the same thing at sunset, because Japanese pilots liked to fly in from the rising or setting sun where they were hard to see."

"This was your first ocean voyage; did you get seasick?" I asked.

"I was sick for four days. I got a pretty bad case of dry heaves, couldn't eat that whole time. But I still had to do my job. The officers took no pity on me. They said fresh air was the best thing for it, and they put me to work topside. The weather decks constantly peeled in the salty water and air, so we had to keep them scraped and painted. After I managed to eat, the seasickness faded. Getting some food down your stomach was the only remedy. I never had any more trouble after that.

"In the sleeping compartment the bunks stood four high, with 200 men or so to a compartment. I had just barely enough room to get in between my bunk and the one above me. We had lockers alongside the bunks to hold our shaving gear, underclothes, dungarees, dress uniforms. A photograph album was the only thing I had from home.

"After Hawaii we sailed for Eniwetok in the Marshall Islands to meet a 150-ship convoy heading west—troop ships, supply ships, everything. Our four small carriers provided combat air patrol and anti-submarine patrol. Then at Manus in the Admiralty Islands we picked up battleships, cruisers, destroyers, and destroyer escorts, until the convoy grew to 200 ships. On the way to Manus at night a destroyer picked up a submarine contact, and our five-inch gun fired a star shell to see if we could locate the sub. The shell lit up the whole convoy and put us all on edge, thinking we were about to get torpedoed. But nothing happened and we continued on our way.

"We took part in the invasion of Saipan, Tinian, and Guam. We got hit with our first air raid on June 15. Our radar picked up a flight of twenty-five Japanese planes coming in, and our combat air patrol flew out to intercept them. Our fighters shot down all but ten of the Jap planes and then had to break off contact before they got in range of our anti-aircraft guns. One of the Jap planes got within a couple of hundred feet of my ship while making a torpedo run on another carrier, and our five-inch gun blew it out of the air."

View from USS *Kitkun Bay* at Saipan, June 1944.

"What were you doing while the ship was under attack?" I asked.

"My job was sky lookout, a plane spotter for the gun crews. I radioed the bridge and told them where an enemy aircraft was, and they told the gun crews to shoot it down. 'This is Sky Lookout Three. There's an enemy aircraft bearing one-six-five on our starboard quarter, altitude approximately 100 feet.' The bridge would respond 'Roger' and relay the information to the gun crews.

"The *Gambier Bay* launched an airplane right into our line of fire as we shot at an enemy plane coming across, and we shot the friendly plane down! Luckily the pilot wasn't hurt. His plane hit the water and he climbed out safely. A destroyer picked the pilot up and transferred him back aboard his ship in a breeches buoy."

"Did anybody get in trouble for that?" I asked.

"Oh, no. Nothing was said. It was just an unfortunate accident, and that sort of thing happened more than people were allowed to know."

"Where was your battle station located?" I asked.

"I did my job from a lookout station on the aft end of the starboard catwalk. These stations were on all four corners of the ship and were manned 24 hours a day. It was an exposed and vulnerable position. Everybody on the flight deck and catwalk was visible to enemy pilots, and if a plane strafed the ship there was a chance I could be hit."

"Did the Japanese planes manage to send any torpedoes your way?"

"Yes, a Jap torpedo bomber dropped one that narrowly missed us. It streaked in on the starboard side. Our helmsman turned hard to port and the torpedo passed right by the bow. Ships didn't always succeed at dodging torpedoes, but we got lucky that time. If the Jap pilot had aimed it better, dropped it farther back toward the center of the ship, we might not have been able to dodge it. But we made it through our first air raid without a scratch. We'd been lucky."

"Was that Japanese pilot's poor aim the rule or the exception?" I asked.

"In my opinion, their pilots weren't all that accurate. They aimed their torpedoes badly and our ships dodged them. Dive bombers dropped bombs close to our ships, but not close enough. Some of the dive-bombers never pulled out of the dive.

"We stood off the shore of Saipan so our planes could cover the troops going ashore. The Navy shelled the beach for three days before the invasion, and at night I could see the sixteen-inch shells flying all the way in, white-hot metal flying through the air. We could hear the booming of the guns, and we saw the flash and the flying debris when the shells landed.

"During our six weeks off Saipan, Jap planes attacked us three times. My ship shot ten planes down in that time. Sometimes during flight operations a plane came in to land just as the ship went down a swell. The tailhook caught, the ship started to rise up on the next swell, and the plane hit so hard it blew out both tires. Sometimes a plane failed to catch the arresting wires, ran into the steel cable barriers at the front of the ship, and flipped upside down. The pilot usually got out and walked away from that. It happened once or twice a week. But sometimes the plane missed the arresting wires, hit the deck and bounced over the side. We lost three or four pilots that way. The plane hit the water so hard the impact knocked the pilot out cold and he sank with the airplane.

"During one of those air raids, the lieutenant in charge of my lookout station reported an enemy aircraft off to starboard. The men on the bridge couldn't find this plane and asked him to confirm, and everybody started looking for it. Before long the lieutenant and I discovered it was a large butterfly flying along with all the shooting going on around it! Let me tell you, that lieutenant had a very red face for a long time. Nobody knew about it but me and him, and I didn't tell a soul!" We laughed.

"Did submarines ever attack you?" I asked.

"Jap subs fired torpedoes at us several times but never hit us. The destroyers in our group always chased them and dropped depth charges. Once they hit a sub near us and we watched the geysers from the depth charge explosions, boiling up 75 to 100 feet high, like Old Faithful at Yellowstone.

"In October 1944 we sailed for the Philippines. The Japanese sent air raids out against our fleet. Air combat usually happened miles away, too far and too high for us to watch. But if the Japs got closer, we had a five-inch gun, 40mm guns, and 20mm guns to defend ourselves.

"At Leyte Gulf the Japs started sending suicide planes. A kamikaze aimed straight for my ship, and we blew it out of the air only 150 feet off our deck. But a moment later a second one hit us on our port bow, killing one man and wounding sixteen. It took about 25 feet of the catwalk with it. It had a bomb, but the bomb didn't explode until it hit the water."

"That must have been a nerve-wracking moment, watching that plane come in," I said.

"That was nothing compared to what came next," Vaughn told me. "On the morning of October 25, as soon as we had secured our routine battle stations, we went belowdecks for chow. About the middle of breakfast the bridge sounded general quarters and we rushed back to battle stations. As I hit the topside catwalk, I looked out and saw shells from the battleships and cruisers of the Japanese fleet splashing around us."

"Oh, my gosh," I said.

"You've heard the expression 'my heart leapt up to my throat?' Well, that's exactly what mine did! Shells hit the water within a few hundred yards of us. I rushed to my battle station as the flight deck crew started launching aircraft as fast as they could. Planes already gassed up launched immediately, then the deck crew fueled and armed the rest and got them up in the air, and the instant the last plane took off, the ships turned around and *ran* from the Japanese fleet. I could see the enemy ships on the horizon, twenty miles away. I saw their guns flash when they fired a salvo and soon after watched the shells splash into the water. The water kept splashing closer and closer to my ship, and I held on for dear life, certain the next salvo would hit us. But at that moment the *Gambier Bay* took some hits right behind us. The Japanese ships concentrated their fire on her, holed her beneath the waterline, and flooded her engine rooms. She stopped dead in the water. The Japs kept shelling her until she sank.

"Every one of the ships in my task group took hits, except mine. The closest they came to hitting us was a shell that landed twenty feet off our fantail, almost directly beneath my station, and the explosion bounced us around so much I thought we'd been hit. When the ship quit shaking the five-inch gun crew radioed the bridge, 'The ship is OK, but we're all wet down here!'"

"How do you deal with the stress of being on a big, slow target in the middle of the ocean, with enemy ships gunning for you?" I asked.

"Funny you should ask," he said. "During the shelling the flight deck crew didn't have anything to do, all the planes were away, so to keep their mind off the situation they started moving equipment from one side of the flight deck to the other. Then they moved it right back where it was in the first place. They carried anything they could pick up, just to keep busy and avoid thinking about those Japanese ships. They'd pick up this box and move it over here, and then a few minutes later they'd pick it up and move it back, right in the middle of the battle. They laugh about it now."

"Wow," I said. "How did you get out of it?"

"The battle took place in sight of the island of Samar, and the skipper decided if the Japanese kept chasing us he would run us aground and abandon ship, because if they got any closer they would blow us out of the water. Rather than having the ship sink with all hands aboard he wanted to give us a fighting chance to get ashore.

"But after two and a half hours of shelling, the Japanese ships suddenly turned around and left."

"What ... why?"

"To this day I don't know. If they had stayed they would easily have destroyed every ship in my task group."

"What happened to the crew of the *Gambier Bay*?"

"Men from the *Gambier Bay* and some sunken destroyers spent two days in the water waiting for rescue. The Navy couldn't find them. Sharks killed a lot of men. We knew at the time they hadn't been found, and we were furious. Our ships had traveled together from the beginning. Those men were like family to us; we spent time with them while on liberty. It turned out somebody reported the wrong position to the rescue personnel. We cussed up a storm when we heard that. Those men deserved better.

"My ship returned to dry-dock at Pearl Harbor. They put us to work scraping and painting the bottom again while they repaired the kamikaze damage. I got liberty every other day. Once I found out a boy from home, Jack McCulley of Brownwood, was in port on his minesweeper, so I took a bus and found his ship in the middle of a long row of minesweepers. I jumped from deck to deck until I got to his sweeper. I found him on his hands and knees painting with his back to me. I snuck up behind him and said hello. He looked around and jumped up and hugged me real tight! He was so glad to see somebody from home. I was glad, too; it was the first time I'd seen anybody I knew. I spent three hours with him, talking about things we did growing up, how we used to go swimming in the bayou. But then it was time to go back to my ship.

"We met a 300-ship convoy going to Luzon in the Philippines for invasion. On the way we stopped in the Solomon Islands and loaded a bunch of frozen goats so we'd have some meat, but when the cooks started cooking them they didn't like the way the goat meat smelled. They didn't know the meat has a peculiar smell when it's cooking. I grew up eating goat meat so I didn't mind it at all. But late one night the cooks threw all the goats overboard, hoping the officers wouldn't catch them. The captain knew all about it but he didn't say a thing. They didn't find out he knew until fifty years later, at a reunion!" He laughed.

"We'd been really lucky up to that point, but luck can't hold out forever. The day before the landings on Luzon a kamikaze plane hit us on the port side, right at the waterline. It knocked a nine-foot by twenty-foot hole in the side of the ship, flooded our aft engine room and machine shop, and stopped us dead in the water. The crash killed one man in the engine room. Then the cruiser *Boise,* off to starboard, fired a five-inch anti-aircraft shell into my ship and killed sixteen men topside. The shell hit right next to a powder magazine for the 20mm gun, and the explosion wiped out a repair party and two 20mm gun crews.

"The ship listed to port at a 12- to 15-degree angle, making it pretty hard to walk on the steel decks. Everybody on the port catwalk moved over to the starboard catwalk to help balance the ship. The explosion had started a fire, but the seawater rushing into the ship put it out. The officers thought she was going down so they ordered everybody to abandon ship, except for volunteers to stay aboard. I started toward my abandon ship station. Two medics came up carrying a stretcher with a wounded man and asked for help carrying him to the fantail where he could be transferred to the destroyer *Stembel* waiting alongside. I helped carry him down the flight deck. When we got to the fantail one of the ship's doctors took one look at the man and informed us we'd just carried a dead man across the ship. We transferred his body over to the destroyer.

"I sorely wanted to go back for my photo album. I had pictures from home in it, pictures of my girlfriend. My sleeping compartment was just forward of the fantail about two or three decks down. It would have taken me fifteen minutes to get to it and get back. I decided not to risk it, because if the ship went down I'd get caught belowdecks.

"The only way to get across from my ship to the destroyer was to jump. We had some moonlight, but not much, and I could just barely see the outline of the destroyer. Its bow was underneath our starboard catwalk, and its crewmembers stood there waiting to catch us when we jumped. This was about three stories above the water."

"You jumped from one ship to another in the dark? How'd you work up the courage?"

"I didn't think about it, I just did it. It's not that difficult to jump off a sinking ship when you're that excited. I jumped out about ten feet, and two guys caught me and pulled me aboard. A couple of guys jumped short, but the men on the destroyer managed to catch them.

"The destroyer crew put us belowdecks in sleeping compartments, to let us rest and to get us out of the way so they could do their jobs. The next morning we awoke to hear the five-inch and 40mm firing rapidly. A kamikaze was heading straight for us. They shot it down.

"Then we found out the volunteers who stayed aboard *Kitkun Bay* had managed to keep her afloat and get steam back. The destroyer crew transferred us back aboard. A little more than a hundred men had stayed aboard, engineers and electricians, and they had counterflooded the ship and returned it to an even keel. We'd lost one of the two engines, so our top speed was only eight knots.

"We sailed to Leyte with a hole in the side of the ship. We only had half-inch plate steel between us and the water inside the ship. At Leyte, frogmen came out from the island and welded a steel patch onto the ship underwater, and then we pumped the water out of the engine room. They found two unexploded bombs inside the ship and called a bomb disposal crew out from Leyte to defuse them and throw them over the side. Then we went into dry-dock to remove the screw from the dead engine so we could go faster. The dead screw was creating drag.

"On the way back to the States for repairs, we only had enough evaporators to make fresh water to run the ship and cook with. That meant we couldn't take freshwater showers. So every time we passed through a rainsquall they'd pass word over the P.A. system, and people would grab soap and towels and run to the flight deck to take a shower in the rain. Now that was a funny sight, a bunch of guys on the flight deck naked as a jaybird soaping themselves up in the rain! We could get a pretty good shower if it rained long enough. But sometimes, it didn't; we'd get soap all over us and the rain would quit.

"Another funny thing that happened... The mess hall was over the compartment where they stored bombs. Sometimes we couldn't set up the folding tables because they might need to open up the floor and get at the bombs in a hurry. When that happened we had to eat sitting on the deck. We crossed our legs and set the trays on our thighs. Well, one time we ate on the floor like this while riding out a typhoon. The water got rough, so when the ship rolled to the left we'd have to raise our left legs to keep the trays balanced, and when the ship rolled to the right we'd all raise our right leg. It was quite a sight, all those men leaning left and right in unison.

"During that same typhoon the cooks needed some pota-toes from the spud locker on the fantail, which was an exposed weather deck with the waves breaking over it. They assigned me and another seaman to go out there in the middle of that typhoon and get two 100-pound sacks of potatoes. So we waited behind a hatch near the spud locker. When the ship reached the top of a wave and broke over the top, the fantail stuck up out of the water, so we made a mad dash to the spud locker, opened the hatch, jumped inside, and slammed it shut just before the ship went down the other side. While the wave broke over the fantail we each grabbed a sack of potatoes. When the ship broke over the top of the next wave, we carried those sacks as fast as we could back to the hatch we'd come out of. We made it, just barely!

"We arrived back to the States in late February of 1945. The ship entered dry-dock and the crew got a twenty-day leave. I went home to Brownwood and married my girlfriend, Wanda White. She wanted to get married so I'd have somebody to come back home to when I got out if I didn't get killed. We threw together a wedding with twenty-five or thirty people; my mother, best man, his wife, a lot of friends from church.

"At the end of my leave Wanda rode the train back to California with me so she could be with me until I went back overseas. We rented a small room, just a bedroom with no kitchen, and went out for dinner when I was able to get off the ship every other night."

"This must have been about the time Iwo Jima and Okinawa were happening," I said.

"That's right. If we had not taken the hit we took, we'd have been in both of those invasions. We'd already gotten the orders. Instead, once we got the ship back in the water, we protected a convoy of tankers that was refueling the Third Fleet while it bombarded the island of Honshu. This was in preparation for the invasion of mainland Japan."

"Were you worried about having to invade Japan?"

"Yes. We knew that landing was going to be rough. We wondered how many of us could expect to come back alive. The

Japanese would throw every airplane they had at our ships. And they still had plenty of submarines.

"But, while we were fueling up at Manus the U.S. dropped the atomic bombs. When we heard the news the men on my ship yelled and jumped for joy. Other ships started firing their anti-aircraft guns into the air, but our commander wouldn't let us do that."

"How did they explain this new weapon to you?" I asked.

"Of course, nobody really knew what the atom bomb was," he said. "They just told us the United States had dropped a very powerful new weapon on Japan and the Japanese had offered unconditional surrender. It was all shrouded in mystery. We wondered what kind of weapon could be that powerful. I only learned more about it after I went home.

"We anchored in Tokyo Bay two weeks after the Japanese signed the surrender agreement. I got a day of liberty and went ashore to look around. I stood in one spot and looked for miles in every direction and saw nothing but rubble. Fires had leveled most of the buildings. People were destitute and homeless and they tried to sell trinkets to American servicemen to make some sort of living out of what was left."

"Were you able to return home quickly?"

"No. We made a couple of trips back and forth across the Pacific to pick up men for transport back to the United States. I got pretty impatient at that point. Finally I got my discharge in January of '46."

He chuckled and said, "When we brought our first load of troops back home to Los Angeles, the fog was so thick we couldn't see the breaker walls and had to find the opening into the harbor with radar. A pleasure yacht had anchored out there to welcome the boys home with the Harry James Orchestra aboard. The Harry James Orchestra was a big deal. The yacht was supposed to sail alongside us, with the orchestra playing songs of the day like 'It's Been a Long, Long Time,' 'I'm Beginning to See the Light,' 'Cherry' and 'I'll Get By.'

"We sailed right past them in the fog and they never did see us, and when we arrived at the dock in Los Angeles, nobody was there to greet us! People were supposed to be there to catch our mooring lines, and the friends and relatives of the boys coming home were supposed to welcome us home. They were all inside waiting for the fog to lift.

"Somebody saw us come up to the dock, and everybody ran out of the big waiting room. Up on the ship we all had a good laugh about the way we surprised them. The gangplank dropped down and the boys streamed off the ship and the crowd swarmed around them, kissing and hugging them. Hundreds of people jammed onto the dock and had quite a celebration.

"But we didn't get to hear any music from the Harry James Orchestra because they were still out there on the yacht, waiting for us in the fog!"

Ron Vaughn
today

218

It seemed like a million years,
even though it was only two

Joe Leeah
El Paso

"**I** was living in Sierra Blanca when the war broke out," Joe Leeah told me. "It's a tiny town eighty-seven miles east of El Paso. I really wanted to join up and go to war at the age of seventeen, but my folks wouldn't sign for me. They said I was too young and I'm sure I was. Now that I've raised a family, I understand exactly how they felt.

"But as I neared my eighteenth birthday I went to visit relatives in Houston, intending to join up there. The very day I turned eighteen I registered and asked for immediate induction, which they granted. The Navy was my preferred choice of the services, but they put you where they needed you and you didn't have anything to say about it.

"But I got lucky and was sworn into the Navy in just a few days. My uncle took me to the train station to leave for boot camp at San Diego, and then he called my folks in Sierra Blanca to tell them I'd be passing through town on the train. As we approached town I got real excited and watched for them. Meanwhile, my sister and my girlfriend had bought tickets so they could ride to El Paso and visit with me for that eighty-seven-mile leg of the trip. The train never stopped there at Sierra Blanca unless they knew some passengers were going to get on, so my sister and girlfriend were the only reason it stopped, and they didn't intend to stay long.

Joe Leeah

"Back then the trains were real long, and my mother had thought if she walked down the track a ways she'd have a better chance of seeing me. But the train only stopped for a few seconds. The old conductor hollered, 'All aboard!' and as soon as they got my sister and girlfriend aboard, the train started moving again, and my mother was all the way down the track. I stepped down in the doorway and saw her. She was trying to get to me, waving and crying and carrying on, but she didn't make it. I stood there as long as I could and waved to her.

"My sister and girlfriend and I had a nice visit and then we had to say a long, hard goodbye at El Paso. This was really a big deal...."

Leeah still sounded awestruck at what he had done. "I was barely eighteen, and back in the thirties people didn't move around very much. I hadn't been hardly anywhere in my life and here I was going to war....

"My father ran an automotive garage so I'd been around engines a lot, so I ended up as an engineer on a landing craft attached to the USS *Bowie*, APA-137. Her name was taken from Bowie County, Texas."

"What does APA stand for?"

"Attack Personnel Auxiliary. It was almost 500 feet long and carried twenty-six LCVP, that's Landing Craft Vehicle/Personnel. The ship was brand new. Old *Bowie* traveled many nautical miles during its time. It seemed like a million years, even though I was only in for two.

"At Honolulu we participated in a mock invasion, landing troops on Maui. It was set up like a real battle, airplanes flying over, smoke generators laying down a smokescreen. Us young buttons weren't afraid of anything I guess. I was just an eighteen-year-old from a little West Texas town. We were out there for a good time.

"After we dropped our troops on the beach and started laying a smokescreen with a generator on our landing craft, my

USS *Bowie*, APA-137, at anchor

Bow of USS *Bowie*, taken from the bridge

crew decided it was time to go swimming. The three of us took turns jumping into the water under the smokescreen, splashing around in the water with this fake battle going on all around us. That's how seriously we took it!

Underway on the bow of USS *Bowie*. Joe Leeah is second from right.

Joe Leeah (second row, right) with buddies in front of the captain's gig.

"The *Bowie* made a stop at Iwo Jima while the battle was still underway. We stood by some distance from Iwo and took on casualties. That battle caused so many casualties, they didn't have enough hospital ships to handle them."

"Was your ship in range of Japanese weapons?"

"We weren't in any big danger at Iwo. Our turn came later."

"Okinawa?" I guessed.

"That's right. We picked up a load of troops at Lingayen Gulf in the Philippines and landed them on Okinawa. That's where we earned our battle star.

"The first wave of men had already landed, so the beach was relatively settled when we landed our troops. But we had another job to do. Every ship available was ordered to anchor in the harbor and help ward off kamikazes until Okinawa was secured.

"The suicide planes came in the evening, out of the sun where they were hard to see. Lucky for us on the *Bowie*, those pilots wanted to hit the big warships, cruisers, battlewagons, carriers. Our ships put up flak so thick a duck could have walked across it. Our fleet fired every gun we had."

"What kind of defenses did you have on the *Bowie*?"

"We had four sets of quad 40mm, two sets of twin 40mm, and several 20mm guns. When we spotted a Jap plane every single gunner turned and fired at it, and the same thing happened all through the fleet, and shrapnel rained down in the water and landed on the decks of the ships. It was really something to see.

"The battleship USS *New Mexico* was anchored off our starboard stern. One evening a kamikaze swooped in right over the top of us, with every ship around us throwing flak at it. It passed less than a hundred feet over us and hit the *New Mexico*, sending up a big cloud of black smoke and killing fifty-four men."

"How close were you to this?" I asked.

"The ships were anchored just far enough that when they swung in the water, they wouldn't collide. No more than a couple hundred feet away. I was at my fire station on the stern of the *Bowie*, directly across from her. We were looking right straight at the nose of this plane when it came in, and we actually thought it was aiming for us."

"What happened to the *New Mexico?*"

"Fireboats and tugs came up to fight the fire. There was nothing we could do to help. The kamikaze attacks continued every evening for several days before slowing down, thanks to our B-29s hitting the airfields on Japan's mainland.

"After Okinawa we went to Honolulu to pick up troops and supplies to take back out into the Pacific. We had just fired the boilers and gotten steam and moved away from the dock. The tugs had turned us loose, and we were about to leave the harbor, and word came that the Japs had surrendered. At that very moment when it came over the loudspeakers, all the ships in the harbor started to blow their whistles, and every sailor that could get up on deck got up there, and everybody threw their hats into the water! If there was one sailor's hat floating in that harbor, there were a million! We were out of our minds, so happy it was over.

"We continued on our way, and the next day we found out that it was just a false alarm! We waited to hear better news. A few days out the old man told us the Japs had surrendered and we would have to land occupation troops on the Japanese mainland. We steamed to the Carolinas to rendezvous with cruisers, destroyers, and troopships to form a convoy to Japan. It was the biggest convoy we'd ever been in.

"Our landing zone was the city of Sasebo, about thirty-three miles from where the atomic bomb had been dropped at Hiroshima. Of course we'd never heard of radiation or fallout so we weren't worried about it.

"We sailed into a natural harbor that would have been beautiful but for the war. It had a very small opening that led into a huge harbor, a big manufacturing and shipbuilding center. We steamed in there, ready to land our troops in the face of resistance if necessary. We didn't know what to expect. Anxiety was very high as we approached the shore. Our ships eased along extremely slowly because we didn't know what we'd find in the harbor. Sunken ships blocking the way? Mines?

"We scanned the city with binoculars. Sasebo was totally in ruins; we couldn't see any buildings intact. Our bombers had done just a super job on it. There wasn't a Jap anywhere to be seen.

"The harbor did turn out to be full of sunken ships sticking up out of the water, so we anchored the ship out a ways and decided to send the landing craft full of troops onto a big seaplane ramp. We encountered no resistance. The place was deserted.

A Japanese aircraft carrier sits in port at
Sasebo, Japan, after the war's end.

"It took us a week to land all the troops and all their supplies; they had to bring plenty of food because there sure wasn't any there. After a couple of days we started to see some people out on the hillsides, looking out at us from behind something."

"They were that afraid of you?"

"They were afraid we were gonna do to them what they would have done to us if they had the chance," Leeah said. "They had fled to outlying areas and buried their possessions, expecting us to pillage. These people were starving to death; they had nothing to eat.

"Still wary and half-expecting resistance, we had landing craft cruise constantly around the ship, circling it day and night, in case any Japs tried to swim out and put a charge against the hull. Every ship in the fleet had small craft circling it. But no incident of any kind ever happened.

"The second time we approached the harbor at Sasebo, with a fresh load of troops from the Philippines, the most amazing thing happened. Outside the harbor opening, we saw a motor circle us and come up on our starboard side. A seaman threw a ladder over the side. Whenever our ship approached land anywhere, anybody who could get abovedecks would be up there to get a look. So we had a good crowd up on deck. A little Jap officer grabbed hold of the ladder, climbed up over the rail, and hit the deck. This man was about five foot two, wearing a black naval uniform with gold braid all over, 'scrambled eggs' on his cap, black wire-rimmed glasses, probably the most typical Japanese you could ever imagine. Suddenly we were staring the enemy in the face, the first Jap we'd seen up close. It turned out he was a harbor pilot, there to bring our ship in. He had to get up to the bridge, and the sailors lined each side of his path, staring him down.

"Steve, you wouldn't believe it. He bowed, and I'm not talking about bending at the waist. This guy *bowed* all the way to the deck, stood up, took a few steps, bowed all the way down to the deck again, and repeated that all the way to the bridge. It was electrifying. I thought any minute one of those sailors would knock the living hell out of him. And I guarantee you, that's exactly what *I* wanted to do. It was an extremely tense situation. I think the only thing that saved him a broken jaw was his bowing all the way to the deck, showing his defeat."

"Wow," I said. "Did you get to go ashore?"

"Yes. But there wasn't much left to see. The only way to get any souvenirs was to find something in the rubble. I did find a Japanese rifle and a sword. I also had a mortar shell that I got at Okinawa. A friend of mine aboard ship had a screw loose—he was from Brooklyn—he picked up a mortar shell and disarmed it and gave it to me. So I kept it in my locker. Some time later, when we ferrying troops after the war, the gunner's mate blurted out on the intercom, 'Will the sailor who has the mortar shell in his locker please lay up to the quarter deck *without the shell?*' They thought it was still live! I didn't even hear it, one of my buddies heard it and told me I'd better get up there. I went up there and he told me to lead him to the shell. I took him to my locker and said, 'It's OK, it's not live.'

"Well, he wouldn't take my word for it. They moved everybody away and snuck up on it like it was about to explode any minute and inspected it very carefully, and found it disarmed, just like I told them. I brought it home with me. I put the rifle, the sword, and the shell on display in a little museum there in Sierra Blanca."

"When did you get to go home?"

"Not for a long time. Our ship was part of the Magic Carpet, bringing boys home who'd been over the longest. We put in at Long Beach with a load of troops. The Navy had started publicizing the dates, times, and places the ships would be arriving, and some of these troops were able to notify family back home which ship they would be on, so their loved ones could greet them at the dock. My mother and father learned the *Bowie* was coming to Long Beach and decided to go visit my Uncle Dick, who lived in San Diego, and try to see me while the ship was in port at Long Beach. But I didn't know any of this.

"I got liberty and went in to town and lost my ID and liberty cards, and if you lost that you were automatically restricted to the base for two weeks. So when I went back to the ship I was restricted. We didn't have cell phones or anything like that back then; the only way we had to reach people was by mail and that took weeks or even months, so I didn't know what my folks were doing. I had to serve on the liberty crew, meaning I manned the boat that took troops ashore for liberty and brought them back to the boat. We tied up at the slip, unloaded the sailors, and we started up to the restaurant at the top of the landing there to get a cup of coffee. A chief bosun's mate from the shore patrol shouted at us, 'Hey, are you guys from the *Bowie?*' We said yes. He asked, 'Do you all know a sailor by the name of Joe Leeah?' And I thought, oh man what have I done now?

"He walked over and told me, 'Your folks were just here, I've been talking to them a long time. They were trying to see you.' He gave me an envelope and said, 'You might catch them if you run out into the parking lot. They literally just left.' I was so excited! I hadn't seen them in so long. I dashed out into the parking lot and frantically looked for them. But they were gone. What had promised to be such a wonderful moment was now nothing but disappointment.

"On the way back I opened the note the man had given me. It had the address and phone number of my Uncle Dick in San Diego. I couldn't call them right then because we were already returning to the ship. The next day when we went ashore I found a telephone and called them. I told them I would try to see them somehow, but I had no idea how. I was still on restriction.

"I went back to the ship to speak to the executive officer about getting off restriction so I could go to San Diego for a day. He wasn't a very likable fellow. He didn't even want to talk to me. Of course, he refused to allow it. I pleaded with him, told him I'd sure like to see my folks, my mother and dad and sister. But he wouldn't have anything to do with it."

I remembered Manuel Palmer's experiences and wondered, what is it about executive officers?

"I went to my division officer for help, and the nice guy that he was, he said, 'Don't worry, I'll let you go.'

"'But how will I get off the ship?' I asked.

"'I'll tell you what we'll do,' he said. 'You put on your dress uniform and wear your foul weather jacket over it. Get in the boat with the crew, and when they come around to pick up the liberty crew, you'll be covered by the jacket.' So I did it. But when we tied up against the ladder and I looked up, and I was looking straight at that executive officer!"

"Oh, no," I said. "What did he do?"

"He didn't recognize me!" Leeah said happily. "The division officer gave me two days. I took a bus to San Diego and got to see my family."

"Did you have to go across the Pacific again?"

"That turned out to be our last trip. We took the ship through the Panama Canal to Norfolk, Virginia, for decommissioning. After we stripped the ship of everything worth saving, we got a thirty-day leave home.

"A buddy of mine, Jack Wakefield, lived in New Mexico, and we decided to hitchhike home and save our money. Back then if you were in uniform, you could just get out by the road, stick your thumb in the air, and somebody would pick you up. Everybody was patriotic. I would never have hitchhiked before the war.

"We caught a ride from Portsmouth all the way to Amarillo. Jack and I parted ways and I came to El Paso. I spent a night at the Hilton, washed up, and caught a taxi out to the end of town so I could start hitchhiking. I had just finished paying the taxi driver when a '41 Ford pulled up behind me. Two Air Force lieutenants were in it, and one asked if I wanted a ride. I hopped in.

These guys had just completed training—they'd missed being in the war—and were on their way to San Antonio. We traded stories the whole eighty-seven miles to Sierra Blanca. About five miles from town I felt the adrenaline; I was real excited about coming home. My folks had no idea I was coming, so I was gonna get to surprise them.

"We pulled into Sierra Blanca. The main street was the whole town, you know. I looked down the highway and said, 'That looks like my father's car coming down the road right now!' The lieutenants couldn't believe it, but I asked the driver to pull over at a little restaurant, El Café, and we watched. Sure enough it was my father, and my mother was riding in the car with him. They pulled into a Texaco station right across from the café.

"I told these officers, 'They don't even know I'm coming. Watch this, I'm gonna walk down the street a little ways and cross over there so they can't see me and surprise them.'

"I walked up behind them so they couldn't see me, and said, 'Pardon me, sir, if you're going west I wonder if I could hitch a ride with you.'

"Without really looking at me he said, 'Well, you sure could if we were, but we live here!' And I just bent down closer and said, 'Well I do too!'"

He giggled. "My mother and father just about had a heart attack! I looked back across the street and the two lieutenants were grinning from ear to ear. One of them gave me a thumbs-up, and they pulled out and drove away."

Joe Leeah with wife, Jean, in Honolulu
for their 50th wedding anniversary, 1996.

Thornton Hamby
Lubbock

I braced myself before I called Thornton Hamby. So far I'd heard many stories of horrific violence, the type of violence that is necessarily a part of war: uniformed combatants trying to kill each other to win a battle.

Now I would hear of something else entirely.

Cruelty.

"When I shipped out to the Pacific the Marine Corps gave me the choice of going to the Philippines or serving aboard the USS *Houston*," Hamby told me. "I chose the Philippines and I'm glad I did, because the *Houston* was sunk shortly after the war broke out.

"I was at Mariveles on the Bataan Peninsula when the Japs attacked the Philippines on December 8, 1941. My officers shipped me up to Imus between Cavete and Manila and put me on an anti-aircraft gun. I had never seen one before. They said, 'You aim it this way, you load it that way. There comes a plane, start firing!' And that was my training."

"That was *it?*"

"That's right. I was a Marine and you did what they asked you to."

"And Japanese planes were attacking at that moment?"

"Yes, Zeros came at us. What planes we had were up there getting into dogfights with them, right over the bay. We had

P-35s and P-36s and a few P-40s. Of course we'd have had more planes, but MacArthur lost our air force for us. He wouldn't let them go up. He kept them on the ground where the Japs destroyed them."

"And what do you think of MacArthur?" I asked.

"Don't get me started on that glory hound," he said curtly before returning to his story. "One pilot had a Zero on his tail and tried to decoy him into our guns, but he came down too close to the water and pancaked into the bay. The Zero spotted us and got away. The water was shallow, so the American pilot just climbed out and waded ashore."

"We shot down a lot of Jap planes. Once we even shot down three planes with only three rounds of ammunition. One day two Jap bombers flew in formation over Corregidor, and a gun emplacement knocked both of them down—with *one round*. The shell exploded in one plane's bomb bay, causing an explosion so big it knocked the other one out of the air, too.

"The first time I got wounded, I was back fighting on Bataan against Japanese Marines, big guys. Every bit as big and strong as us, not small like you'd expect. One of them threw a grenade at us, and the shrapnel sprayed me in the right side of my face. The guy on my left got two middle fingers and a thumb cut off, and shrapnel cut through his forearm. The guy on my right got hit in the leg.

"Navy doctors worked on me for a couple of days in a hospital tunnel there on Bataan. I had more than 200 pieces of black powder in my eyeball and twelve pieces of steel. In fact I've still got a piece of steel in my eye. The doctors couldn't remove it without completely blinding me."

"Does it affect your vision?"

"No, it just healed over it. The second time I got wounded, I was being strafed by a Zero. I was running as hard as I could, trying to dodge them bullets, and I hit something and fell, hard. I tore up my right arm and shoulder."

"How close did the bullets get to you?"

"Oh, I could feel them passing by me in the air. Anyway, when the Bataan Peninsula fell, they sent me to a trench on the island of Corregidor. I looked out over Fort Hughes and Fort Drum from my position. The Japs bombed us constantly. A dud landed right by us and I helped another guy roll it down into the ocean.

"The Japs took the island from a different direction, and I never even saw them before General Wainwright surrendered. We got word that we must gather at Malinta Tunnel to be taken prisoner."

"What did you think of the decision to surrender?"

"I didn't have any say in the matter. We had to go, unless we wanted to fight until we died."

"Was there grumbling among the troops?"

"There was always grumbling about something."

"What happened when the Japanese took you prisoner?"

"We lined up and the Japs came marching down through there, staring at us. They taunted us and laughed at us because we had surrendered. They didn't believe in surrendering. They'd die first.

"As you may know, at the beginning of World War II we had World War I equipment and uniforms there in the Philippines. We had 1903 Springfield rifles and grenades you could play catch with for twenty minutes before they'd go off. And we wore those flat metal helmets, not the ones that came later. Just like in World War I.

"One little bitty Jap was carrying a wooden baton of some kind. He saw Sergeant Pinto standing right next to me, and he took that stick and conked him over the helmet, and that helmet just rang like a bell. They thought that was really funny. But there wasn't anything we could do about it.

"A buddy of mine, Tiger Barnes from Mississippi, wasn't gonna give up, and the Japs bayoneted him in the stomach. He dived off a cliff and swam out to an American barge anchored out there and hid there all night. But the Japs got him the next day. A doctor said swimming through the salt water saved his life by cleaning out his wound."

"Tell me about the food the Japanese gave you."

"What food? We went three days without any. Then a Jap found some cans and took me and another prisoner to carry them for him. It turned out to be canned tomatoes. The Jap opened one, tasted it, sputtered and spewed. He didn't like canned tomatoes. He told us we could have it all, and that was the first food we got."

"And you were already short on food even before your capture, isn't that right?"

"Funny you should mention that. The Navy fed us Marines, and Army troops would stop by to ask for food because their leaders never sent them anything to eat."

"Did they have anything to send them, though?" I wondered.

"The Japanese put me to work on Corregidor loading boats, and I helped load three ships full of frozen food the Japs found on the island. It had been there the whole time! Meanwhile the GIs had been eating cavalry horses and mules that got killed by the bombing.

"The Japs marched us down the streets of Manila, parading us in front of the Filipinos and bragging about how they'd captured the big Americans. The next day they loaded us on a train to Cabanatuan, and then hiked us about thirty kilometers to a camp."

"What was the march like?"

"This was late May and it was steaming hot. Men staggered and fell around me. Others picked them up and carried them.

"Cabanatuan Camp No. 1 was a death hole. Nothing to eat and everybody was sick. Beri beri, dysentery. Some of the worst brutality I saw in the entire war was at Cabanatuan."

He now spoke slowly, softly.

"Three guys got lost out on a work detail and wandered back into camp. The Japs tied logs back behind their knees to hold them in an uncomfortable squatting position, and made them stand out there in the steaming hot sun. They told them if they couldn't stand that way for 48 hours they would kill them."

"How long did they last?"

"Most of one day."

"What happened?"

"The Japs made them dig their own graves, shot them, and covered them up."

"You saw this?" I asked after a few seconds of silence.

"Yes. I witnessed it."

I couldn't think of anything appropriate to say. After a moment, he continued the story.

"The Japs organized us into groups of eleven people. If one of the eleven escaped, they shot the other ten. Well, a man from my group escaped.

"The Japs stood me up in front of a firing squad because of this, along with J.W. Hough, a friend of mine who lives here in Lubbock. If you don't think you can freeze to death in 120-degree weather, you've never faced a Japanese firing squad."

"How did you survive?"

"A young captain in our camp named Fleming buffaloed them out of shooting us."

"How in the world did he accomplish that?"

"He made more noise than they did. Got into a fierce argument with them, told them it was against the Geneva Convention. They backed down.

"I spent two years as a prisoner in the Philippines, working at Clark Field, before they took me to Japan. They put me to work in a coal mine outside of Hiroshima. I'll tell you one thing, after doing that, there's not enough money in the United States, Canada, and Mexico to get me down into Carlsbad Caverns.

"I narrowly survived a cave-in down there. My job was to build what they called 'castles,' which were log frames that we filled with coal to hold the roof up. There's always a cracking noise in coal mines, but when it starts to cave it's a different noise altogether. I heard this horrendous noise and I hollered to the guys digging the coal up above me in a lateral tunnel. I hollered, 'It's fixin' to cave, get out of there!'

"A moment later the ceiling came down and knocked me down into a chute that takes the coal away from the laterals and dumps it into the carts. I tumbled down the chute, a long, high-speed slide with coal rushing down around me, and climbed out of the mess down at the other end. A Japanese officer ran up and asked me what had happened to the others. I said, 'I don't know, I hollered at them.'

"It turned out my buddies made it out safely. But that coal carried me down that chute so fast, it knocked the doors down at the bottom clear off."

"How far underground were you?"

"About half a mile underground. My feet are still messed up today because of the water that always covered the floor of the mine. It had such a high mineral content that it ate up your feet. I draw compensation now because of it. The skin peels off them and the toenails are thick and heavy. You take one swallow of that stuff and it would be like drinking a whole bottle of Epsom salts and castor oil."

"What was it like working down there?"

"It was real confining, digging in those little laterals. There were some jackhammers but mostly we used hand tools. We wore lamps on our helmets. We worked ten, twelve, fourteen hours at a time and came out of there covered in black. They kept our heads shaved the whole time to keep the lice down."

"How did the Japanese treat you?"

Photo taken of Thornton Hamby while
he was a prisoner of war in Japan.

"One broke eight of my ribs with a pick handle—just waded in and hit me."

"Why? What was he mad about?"

"I don't know. The *Japs* didn't even know." His voice rose and he seemed surprised that I would expect the Japanese guard to have a reason. "Some of the Japs there in the mine were pro-American. I asked one friendly officer, 'What in the world was he mad at me for?' He said, 'I don't know, I couldn't understand a word he said. He was just ranting and raving.'

"The man who hit me was a schoolteacher, and I guess he was mad because they made him work in a mine instead of letting him teach school.

"One of the worst beatings I got was with a wooden saber after the war was over. A Jap saw me and attacked without warning. I only weighed eighty-five pounds at that time."

"Any particular reason?" I asked.

"*No,*" he said stridently, and I realized I'd done it again. "They didn't need any reason. They just *did it.*"

"How often did it happen?"

"They got somebody every day. That was their normal way of treating Americans."

"Just beating people and screaming at them for no apparent reason?"

"Yep. They might have thought in their own minds they had a reason, but it was a mystery to us."

"What happened after the schoolteacher broke your ribs?"

"Medical attention was not available. I kept working the rest of the shift and then walked out of there."

"You had to keep working? You had to *walk* out with eight broken ribs?" I asked, trying to imagine even standing in that condition. If I get a bad headache I have to lie down.

"That's right. Every time I go to the doctor they see the X-ray and ask me, 'What in the world happened here?' And I have to tell the story all over again.

"After the war they wanted me to go back to Japan and testify against him in his war crimes trial, but you had to remember the day and the time. Day and time meant *nothing* in that mine. I told them, I can barely remember the year, much less the day. So I didn't go testify."

"What were your living conditions in the camp like?"

"We got 250 grams of dried food a day. The Japs gave us three bowls of soup and three pieces of bread a day. The soup was made of dried cabbage or beans."

"What was the bread like?"

"You could knock a window out with it and not dent the bread."

"How did you eat it, then?"

"We soaked it in the soup to soften it up. When the Americans bombed the ships out in the bay, the concussion killed a lot of fish. The Japs wouldn't eat them for some reason, but they'd bring them into camp for us to eat. We always enjoyed seeing those bombing runs because it meant we were about to get fish soup!

"We slept three to a room that got freezing cold. *Boy* was it cold in Japan. To make matters worse the sliding doors were made of paper. We had no heat in the building. Each room had a grass mat full of big fleas, and that's where we slept. We each had one blanket to roll up in."

"Just how cold did it get?"

"We didn't have a thermometer! Colder than it does in Plano, I'll tell you that."

"Did they torture you?"

"The Japs made prisoners stand for hours holding a heavy log over their heads, and if a prisoner gave just a little bit they'd hit him across the back with wooden sabers."

"Did you or anybody you knew ever try to escape?"

"We had some men escape in the Philippines, but in Japan it wouldn't do any good. We'd stand out like a sore thumb in Japan."

"Did you see a lot of bombing raids?"

"Oh, yes. One day I was sitting with three British guys and two other Yanks and we heard a deep, low groan behind the hills. One of the guys said, 'Wonder what kind of plane that is?' A British airman said, 'That's some kind of American plane.'

The American asked how he could tell. The Brit said, 'Well it's not one of these Jap planes with their washing machine engines, and it's not a British engine because I know all the sounds they make.'

"Then we saw 200 B-29s come over the hill, wave after wave. Three Japanese pilots decided they were gonna be heroes and flew up there. The first Zero attacked from below and the gunners knocked him out of the sky, and the second went after a top gunner and he cut that Zero to ribbons. The third one immediately turned around and returned to base.

"These little Navy planes would hang around in the clouds over our camp, putting on a little air show for us, and here come the Zeros. It turned out every one of those big clouds had two or three Navy or Marine Corps fighter planes hiding in it, and they'd jump out and chew up those Zeros. Fifty-millimeter slugs landed in our camp during those dogfights. After a while the Jap fighters stopped taking the bait when those Navy planes were up there.

"Did the soldiers cheer when they saw these kinds of things?" I asked, remembering the stories of men cheering in German POW camps.

"No!" he exclaimed, shocked at the idea. "You didn't cheer, good gracious. The Japs would *really* beat up on us if we did that. We were too exhausted from working in the mines to cheer anyway."

"You mentioned you had dropped down to eighty-five pounds. You must have been extremely weak. How did you find the will to keep working?"

"You *had* to work regardless of how weak you felt. When he broke all those ribs I never did stop working, they kept sending me back down to the mine. A doctor here in the States told me that was the best thing that could have happened to me. If they'd tried to treat me with their poor medical facilities, they would have messed me up worse."

"The pain must have been terrible," I said, unable to think of anything else to say.

"Yes, very painful. More pain than when I got hit in the face by the grenade fragments."

"Tell me about the end of the war," I said.

"The Lord told me about two weeks before the war ended, that it would be over soon," he said matter-of-factly.

"Tell me about that."

"When the war first broke out I talked to the Lord and said, 'I've always heard about World War I. I'd really like to live to see what people are going to say about *this* war.' And He told me, 'You don't have to worry. You're going back home. You're not going to die.' But He didn't mention what I would have to go through over the next four years!

"In Japan it came to me plain as all get-out that the war would be over in two weeks, and that's what came to pass.

"Our camp was located about sixty miles from Hiroshima and not much farther from Nagasaki. We came up from the coal mine and saw what looked like burning paper falling into the camp from the sky. Some kind of ash. We'd never heard of fall-out, so we didn't know what it was. The Japs told us the Americans had attacked with chemicals.

"We saw the people from Hiroshima come over the mountains, fleeing the destruction. The people and livestock had their hair burned off. The people walked along with just the clothes on their backs, burned and pitiful looking. Their skin looked all dried out. We knew something powerful happened, but we had no inkling what it was.

"We got out in September, about a month after the war ended. The Army Air Force had dropped fifty-five-gallon drums filled with food and medical supplies down on parachutes. We knew something was up because a real old Japanese captain arrived, a real nice man, and all the Japanese soldiers were in awe of him. I think he must have been a war hero. We heard this Jap car bring him into camp, and a guard gathered all our officers to go meet him. He told them the war was over.

"The Japanese brought in a radio for us, and we listened to broadcasts out of Saipan containing messages for POWs. It was my job to write down the messages and give them to the officers. On our last morning in the camp, the Air Force sergeant on Saipan told us, 'This will be my last message to you before you start the first leg of that long trip home.'

"He said, 'Go get your officers in the room and I'll give them instructions.' We brought in two British and two American officers. He told us to walk down into town there and take a train to Wakiyama. There we would meet the Navy.

"We walked out of the gates of the camp, got on the train, and rode all that night and most of the next day.

"Wakiyama had been a resort town. The Americans had pattern-bombed it, leaving the railroad depot, the hospital, the church, and one hotel standing. The Navy had taken the hotel over as a headquarters building. They loaded the men in the best physical condition aboard a destroyer escort and took us to Guam. There they deloused us and gave us fresh clothes.

"A hospital ship carried us to Manila. On the way we hit that famous typhoon that wrecked all those ships off Okinawa. Everybody on the ship got sick but me and two sailors. We were the only ones who could eat anything. When the water gets rough I get hungry!" He laughed.

"I will never forget what the cook made for breakfast and supper that night. He had pancakes and ham for breakfast. I showed up and he gave me three pancakes, a slice of ham, and a cup of coffee. I got through and was about to put my tray up and he said, 'You want some more? Nobody else is eating any of this.' I said, 'Sure!'

"He asked, 'How much?' and I said, 'Let your conscience be my guide.'

"He put on a big stack of pancakes and two more slices of ham.

"I don't remember what he fixed for lunch, but I definitely remember he made smothered steaks that night! I ate a *bunch* of them. When I came in for dinner he said, 'Here comes my only friend in the Navy, the only man who can eat my cooking!'

"That night after I got done eating, he said, 'You know how many men's rations you've eaten today?'

"I said, 'I haven't a clue, but I've enjoyed every bite of it.'

"He said, 'You've only had twelve men's rations!'"

We laughed.

"What kind of effect has your captivity had on your health?"

"I lost some teeth afterwards due to malnutrition. I draw 100 percent disability. Eleven service-connected disabilities, including my eyes, my ears, my feet, my stomach, my arm and shoulder. It's all because of malnutrition, slave labor, brutality, and disease."

"How do you feel toward the Japanese now?"

He took his time considering his answer.

"I hold no animosity toward the Japanese *people*," he said finally. "It wasn't their fault. But I have no respect whatsoever for the Japanese government. I avoid buying Japanese products as much as possible. I think any American car dealer who's got a Japanese car on the lot should be fined a thousand dollars every day he's got one on his lot, and our government should put a 100 percent duty on those cars. I don't care if it *is* made here in the United States, because that money goes to Japan. And they treated me like hell. Forced me to work, starved me, beat me."

"What made them capable of doing such things, in your opinion?" I asked.

"They were able to do it because they had no respect for anybody or anything," he said fiercely. "Life meant nothing to them."

"What's the biggest thing you think younger people today don't realize about the war?"

"Our young people don't understand *any* of it because nobody's ever explained it to them. They don't know what it meant to be a prisoner of war. They don't understand why we bombed Hiroshima and Nagasaki. They can't believe their ears when they find out the truth of what happened back then. I recently spoke to the entire ROTC class at Texas Tech. What a pleasure that was! Those kids were fabulous. They sat there and listened with their mouths wide open as I told my story. It was all news to them."

"What about the debate on whether we should have dropped the atomic bomb?" I asked.

"Let me tell you something," Hamby said, and his voice became a growl. "Outside of our camp in Japan, they had already dug our burial trenches. If the United States had landed on mainland Japan, the Japs planned to run all us prisoners into those holes and shoot us. Our country's losses across the entire Pacific would have been *nothing* compared to what we would have lost in Japan."

"Could America today do the same thing over again, if it had to?"

No hesitation. "Our leadership will have to improve first. Our military now is just as unprepared as it was before World War II broke out. Our young people need to know they wouldn't be here, doing what they're doing now, if it hadn't been for our armed forces. Let's keep our military strong so nothing like that will ever happen again."

Left to Right, General Fred Woerner,
Thornton Hamby, Governor George W. Bush

LuQuincy Bowers
Fort Worth

"I was born in Franklin in 1925, but my family moved to Fort Worth in 1933 when my parents split up," LuQuincy Bowers told me. "My mother supported me, my sister, and two younger brothers by ironing and washing. When I was old enough I got a job at the Rock Island Railway and helped out.

"It was a different time back then before the war," he said. "You know the electric streetcars, when they got to the end of the line, they didn't have a way to turn around. Instead they had controls at each end, so at the end of the line the driver switched places and drove the car in the opposite direction. Problem was, the black folks were supposed to sit in back, and if the car went in the other direction, they'd be in front. So everybody got out and switched places. The white folks moved to the front and the black folks moved to the back."

"You're kidding," I said naively. Of course I knew segregation existed back then. What surprised me, as I imagined the absurd scene of everybody getting up and changing seats, was the inconvenience that people would go through to maintain it.

"That was the way everybody was brought up back then," Bowers said. "Nowadays people understand that's wrong, but at the time that was the way we all thought it was supposed to be. People didn't know any different."

"How did you come to be in the military?" I asked.

"I was first drafted in 1943, but they wouldn't take me because I was working for a railroad, which at that time was considered an essential industry for the war effort."

"How did you feel about that?"

"I was disappointed. All the men I knew were going into the military. We knew we had a responsibility, and we were ready for it. So I kept working at the railway until 1945, when they drafted me again. By this time, the war was going very well, but nobody knew for sure when it would be over, and the military still needed lots of men to replace its losses. I was inducted in April, just weeks before the war ended in Europe.

LuQuincy Bowers in uniform

"I rode a train from San Antonio to Fort Leonard Wood, Missouri, for basic training. It took that train four days just to get to Amarillo from San Antonio, because the trains took unpredictable, winding routes so enemy spies couldn't tell where they were going. A train would leave the station in the opposite direction of where it was really headed.

"Somewhere on that train ride, we learned that President Franklin Roosevelt had died. Word spread by mouth down the length of the train. It was a very sad day for us. Many of the soldiers cried. At our age, Roosevelt was the only president we remembered. Back then there wasn't a two-term limit on presidents, and Roosevelt was well into his third term. This was the man who had brought us out of the Depression years.

"We were in the middle of a war, and our president had died. People didn't know what to expect. There was a lot of uncertainty."

"What was basic training like?"

"It was very disciplined. I liked the discipline, but it took a lot of getting used to. Everything was strictly timed. When the bugle blew in the morning, we had ten minutes to get up, make our beds, wash up, and put our clothes on. We had to be outside in line for inspection before the second bugle blew. This was before you got to eat breakfast. In the meantime, they'd inspect your bed and if the officer of the day found a wrinkle, he would pull the covers off and pile them on the bed and you would have to go back and redo it.

"At meals, they allowed no waste. A sign in the mess hall told us, 'Take what you want, but eat what you take.' An officer of the day would stand at the door and wouldn't let us throw any food away. I mean, if you took two extra pats of butter and didn't use them, he would make you eat them. You didn't leave until you ate everything.

"Our first hike was pretty rough. It was actually a twenty-five-mile hike, but they told us it was a five-mile hike. You see, we had to walk twelve miles to get to the starting point! Then we walked the five miles, and we still had to walk home! When you added it all up we had walked twenty-five miles.

"I learned to walk in my sleep. When I was given guard duty, I had to walk guard for two hours, then sleep two hours, then walk guard another two hours. I had to walk around all the barracks in the camp, and I slept through a lot of it.

"After we took a class in compass reading, they woke us all up at night and took us up into the Ozark Mountains. They gave us each instructions on a sheet of paper and told us to follow the instructions, using our compass, to find the next set of instructions, which would be attached to a tree, and so on. Everybody had different instructions. If you did it wrong and missed your tree by just a few feet, you'd be lost out there in the woods all night."

"How'd you do?"

"I did all right. I might have gotten lost but a buddy of mine was nearby with similar instructions, and we worked it out. But a lot of soldiers did get lost, because they didn't pay attention in class. The instructor would be teaching us how to use the compass and a lot of these guys would be talking to each other, cutting up.

"After we finished the course we had to walk back to camp for breakfast. Well, the next evening a bunch of the men still hadn't made it back yet! Some of them ended up clear over in Jefferson City. We learned our lesson: you must *always* pay attention.

"Then there was the obstacle course, man that was rough. We had to crawl under barbed wire with our packs on, and they had men firing machine guns right over us, just sweeping left and right. And they were firing live rounds. We couldn't get up even a few inches. Even if you found yourself face to face with a rattlesnake, you couldn't afford to get up."

"Did that ever happen?" I asked.

"I heard stories," he said.

"How were you treated, as a black soldier?" I asked.

"Everything was strictly segregated," he said. "Separate barracks for black and white soldiers, separate mess halls, everything. Our officers were white, but our non-commissioned officers, our drill sergeants, were black. Because we were black, I had no contact with any white soldiers."

"Where did you go after basic training?"

"I became part of a quartermasters unit and we were sent to the Aleutian Islands to relieve the soldiers who'd been there. I lived and worked on Adak, Amchitka, Shemya, and Attu."

"What were those islands like?"

"Cold. It got down to thirty below. The islands were mountainous and didn't have a single tree on them. Which was disappointing, because back on the mainland, when other soldiers heard we were going to the Aleutian Islands, they'd laugh and say, 'Oh, you'll love it up there. There's a woman behind every tree!'" He chuckled.

"What were you doing there?"

"Loading and unloading ships, stocking supplies, things like that. A lot of men stationed there were going home from the war.

"I've never seen so much snow in my life. It could be crystal clear when we went to bed at night, and by morning it snowed so much the Quonset huts would be totally covered and we'd have to dig our way out."

"Did you ever have frostbite or anything like that?"

"No, we did fine because we had proper winter gear. We just had to be careful. At night, if you needed to go out to relieve yourself, you could request any one of the other men in the hut go with you and they had to go, whether they needed to or not. That was the rule, because they wanted two people traveling together at all times so nobody got swallowed up by the snow. See, the snow would look perfectly flat, but the ground beneath might have a hole or a ravine, and if you stepped on it you'd disappear. We had one soldier that I knew of disappear like that and we never found him.

"One night we got word that a tidal wave was expected to hit Adak in a matter of hours. We evacuated the huts and marched up into the mountains in the dark. The island had no caves, nowhere to go for shelter, so we dug holes in the snow and waited through the night. But the tidal wave passed us by."

"The Japanese were on a couple of those islands for a while during the war," I said. "Did you see any traces of their presence?"

"Yes, I saw the wreckage from the fighting on Attu. Twisted, burned out vehicles. Just like you see in the movies."

"How long were you on those islands?"

"Until 1946, when I got out," he said. "After that, President Harry Truman gave an order that there would be no more segregation in the armed forces. But I missed that."

"What do you think of the Army, then?"

"I think that even though it was segregated, the Army brought the races together," Bowers said. "I think a lot of soldiers went over there and saw black units fighting the same enemy. Soldiers didn't care about black and white when they were fighting, they just wanted to win the war. A lot of white soldiers came back home after the war with a new viewpoint. That allowed acceptance to start spreading. I think the Army is good in that way. You know, both my brothers, Freddie and Elijah, went into the military. Elijah was in Korea and Vietnam.

"But, things don't change overnight. After the war, I was passing through Amarillo on the way home. We had some time off and I went to a restaurant in town and waited. Nobody came to help me. Finally I asked for service and they apologetically told me, 'I'm sorry, we can't serve you. But if you'll go around to the back we'll get you something.'

"I had thought with the war over, things might be different. After all, we had done our part to help. But to a lot of white folks, it didn't matter."

"Did you go around to the back?" I asked.

"You know, I just wasn't hungry enough to do that," Bowers said. "I skipped that meal."

LuQuincy Bowers today

Rip Collins
Houston

I met Rip Collins and his wife, Marilyn, outside the Café Portobello in Coppell. We shook hands and Collins said, "Come over and meet our kids."

He led me to the side of his minivan and slid open the door, smiling proudly. I saw a dark, furry face, two perfectly round eyes, and a little tongue. Ears perked up. Another canine face appeared behind the first.

I grinned and extended my hand. The dogs sat calmly, allowing me to pet them, neither overly excited nor disturbed by the presence of a stranger.

"Their names are Patrick and Kiltee," Rip Collins said.

"What kind are they?"

"Full-blooded Scottish terriers."

He left the engine running so the dogs could enjoy the air conditioning and locked the door. We headed into the restaurant.

"You must be a real Italian," Collins said, studying the waiter who greeted us. "You're a very handsome young fellow."

"*Very* Italian," the waiter said with a confident air.

Collins looked at me and nodded. "This place will do."

He asked for a quiet table and the waiter led Collins, his wife, and me to a corner. We sat down and I glanced at the shiny golden cross hanging from Collins' neck, placed over his shirt for visibility.

"I drink a beer maybe a dozen times a year," he said to me, "but I think I'll have one now." Turning to the waiter, he asked, "Do you have any dark beers?"

The waiter shook his head. "No, I'm sorry, none of our beers are dark."

Collins looked disappointed. "Well, bring me the darkest one you've got."

The waiter soon reappeared with a bottle whose label read Birra Moretti. Collins turned the bottle in his hand, eyeing the label dubiously before telling the waiter, "OK, this is good enough."

When we were alone again, he looked at me and said purposefully, "Tell us about yourself, Steve." His tone was gentle but commanding, and I recognized officer material. We exchanged pleasantries for a few minutes. Collins and his wife lived in Houston but had driven up to visit his family and attend a Promise Keepers meeting in Dallas.

It was time to begin the interview. I turned on the recorder and placed it near him on the table, hoping it would isolate his soft, deliberate voice from the background clutter of clanging plates and laughter.

"Tell me what you liked about being a fighter pilot," I said.

Collins smiled mischievously and contemplated his answer. I could tell he liked the question.

"The main thing I liked about it was this: You're the pilot, the navigator, and the bombardier. You're the whole show. I liked the individuality, the freedom, the ability to do your own thing and complete the mission in your own way."

"And what did you like about fighter planes?" I asked.

"I liked the speed and maneuverability. Airliners will bore you to death. In a fighter you could always do what you wanted to do. Flip it, dive it, loop it, roll. It was the only kind of plane that would do all those things. Fighter pilots like to fly aggressively. They're the competitive type. They want to go out and do the job and get it done now, get right to the point."

"Do you remember when you first decided you wanted to be a fighter pilot?"

A fond memory lit up his face. "A fighter buzzed the campus of Texas A&M. I stood there and watched it fly over and knew right away that was what I wanted to do. I was in ROTC, coast artillery, and bored with it. I called my dad, who said, 'If that's what you want to do, do it.'

"I still remember my first flight as an aviation cadet. The instructor got me up in a plane and flew me around a while and asked if I was feeling OK. I guess a lot of people got sick their first flight. But I said, 'I'm fine. Can we do a loop now?' I loved flying from the beginning.

"I soloed and practiced cross-country flying in Vernon, Texas. Chased some farmers up near Oklahoma along the Pease River. Scared a few cows, too!" He grinned. "We went to Garden City, Kansas, that winter. It was so cold up there, we had to knock ice off the wings of the trainer to make it flyable. We flew a basic trainer they nicknamed the Vultee Vibrator. As we went through training the instructors began to separate us in their minds, figuring out who was best for which type of aircraft. You see, when we moved up to advanced training we got assigned to either multi-engine or single-engine aircraft. Fortunately I got single-engine like I wanted.

"I graduated and got my silver wings at Aloe Field in Victoria, Texas. Before I left to enter the war, I got married, because the Collins family didn't have any boys other than myself. All the others were either girls or didn't have any kids, so the family encouraged me to get married in case I didn't come back. I was trained in P-47 Thunderbolts in Windsor Locks, Connecticut.

"I got on a troop train to Richmond, Virginia, with the pilots from my class. We got our assignments there. I got separated from all the guys I trained with, because when I took a high-altitude test in a vacuum tank, I got the bends at around 30,000 feet. The corporal running the test saw my condition through the window and said, 'I better bring you down.' I'd had a tetanus shot the day before and that spot was really hurting under the pressure. I got delayed because I had to take the test again, so I joined the next group of pilots to come through. I would have gone with my buddies to the China-Burma theater if that hadn't happened.

"Instead I ended up at Suffolk Air Force Base on Long Island where I again flew P-47 Thunderbolts, we called them 'Jugs,' tired old birds that had already seen plenty of action in Europe. We did a lot of gunnery training. For aerial gunnery we took turns being the 'Tojo,' meaning we towed the target sleeves through the air."

"How did that work?" I asked.

"The P-47 would line up on the runway with a flexible cable attached. The cable looped back and forth in a big 'U' and was attached at the other end to the target, which was lying almost parallel to the plane. I'd roll down the runway and feel it taking up the slack, and the plane would jerk as the cable went taut. They told us, 'This is very important: You have to keep that stick back in your gut, because if you don't the weight of the cable will pull the nose into the ground. It'll be against all your training and instincts, but do it! Keep that stick all the way back until you get flying speed.' Once we got the targets in the air the other pilots would shoot at us. We took turns, hoping the other guy wouldn't shoot *us* down.

"One night, really late, I heard a knock on my apartment door in Riverhead, Long Island. I opened the door and an official-looking man asked me, 'Are you Rip Collins? I'm with the FBI. May I speak to you for a minute?'

"Well, what else are you gonna say to that but 'Yes, sir?' I let him in. It turned out he was investigating sabotage. Somebody had sawed the steel cables that controlled the foot pedals to the elevators in the P-47 I had flown that day. The guy who flew it right after me got killed when the cables broke in flight. We were right in the middle of all that hysteria about German sabotage at the time. The FBI man asked me for all kinds of details. Did the plane fly normal? Did you notice anything unusual? I said as far as I knew, everything was normal."

"Tell him about what happened over Hartford, Connecticut," Mrs. Collins said eagerly.

"Oh, yes," he said. "We'd completed our training and were getting ready to go back down to Richmond to be assigned to a combat theater. I got a phone call in my apartment. A sergeant told me, 'Lieutenant, I hate to tell you this, but you're short some flying time on your log. It's not your fault, it's just a mistake we made. But you have to fly another fifteen or twenty minutes.'

"I said, 'That's fine with me!' I certainly didn't mind another chance to go up. He said, 'The good news is you won't be flying a beat-up old plane from Europe on 80-octane fuel. This one is right off the production line. It even flies on 100-octane gas. So just go out and have at it, see what she can do.'

"We'd all been told how the Jugs would out-dive other fighters. I thought, 'I've got all this time to kill, so I'll get way up there.' I climbed well over 40,000 feet. The clouds were pretty thin up there, just a little cirrostratus, and when I looked back I could see the clouds ruffling in my wake. I looked at my watch and realized it was time to go home. But before I returned, I decided, 'We're going to find out if all these stories about how she dives are true.'"

"Oh, boy," I said. I could see where this was going.

"Well...she got away from me. That plane got real close to compressibility, which means you're right up against the speed of sound but not quite there, and that plane got shook up real good because it wasn't designed to blast through the sound barrier."

He shook his head and grinned ruefully. "The plane screamed down from the sky and by the time I pulled out of it, I was over the city of Hartford. I will never forget the sight of that big gold dome in downtown Hartford rushing up at me. I pulled out at about 1,500 feet and rocketed out of there, and before I got my nerves back together I was durn near down to Brooklyn."

His wife chuckled.

"*Brooklyn?*" I echoed.

He nodded. "It's not that far to go when you're moving at 500 miles an hour."

"Wow."

"I got back in one piece and taxied up from the runway. The crew chief took one look at me and said, 'Lieutenant, what's the matter? You're white as a ghost!'

"I said, 'Aww, nuthin'. I'm probably just a little excited about flying this brand new plane.'"

The waiter returned to take our dinner orders, glancing curiously at the tape recorder.

"We went back to Richmond Virginia, to get our assignments," Collins continued. "The choices were England, China-Burma, North Africa, Alaska, or Southwest Pacific. During World War II the Pacific Theater was called 'Swapa', SWPA, for Southwest Pacific Area. But we didn't know where we were going, we just went.

"We took off in a C-54 transport from Hamilton Field near San Francisco and headed out over the Pacific Ocean. We'd been given secret orders and were told to open them after several hours. That's when we found out we were on the way to

SWPA for combat duty. We stopped at Hawaii and then flew a *long* way out to a little bitty atoll called Canton Island, then Guadalcanal, then Port Moresby on the south side of New Guinea opposite Australia.

"After two months at New Guinea, my combat duty began at Morotai, a tiny island in the Halmaheras. We'd captured just enough of a piece of the southeast corner to set up a perimeter, and the Japs ruled the rest of the island. Ground troops protected our little air base. We held enough ground for the airstrip and our tents, and that was it. The Japs bombed us every night. When the Jap planes came in and our lights picked them up, our guys would fire a 40mm gun three times to sound red alert. That meant it was time to get out of your tent and into a hole real quick.

"One night," he said quietly, "they put a bomb directly into a foxhole and blew three pilots to smithereens. But during the day, it was our turn. We'd go up and bomb and strafe the airstrips they used to attack us.

"Our next base was at Lingayen in the Philippines. We were the first fighter group to go in after MacArthur returned. We didn't have a real airstrip; we flew off of steel mats they laid down to make temporary runways. But it rained so much, the mats became slick and muddy and dangerous. We lost pilots who tried to land and slid right off into the trees."

"Were you in close proximity to the Japanese?" I asked.

"Definitely. They still had powerful forces there. We attacked ground troops, supply ships, and combat vessels. We even attacked a battleship. Sometimes we went up two or three times in one day to support our own ground forces. For example, a huge number of Japs had concentrated in the Ipo Dam area, and we flew up there and dropped napalm firebombs on them. We couldn't see anything in the jungle, so light planes would go ahead of us, flying low and slow, and fire smoke bombs when they spotted the enemy, and we'd go in behind them and tear up any place we saw smoke.

"We lost men there," he said, and paused, deep in thought. "I almost lost a wingman. We were up in P-47s, strafing Japanese troops. His electric prop ran away on him. The prop started spinning too fast and he had to crash land.

"It was no problem for the Jug to survive a crash landing; it was one tough airplane. We saw him climb out of the cockpit and run for the trees. We stayed there as long as we could to cover him. Japs were all around. We strafed the crashed plane and set it on fire so the Japs couldn't get it. We saw him make it to the trees and disappear but had no idea what happened to him after that.

"Several weeks later this guy walked up into the camp from the jungle, in great shape! The Filipino underground had picked him up and brought him through the jungle to us. Those Filipino rebels were brave, they helped us a lot."

The waiter brought our food. Just then piano music invaded our airspace from the other end of the restaurant, around a corner. We hadn't realized the place had a piano. Collins glared in its direction, displeased. I watched the tape recorder, wondering how it would perform in such adverse conditions.

"Where else did you fly missions?" I asked, determined not to let the plinking noises interfere with my historical research.

"After a while we moved to Clark Field and attacked targets at many places on and around Luzon, the Philippines' largest island, including Corregidor, Manila, and Baguio and others. Baguio had been a popular resort before the war. We could see its swimming pools from the air. The Japs used it as a headquarters, which meant lots of targets for us. Our 35th Fighter Group now flew P-51 Mustangs rather than P-47s. I had gone to Sydney, Australia, on R&R in March of 1945, and when I got back the 35th Fighter Group had exchanged our Thunderbolts for the Mustang. I was given fifteen minutes of ground instruction

Rip Collins poses in front of a P-51 Mustang.

on the new aircraft type and then they sent me up on a combat mission."

"How many combat missions did you complete during the war?"

"Ninety-two," he said matter-of-factly, failing to notice my surprise at the number. "Lots of different kinds of missions. Dive bombing, ground strafing, troop support, Cat cover."

"What's Cat cover?"

"We protected Catalina flying boats when they landed in the water to rescue American airmen. We circled overhead while the Cat crews tried to pull people in, which was pretty tricky in choppy water."

"Tell me about the time you attacked a battleship," I said.

"We lost a real nice boy we called Smitty going up against that big thing. Herbert Smith Jr. was his name. It was in the Philippines on June 3, 1945. Battlewagons could put up a terrible amount of flak. I stayed more out to the side and made it out of there alive. But Smitty came down right over it and tried to put a bomb down one of its funnels. He took a direct hit and went straight down into the water. That was the only time we attempted to attack a battleship."

"What was dive-bombing like?"

"We'd get in line and wing over, going down at an angle, and we'd kick our rudders to throw their gunners off if we saw flak. I didn't have a bombsight. Dive-bombing was based on judgment. I knew I was part of that plane, and if I aimed that plane at the right place at the right angle and let go at the right moment, chances were the bomb would land where it was supposed to. And I got pretty good at it. Once I released the bomb I'd get the hell out of there, usually peeling off to the right or left. I'd go in from 2,500 feet and pull up at 300 to 500 feet. I'd see the ground coming up at me. What's amazing is, I was concentrating so hard on what I was trying to accomplish, that I had no time to think, 'Am I going to get hit?' or 'Will I be able to pull up in time?' I was thinking, 'I want to drop this bomb right in the middle of that runway.' Discipline and training took over and became much stronger than the fear of getting hit. It's strange, and may be hard to believe, but it is true.

"Once I pushed the button to let that bomb loose I felt the plane jerk up, and I'd start pulling G's, so that instead of weighing 140 I weighed more like 280. At that point I focused on pulling up fast enough to miss the ground and on getting away without getting hit. I didn't think consciously about doing things. I just did it. You know how, when you're driving a car, you don't stop and think, 'OK, I need to turn the steering wheel to the left now.' You just do it. That's what it was like, second nature.

"One time in the Halmaheras we attacked a runway that had a white church down at the end of it. Being a good Christian boy, I wasn't about to hit that church ... until I saw red splotches coming out of the steeple! At the end of my dive bomb I pulled up over the runway and hit that church with my eight .50s. I blew the whole top of that steeple off.

"I've strafed trains, blown them up, seen men jump out of the cars and scatter. I've shot up boats. Strafed troops, trucks, a few tanks, but not many. The Japs didn't have many tanks. When I strafed ground troops I'd see the Japs scurry away in every direction. All except the anti-aircraft gunners, who were paid to shoot back. It was just a question of who shot who."

"What was your worst day of the whole war?" I asked.

"June 10, 1945. That was when I lost my wingman, Hulen Leinweber, over Formosa. He was only thirty feet away, right under me when the flak hit him. I watched the plane go down, and I saw a parachute, but he was already so close to the ground it didn't open all the way. It really shook me up. I felt sorrow, anger, fear, gratitude, guilt. Why did he get hit and not me? It was the same way a week earlier when we lost that boy Smitty, such a nice quiet kid from Virginia. It's hard to describe the emotions you go through when you see his cot empty, with all his personal belongings around, and you have to gather up all his stuff and turn it in to be sent home.

"I tell you, that time the fella's prop ran away and he set the plane down in the jungle, and there were Japs all around, and we wanted to stay but were running out of gas, I was worried sick the Japs would get him. But there was nothing more we could do to help and we had to go. When he appeared in camp ... there's no better feeling in the world.

"Another emotional moment I remember ... We had built our own makeshift shower by poking holes in wing tanks one evening after we landed. We took showers and were drying off in our tent. I was standing there with shorts on and a towel around my waist and I noticed an elderly little Filipino lady walking by outside. She could have been fifty or sixty but to a twenty-year-old kid she looked seventy. She stopped and stared at us. We wondered, why would this old lady be staring at American fighter pilots in a tent, wrapped in towels?

"Then it occurred to us she wasn't looking at us. She was looking at our *towels*. I took my towel over and gave it to her. She just broke down crying and cradled this towel like it was the most precious thing on Earth. She must not have had much. It was very touching."

He grew thoughtful. "We was just kids," he said. "I look at my grandson who's about the same age now that I was when I was over there, halfway around the world, and it's remarkable to think about."

I thought I knew what he meant. I remembered myself at the age of eighteen or twenty. Then I tried to imagine that at that age, the central purpose of my life was not getting an education or taking girls to dances or saving money for a car, but saving the world, at the cost of my own life if necessary. It was a sobering thought. Could I have done it? Could you?

"Tell me about some of your close calls," I suggested.

"Once we attacked an airstrip on Formosa. We lined up our Mustangs almost wingtip to wingtip and made high-speed passes over the strip, flying extremely low. A big metal building loomed up in front of me just off the runway. I cut loose on that thing and the whole building blew up! It must have been an ammo dump. Well, it had been raining real hard that day. I looked up after I made it past the explosion and saw *mud* splattered on my windshield!

"I got out of there OK and returned to base. G.J. Kish, my crew chief, inspected the plane after I killed the engine and climbed out. He said, 'Lieutenant, did you know you took a hit?' I said, 'No, I didn't. I know I got mud on the windshield, and you can have some for a souvenir. That's Formosa mud.'

"He said, 'Sir, you took a hit in the coolant tube that runs into the radiator.'

"I said, 'My goodness, how in the world did I keep flying?' The P-51 had a liquid-cooled engine, which will seize up if it runs out of coolant.

Rip Collins and his crew chief, G.J. Kish,
pose on the wing of a P-51 Mustang

"He said, 'You got lucky. The bullet went through the middle of the tube and sealed it, rather than hitting the edge and leaving a hole. But I'd give you about another ten minutes before the engine would have died on you.'

"That's the difference between a Jug and a Mustang. I remember a time when we were on Morotai, a guy flew back from Balikpapan in a Jug, with his master cylinder blown out. We could hear him coming from a mile away, *clunk clunk clunk*, just barely managing to stay in the air. He managed to get his plane back that way! A Jug could fly with a major problem like that, whereas just a pinhole in the coolant tube of a Mustang, and you're in big trouble."

"What about the Japanese planes? What did you think of them?"

"Most people don't realize just how many different kinds of planes the Japanese had. Everybody's heard of the Zero, but the Japs had much more. They had the Oscar, a very good fighter. They had the Mavis, which was a copy of the Short Sunderland flying boat. The Japs were real good at copying our planes.

"They had the Judy, a three-man bomber; the Paul, a very well-built floatplane. We had these codenames for their planes because we couldn't pronounce Jap very good. The George and the Frank were two of their latest fighters. The George was similar to our P-47. The engine on it had 1990 horsepower, very powerful. Unfortunately for them those planes came very late in the war.

"They had planes called Nick, Nell, Randy, Lily, Claude, Jack, Sally, Dinah, Tony, Peggy, Jill, Kate, and Tojo. They had one we originally codenamed the Hap, but since we had a general named Hap Arnold, we changed the plane's codename to Hamp."

"What kind did you see most often?"

"I saw more Oscars than any other plane. It was a very maneuverable fighter, could turn on a dime, but it had no armor protection for the pilot. I also saw a lot of Big Butt Bettys. The one I shot down was a Judy. I was the youngest in the group and was flying as wingman for an older pilot in the Philippines. The Judy tried to land, and my leader dove down toward the ground to chase him. I could see he was about to overshoot the target because he was flying too fast, so I cut back on my engine and fired. I watched the tracers go right through its fuselage, and it went straight down. I was in a Thunderbolt with eight .50s."

The waiter came to check on us and Collins asked him pointedly, "Is that music going to be playing for long?"

"We have live entertainment here this night every week," the waiter said apologetically. Collins looked annoyed, and I couldn't blame him.

"Our next base was on Okinawa," he continued, raising his voice, determined to prevail over piano music and boisterous conversation. "On the way up there my P-51 got an oil leak and the front windshield got completely covered in it, and I had to fly the plane looking out the side! We stopped at the little town of Laoag on Luzon, and a mechanic said he'd take care of the problem right away. He let the plane cool down a few minutes and the next thing I knew, he was spraying 100-octane gasoline all over the front end of my plane! I cringed and demanded, 'What in the world are you doing?' And he said, 'I have to find out where the leak is!'"

Collins shook his head in wonder. "Why the plane didn't catch on fire, I don't know," he said. "And I don't know what spraying gasoline on it had to do with finding an oil leak. But he found it and fixed it, and we went on our way to Okinawa.

"I remember a Marine pilot took off one day at our base on Okinawa. He didn't bother to get clearance from the tower. A B-25 happened to be taking off in the other direction, with clearance. They rammed together at midfield. It was a terrible, terrible accident. Another time one of my bombs hung up when I was out on a mission, so I had to land with that thing hanging there. When the tires hit, the bomb tumbled off and bounced down the runway. Fortunately it didn't explode, but my heart just about did."

"What were you attacking from Okinawa?" I asked.

"We shot up a lot of gunboats and supply ships. We flew over Kyushu, Honshu, the China coast, and a southern island of Korea. These were long flights over water. When you fly over water you lose all sense of direction, so we'd follow the flight leader who had a radio compass. One time we had to fly around an entire storm to reach our base and almost ran out of gas.

"One night just before the end of the war a Jap ventured down from the hills on Okinawa and snuck into our camp. I'm sure the poor son of a gun was hungry, he wasn't trying to disturb anything. He just wanted to sneak between our tents to get some food. But he stumbled and fell into our tent! Everybody jumped up, and he dashed out toward the shore, and all hell broke loose. Guys grabbed their .45s and fired like crazy at him.

"After we expended all these hundreds of rounds of ammunition, when he floated up on the shore the next day, he had exactly two bullet holes in him. I'm sure he meant no harm, but at the time, we thought he was coming to get us."

The music intertwined itself into our conversation ever more persistently. Finally, we gave up. "Let's go down the street to my daughter's house and finish this," Collins said in exasperation.

We drove perhaps a mile until we reached a narrow residential street that greeted us with a neighborhood watch sign. Collins' daughter and son-in-law welcomed us into their home. We watched the dogs run around in circles in the front yard for a minute or two before heading inside, where Collins and I sat at the dinner table to continue.

"Let's see, where was I? In early August, we heard rumors about an incredibly powerful bomb dropped at Hiroshima. We didn't know any more about it. Of course we'd never heard the term 'atomic bomb.'

"Three days later, on August 9, our 40th Fighter Squadron was covering B-24s on a mission back to the Hiroshima area, where many military targets had survived the nearby atomic blast. We were out over the ocean east of Kyushu, flying north, and my flight spotted contrails way up high in the sky above us. We didn't know what it was, but it was moving northwest. About halfway up the length of Kyushu, the group commander ordered me to take my flight and go back to cover a B-24 that was having trouble and lagging behind the formation.

"I said, 'Roger,' and started to turn left, and at that precise moment I saw the Nagasaki bomb cut loose. It was an unbelievably large explosion. I knew, from hearing the earlier stories, what it must be: the same weapon that had destroyed Hiroshima. I immediately got on the horn and shouted, 'Look at 6:45!' The other pilots looked back and saw the mushroom cloud. But they didn't see it at the exact time it detonated, like I did."

"Describe it," I urged.

"Nagasaki had cloud cover at seven or eight thousand feet, and I could see the fireball pushing up through the clouds. This bomb was different from any other bomb I'd ever seen or heard of. It wasn't just a quick boom. It didn't go off like a firecracker. It *boiled*. The fireball kept growing larger, in thousands of different colors. Purples, oranges, pinks. It just kept getting bigger and bigger, and suddenly it went out just like that."

He snapped his fingers.

"Just like you blow out a match," he said. "I later learned that it was an implosion, rather than an explosion."

"How far away were you?"

"About 125 miles away. The only reason I saw it was because of that plane falling behind. If I hadn't turned left at that precise moment and looked over my shoulder, I would have missed it. Have you ever stared into the glowing embers of a campfire in the dark? It looked sort of like that. It was actually beautiful, all those different colors. The ball wasn't a perfect oval shape, it had bumps writhing around in turmoil. We kept looking back at it as we moved farther away. All the dirt and debris began to rise into the air, like a giant dust storm. It climbed to what must have been 30,000 feet, where the winds aloft started to carry the top of it and shape it like an anvil. I heard some 'Wows' and other comments on the horn, but not much. I guess we were speechless. We could see it until we passed the southern tip of Kyushu on our return to Okinawa."

"And what were you thinking as you saw this?"

"Amazement," Collins said. "And, 'This war's over. This baby's *finished*.' I felt a combination of awe, surprise, and satisfaction. And of course, relief that there would finally be an end to all the violence."

"You must have talked about it quite a bit when you got back to the base."

"Yes, we predicted the war would end soon and we wouldn't have to invade the Japanese mainland and lose hundreds of thousands of our men."

"Was that your last mission?" I asked.

"After the Nagasaki bomb I flew one more mission, one of the last combat missions of the war. Then the announcement came that the war was over. At that moment everybody cut loose. Men fired everything from .45s to anti-aircraft guns straight up into the air. It was a big fireworks show. People had to run and get their hard helmets because of the shrapnel falling all over the place!"

"How soon did you get to return home?"

"They gave me a choice to become a captain immediately and go to Japan with the occupation forces, or to return to the States. I had a ten-month-old son I'd never seen, so I chose to go home."

He paused and looked at me questioningly. "Well, that's my story. What else can I tell you about?"

"Let's talk about the atomic bomb a little more," I suggested. "In recent years there has been an ongoing debate about the morality of dropping that bomb. Some have even suggested it was militarily unnecessary. What do you think about that?"

Collins became stern and chose his words. I got the sense his preferred response would have been unprintable.

"None of us were glad we burned up women and children," he said. "That wasn't the point. But you have to remember the Japanese came over and killed a lot of us while we worshiped on a Sunday. And you don't forget that kind of thing. When we dropped that bomb, I know a lot us were thinking, 'I'm glad we're the ones who got the bomb first, and now we won't have to lose a bunch of men going in there the hard way.' We had already lost enough people in that war."

For the first time in the interview, this soft-spoken man raised his voice a notch.

"What upsets me about those critics' way of thinking is that it's *illogical*. When people talk about a certain type of bomb being a more horrendous way of killing people than another, how can that be? How do you set a limit on how to defeat a dangerous enemy who attacked *you* in the first place? That's absurd. If a stranger invades your home and intends to kill you, rape your wife, kill your kids, and burn down your house, if you've got a way to defend yourself you're not going to stop and think about whether it's the *nice* thing to do. You're going to protect your family the best way you can. The atomic bomb was the best weapon we had. The Germans were trying to get it. The Japanese would have bombed us with it *dozens* of times if they had it.

"My understanding is that our incendiary bombs killed a lot more people than the two atomic bombs. Those B-29s flew in, hundreds at a time, dropped those incendiaries, and set whole cities afire. Can you imagine the ways people died in that? What makes the atomic bomb worse?

"I guess it's hard for somebody of my generation to understand the thinking of these people. They have no common sense. Take abortion, for example. It doesn't make any sense to claim that an unborn child living inside a mother is not a person. And these people want to question *my* generation's morality!"

"What effect did the war have on your religious beliefs?" I asked.

"I wasn't as involved in church as I am now. I'd been brought up with religion, but I was in my twenties and hadn't matured. Sure, I had my Bible with me overseas and read it and prayed when the war weighed down on me. I always remembered there was a Creator, but in wartime there's a lot going on that takes up your time and keeps you from worshiping as much as you want to.

"But war helps you see the true value of life. It is not something to be treated trivially. We're created in God's image. You're reminded of that when you're up against such massive slaughter and inhumanity. The Japanese were a real bad group of people. The way they treated the Chinese when they invaded, the way they treated American prisoners, the way they shot pilots coming down in parachutes ... We never cried about it when we killed some of them."

"Are you still angry at them?" I asked.

"Time heals, but sometimes I'm still angry. I remember the first time I bought a Japanese car, a Mitsubishi, back in the sixties. I had strong feelings about it. I thought, 'What am I doing buying a Japanese car?' The answer was, I bought it because at that time American cars looked like they were made in a sheet-metal shop.

"But ... why would you make a nation better off after it did what Japan did?"

Rip Collins with his Scottish terriers, Patrick and Kiltee

Lloyd Groce
Willis

"I landed on the beach at Salerno, Italy between 9 and 10 A.M. on September 9, 1943, the first day of the invasion," Lloyd Groce said. "We got dive-bombed on the way to shore. My truck was parked next to my buddy Mackey Yoakum on the LST. Mackey had a machine gun ring mount on his truck, and he was firing away at the German planes as they bombed and strafed us, and I was standing next to his truck watching his tracers. Suddenly I felt something whack me in the helmet, and I fell to the deck, terrified.

"Mackey stopped shooting long enough to look down at me and say, 'Groce, get up. You're not hit. That was the ammo clips flying out of my gun.' I tell you, it scared me to death.

"I could only get my two-and-a-half-ton GMC truck 100 yards before my sergeant told me to dig in and stay there. As I dug my foxhole next to the truck I could see the fighting less than 1,000 yards ahead of me. A railroad ran parallel to the beach, and running up and down that railroad were German tanks, and of course artillery shells were coming in and German planes were bombing and strafing us. Our infantry was barely dug in between me and those tanks. I could see the tops of 'em sticking up out of the ditch beside the railroad.

"The half-track in front of me hit a mine and blew up, and one of its front tires went flying away. Two men inside it died.

Lloyd Groce at Camp Edwards in 1943

280

Lloyd Groce in Italy

We had a mat laid down on the sand that we were supposed to drive the truck on, and my sergeant told me, 'Groce, don't you get off that mat!'"

"Did your truck come pretty close to getting hit?" I asked.

"Oh, yes," he said. "Artillery was exploding everywhere, and we were in the line of fire of Stuka dive-bombers that were trying to bomb the ships out in the harbor. When they pulled out of the dive and passed over the beach they opened up with their machine guns. The bullets came very close, I could see them kicking up sand. I crawled down into my hole as low as I could get."

"What was your truck loaded with?"

"Ammunition," he said matter-of-factly. "They had loaded it up with a variety of different types, so in case my truck blew up they wouldn't lose their entire supply of one type of ammo."

"And how far from this truck was your foxhole?"

"Right next to it."

"You must have been nervous," I astutely observed.

"My sergeant had told me not to leave that truck, and you *obey* a command," Groce said. "But I knew if anything hit that truck…" He left the sentence unfinished.

"I stayed there in that hole all day and into the night. Our troops managed to push forward onto a small mountain beyond the railroad. My sergeant told me, 'We're gonna unload the ammo from your truck and haul bedrolls up to the men so they can try to get some rest tonight.' So he and I started up the mountain with the bedrolls. We didn't get very far before we started hearing sniper fire outside the truck. We could hear a lot of small arms fire not far ahead of us on the other side of the mountain. Our trucks had a white star painted on the door. We immediately covered those with mud once we figured out they made a perfect target for a sniper to hit the driver.

"When I looked back on the beach from the mountain that night, it was lit up like a Christmas tree. The Germans flew

over and dropped flares to light up all the ships they were trying to sink. They bombed one ship and it caught on fire, and the
next day an American ship deliberately sent salvos into it to
sink it, because the flames had been lighting up the whole area.

"You know," Groce said with wonder in his voice, "I will
never understand … That was the first day of the landing, I was
one of the first to drive a truck off the ship, and we were right
in the middle of all that enemy gunfire, planes strafing,
artillery … and my sergeant and I never got hit.

"I could see the wounded and dead lying on the beach.
From my foxhole I watched a weapons carrier drive along the
beach, and I watched the men pick up the dead bodies … I
haven't talked to many people about this. It gets to me. They just
picked the bodies up and loaded them, like they were *objects*.

"I had a friend in K Company, a platoon sergeant named
Gus. His last name escapes me, it's been so long. Our division,
the 36th, was a National Guard division, and those often had
brothers in the same division, and he had a brother named
Charles in the same company. Gus's platoon surrounded a German machine gun nest, and the Germans put a white flag up on
a bayonet. Gus said, 'I'll go over and take them prisoner.' The
Germans let him get halfway, and then they cut him in half with
that machine gun. It really tore me up when I heard about it.
He'd ridden in my truck a time or two when I was hauling his
men, and he'd get up in the cab with me. Said he liked riding
with me because I was good company and he felt comfortable
enough to sleep. They say that boy Charles, his brother, went
for days without speaking to anybody.

"After the troops established a beachhead, we began to haul
supplies in for our regiment. One of my first jobs was to drive a
wire crew up to the front lines."

"What's a wire crew?" I asked.

"A wire crew handled communications between the different units. I never saw so much wire in my life. They strung it

between each company headquarters and from each company headquarters to the battalion headquarters. Sometimes they would even send one wireman with a telephone as far toward the enemy as he could go, and he would be a spotter for our artillery.

"I was carrying the wire crew north along that railroad I told you about and came to an intersection and turned to cross the railroad. That turn put us in close proximity to the Germans, who were keeping this whole field in front of us under observation. I saw several of our tanks out there in the field, waiting to go forward, just sitting ducks for the German artillery that was coming in. To keep the Germans from getting the range on them, the tanks constantly moved up, moved back, moved up, moved back.

"I took the wire crew forward until I couldn't take the truck any farther. A lieutenant was driving ahead in a Jeep leading me, with a 150-yard interval between us. He stopped to ask directions from an MP standing by a foxhole. As they spoke an artillery shell exploded right behind a house just off to our left, and we knew the Germans had spotted us.

"The lieutenant ducked down to the right, jumped the Jeep into a ditch, and hid it behind a huge embankment. All the men riding on my truck saw that shell explode, jumped off, and ran for cover. I was left there alone with that big truck! So I followed the Jeep behind that embankment, hoping the Germans wouldn't be able to see me back there. They continued to bombard us. But they didn't get us.

"I did go all the way forward to the front line a few times. My primary job when the regiment moved was to haul K Company's kitchen. We had a mail clerk who went forward with a mailbag in a Jeep as far as he could drive it, and then he would get out and crawl with that mailbag to get the soldiers on the front line their mail. One day he asked me if I wanted to go with him, and I wasn't busy, so I said OK.

"As we drove closer to the front, I began to smell smoke and hear mortars and small arms fire. The mail clerk said, 'Groce, we're gonna have to get out here and crawl.' We crawled on our hands and knees more than a hundred yards across open field, dragging that mail in the middle of all that small arms fire! I could hear shells going off not too far away. You never know when one of those mortar shells is gonna hit right by you, so you don't stand up. There was smoke everywhere. I told him, 'This really isn't my job. I don't think I'll be doing this again.' We carried that mail up not far behind the line of foxholes.

"Funny thing happened with one of my buddies, C.D. Jones from Dallas. We had pulled back for a rest in a little town called Prezenzano, south of Naples. An old Italian allowed me, Sergeant A.B. Chaney from Houston, and a boy named J.D. Pittman from Eastland to stay in a side building next to his house and keep out of the weather. The Italian people were real friendly to us. We met two darling little girls, Maria and Jopina, ages six and nine. They were the granddaughters of the mayor of the town, an old man named Petrillo. Their father had died in a bombing raid, and everyone in the family, including the little girls, wore black continuously.

"The Italian government had surrendered and joined us a few months earlier. Their army had been hauling something in trucks up the side of this mountain by Prezenzano. German observation planes constantly flew overhead, and I'm sure they spotted these trucks. The next day as we sat in this little building, German planes dive-bombed the town.

"The Germans hit the side of the mountain where these trucks had gone with 500-pound bombs that shattered glass and blew in the door to the house. Plaster flew around the room. Maria and Jopina ran into the room with us, screaming and crying, and the sergeant grabbed them and held them down on the floor with him. He kept trying to console them, though they didn't speak a word of English. He held one under each arm to keep them from running back outside. We could hear something hitting the pavement outside, and we were sure the planes were strafing.

"'Where did Jones go?' we wondered. It turned out he was down in a basement with a bunch of Italians. They kept telling him, 'Jones, comrades, comrades!' They didn't speak much English but they were trying to tell him to come get us and bring us down there where it was safe. Pardon my expression, but he said to them, 'To *hell* with the comrades. I'm not going back up there!'

"The same time this happened, another buddy of mine was down beside the mountain close to a bunch of olive trees. Italy is full of 'em, you know. The explosions were so powerful they knocked the olives off the trees, and they hit him in the back so hard, he jumped up swearing and shouting that he'd been hit. The other men couldn't see any blood on him. But he insisted, 'I've been hit, I've been hit!'"

The laughter faded. Groce paused and his voice grew somber. "There were a lot of sad things ... I can't hardly talk about it. I had a good friend from Tenaha, Tim McCoy, we called him Tenaha Tim. He drove M Company's kitchen. After he had driven the kitchen up and gotten it unloaded, the men were sitting around by the truck and a mortar shell landed right in the middle of them. It killed him outright, along with two of the cooks....

"You have to understand, it's hard to describe the bond that develops between the men. You stay with a group of men almost five years, live, eat, sleep, and share, you become like brothers. When we lost one it was awful...."

"Were you nearby when it happened?"

"No. Didn't hear about it until two or three days later. And we couldn't dwell on it, or it would get in the way of fighting the war. It's impossible to disregard, but we couldn't let it get to us because we had a job to do. I think about it now more than I did then. It brings me to tears sometimes."

"Salerno was not the only landing you took part in," I said.

"That's right. I was in Dragoon as well. On August 15, 1944, we invaded southern France, along the Riviera near Nice and Cannes. Once again, I landed on the very first day, but it wasn't nearly as bad as what we went through at Salerno. Not as much resistance. In Italy we fought troops that had been under Rommel. The troops in southern France were not as highly trained, and we cut through them much faster.

"From there we went straight up through France, moving incredibly fast, with the Germans retreating before us. We skirted around Switzerland and entered Germany around Stuttgart, and headed southeast to Austria. This was a different war from the one we fought in Italy. This was a much faster-moving war. In Italy we had mountains, one after the other, we'd take one mountain and there would be another one staring us in the face. Southern France was different.

"Our supply lines through southern France got so long, between August 15 and September 15 one of our trucks drove 9,000 miles, rushing back and forth to get supplies from Marseilles up to the front line, which kept getting farther and farther away.

"Once we got into Germany and started southeast toward Austria, we moved so fast, instead of having the trucks follow behind the front line troops, the troops would load up on the trucks and we'd hurry down the highway until we hit some resistance. Then the GIs would get off and fight, and when they were done they'd load back up and we'd go on our way.

"I brought home an SS soldier's helmet, with the lightning rods on the side. The Germans had set up a machine gun nest on the side of the road. When I passed by the Germans were dead, and the helmet was laying there by the road, so I picked it up.

Lloyd Groce in France

"My regiment, the 141st, spent 361 days in combat. The 141st had more than 1,100 killed, about 5,000 wounded, and 500 missing."

"That's just one regiment?"

"That's right. I can't say I was a brave soldier. I never got into a fight. When you go into the military you fill out an application form, just like any other job. I had driven a half-ton truck for a refrigeration company, so I marked 'truck driver' on the form. I didn't know that was going to land me in a service company.

"There were so many times I felt like I wasn't doing my part. I carried a BAR but never fired it because I never got close enough to see the German soldiers. Even though I got dive-bombed and shelled, I never went through the fire some of those men went through. When I saw all those replacements coming in because of all the men we'd lost, I didn't feel like I was doing enough, driving a truck."

Hearing him say that left me speechless for a moment. I thought of the stories he'd just finished telling me: about shells landing in close proximity to his truck loaded with explosives; about driving the truck up to the front lines with German artillery gunning for him; about huddling in a small building while 500-pound bombs exploded outside.

I wanted to assure him he had done his part but was afraid anything I could think of to say would just sound ridiculous. I wasn't there. It wasn't my place to debate with him how he should feel about it.

"Are you saying you wanted to be on the front lines?" I asked.

"I just wanted to do more, is all. I felt too safe, too protected."

"What do you think of the Army?"

"You will never see a finer Army than the one we had in that war," he said firmly. "The men, the friendship...it will never happen again. We were like brothers. To be thrown together for such a long time under such stress … what he had was yours, what you had was his. And we never shirked a duty. Never did I ever see a man in our company shirk a duty. When he was asked to do something, he *did it* without question. I don't believe we'll ever see it again."

"Why were they like that?"

"I'll tell you my theory. Most of these men grew up in rural areas and survived the Depression. They'd known hard times. They knew you have to fight for some things. They knew you're better off if you work together.

"See, the children of today don't know what it is to do without. We *knew*. We had a lot of dedicated people doing difficult jobs because we knew we'd all suffer a lot more later if we didn't win the war. We knew we had to go all out."

"What if it happened now?" I asked. "Do you think we could do it again?"

"I honestly believe," Groce said with conviction, "if the same situation arose today, it might take some time, but once it registered with the young people of today what would happen to them if they didn't get the job done, *in time* this country could do the same thing over again. I just don't believe the American people would ever let one another down. I can see some of the faults of the young people of today, but I'm not going to put them down.

"When our back is against the wall, the American people will stand up and fight."

Lloyd Groce today, holding an SS helmet
he picked up off the ground during the war.

Index